Ethics and Culture
Some Indian Reflections

Ethics and Culture
Some Indian Reflections

Edited by
Indrani Sanyal
Sashinungla

Department of Philosophy
Jadavpur University
Kolkata

in collaboration with

Decent Books
New Delhi

Cataloging in Publication Data — DK
[Courtesy: D.K. Agencies (P) Ltd. <docinfo@dkagencies.com>]

Ethics and culture : some Indian reflections / edited by
Indrani Sanyal, Sashinungla.
p. cm.
Contributed articles.
Includes bibliographical references.
Includes index.
ISBN 13: 9788186921524 ISBN 10: 8186921524

1. Ethics — India. 2. Values — India. 3. India — Intellectual life. I. Sanyal, Indrani, 1950- II. Sashinungla, 1975-

DDC 170.954 22

First published in India, 2010
ISBN 13: 978-81-86921-52-4 (Hb) ISBN 10: 81-86921-52-4

Published by:
Department of Philosophy
Jadavpur University, Kolkata

in collaboration with

Decent Books
D-36/A-1, Mohan Garden
Najafgarh Road, New Delhi - 110 059
Ph. (011) 2535-3435

Distributed by:
D.K. Printworld (P) Ltd.
Regd. office : *"Srikunj,"* F-52, Bali Nagar
Near: Ramesh Nagar Metro Station, New Delhi - 110 015
Phones : (011) 2545 3975, 2546 6019; *Fax* : (011) 2546 5926
E-mail : indology@dkprintworld.com *Web* : www.dkprintworld.com

Printed by: Decent Books, New Delhi.

Preface

THE contribution of each and every individual author of this volume has added to its enrichment. None of the initial obstacles could succeed in deterring the functioning of this Group Research Project. We are happy that we have been able to bring out on time this research publication of the Research Group. We acknowledge our indebtedness to each and everybody who has helped us in one way or another in bringing out this volume. In the preparation of the manuscript we are extremely grateful to Sudipta Samanta, Anamika Halder and Doyel Mukherjee, Project Fellows, Centre for Sri Aurobindo Studies, Department of Philosophy, Jadavpur University. We are thankful to the University Grants Commission for providing us financial support in bringing out this anthology. We are also indebted to Jadavpur University for providing us all sorts of administrative support. Two persons have been included who are not directly members of the value-research group. Their contributions fall very much within the theme of the anthology and add to the debates raised by the members. "The Ideal of Human Relations: Sri Aurobindo's Global Perspective" included in this anthology, was presented by Aparna Banerjee in the National Seminar on "International Affairs and Morality," organized by the Department of Philosophy, Jadavpur University during 2007-08. Anirban Ganguly who has contributed a paper titled "Values in Politics: In the Light of Sri Aurobindo's Early Political Thought" is at present a research scholar in this department. We would also like to thank Manjusri Chowdhury, former Professor of Philosophy, Rabindra Bharati University and Kumar Mitra, Professor of Philosophy, Rabindra Bharati University for their kind advice and suggestions in their capacity as referees of this volume. We must convey our gratitude to Rajendra Agarwal of Decent Books, New Delhi for completing the publication on time. Finally, we convey our heartfelt gratitude to Susheel Kumar Mittal of D.K. Printworld (P) Ltd., New Delhi for his kind assistance.

Kolkata
30 March 2009

Indrani Sanyal
Sashinungla

Contents

Introduction

Indrani Sanyal

THE anthology, *Ethics and Culture: Some Indian Reflections,* is an attempt to explore values that surround man's existence and his interrelations with others, including men, women and non-humans. No conscious attempt has been made here to define value or to provide any clear-cut criterion for differentiating values from disvalues. Values are difficult to subsume under any universal characterization. One common trait may be that values are something we desire or hanker after either for its own sake or as a means to reach some goal. In an endeavour to say something concrete, positive and tangible about values the articles remain confined to the domain of ethics and culture. Mainly from Indian perspective — classical and contemporary, aboriginal and non-aboriginal — the authors have deliberated upon various domains where values are predominant. We are not, however, venturing to provide a detailed explanation of an Indian reflective viewpoint on values. The very existential situation of life — social, moral, political, economic — of yesterday, today or tomorrow, in urban, rural or in whatever setting, cannot ignore the influence of values. It is needless to point out that it is a Herculean task to make room for all or most of the Indian views on the subject in a single volume like this. Some of the important views, but not all, have been discussed in this anthology. A holistic world-view, contrasted with the fragmented view of the world may be taken to be the common presupposition in most of these articles as one of the major Indian reflective viewpoints. Articles that are included in this anthology follow no uniform pattern in projecting values from different spheres of our life. As the notion of value appears to be a slippery one, we have tried to avoid hovering around any preconceived notion of value with a certain preset methodology. Issues relating to values presumably persist from time immemorial.

The concern for value is nothing unique for Indians, nor do we make any such absurd claim. The Sophists believed that good and bad, right and wrong, reflect subjective opinion and desire. Plato and Socrates believed that good and bad, right and wrong are part of the objective nature of things — of how the world around us is. We deliberately avoided discussions on debates relating to whether the study of values is of paramount importance for all social sciences or whether value-free social scientists are more scientific? Neither did we open a Pandora's box to answer whether there is a difference between the world of values and the world of facts, between *nomos* and *physis*, between statements of values and statements of facts. A committed approach towards values, though not exactly definable, and a belief in value-orientation in the social-scientific perspective are, what I observe, the common bonds that bring closer all the authors of the present volume. Some authors are more straightforwardly engaged in the analysis of character traits of a personality and through such analysis and description they tacitly enter into the discussion of values. Some articles are more focused in their analysis of values in either the economic realm or the social realm or the political realm by discussing views of distinguished thinkers of India.

We frequently hear about the need for the introduction of value education in our curricula, we hear about the tremendous degeneration of values in every sphere of life, we also hear about the clash of values, but we often appear to be unsure and lacking in confidence about what are values and disvalues and how to sustain values and eliminate disvalues. The Research Group on Values at the Centre of Advanced Study in Philosophy, Department of Philosophy, Jadavpur University has tried to initiate a move for substantial research on the conceptual understanding of values and on mapping domains for the applicability of values. The present study hopes to regenerate more and more values in our life and in our surroundings.

The first article, "Sri Ramakrishna: Embodiment of Pure Simplicity" by Krishna Roy presupposes simplicity as a value while identifying it as a character trait. In the *dharma* literatures, especially in the *Mahābhārata* there are passages mentioning *ārjavam* (simplicity) among others as a *dharma*, worthy of pursuit. However, no detailed analytic exposition about this quality is available there. Roy focuses upon Sri Ramakrishna as the repository of the values of simplicity and purity. Ramakrishna led a very simple spiritual life that was devoted towards the unification of religion with philosophy. He conveyed a profound philosophy of Vedānta and other classical schools through his advice to, and dialogues with, his disciples. He was influenced by the Tāntric trend as well and to him *Brahman* is not distinct from Kālī or Śakti. The antagonism between matter and spirit was not recognized by Ramakrishna. He was always in the habit of communicating difficult philosophical ideas with the help of simple examples. The single reality can be described in different ways. Similarly, there are different ways to reach the ultimate. Ramakrishna instead of emphasizing the role of *jñāna* and *yoga* laid much importance on the *bhakti-mārga*. He was tolerant towards all religions so Islam and Christianity were respected by him. He attempted a unification of all religions. The author believes that the simplicity of Ramakrishna gave a unique dimension to the concept of religion as such. His aim was not only that of obtaining *samādhi* for himself alone; he was also eager in eradicating the poverty of the masses. Sri Ramakrishna was very transparent in his thought, speech and action. His aim was to convey subtle messages of Śāstra in a layman's vocabulary. He was able to convey his messages in a simple language and in a simple style. Profound philosophical and mystical experiences were communicated by Sri Ramakrishna in unambiguous and clear languages that would touch the hearts of all men. From Roy's article it is clear that simplicity as a character trait is not very easy to possess. However, in the context of the present-day society one may grow suspicious about regarding simplicity as a value. Today simplicity is often equated with a dull intellect.

What about positing a value-norm for all men or for all women? Is there any such absolute eternal model for all men of all periods? Are values the same for both men and women? Similar vexing questions are no doubt difficult to answer in one or two words. Rubai Saha in her article, "Saradamani Devi: An Eternal Image of Traditional Indian Values," has vividly sketched the character traits and chores of daily life of Saradamani Devi, originally an ordinary village girl of Bengal, married to Sri Ramakrishna at the age of five and finally was transformed into a Universal Mother and embraced everyone ignoring their class, caste or social status. From Saha's observation about Saradamani Devi, we are able to identify the value-ideal associated with the good character of a person, especially of a woman, in the traditional Indian context. Saha draws out the picture of Saradamani as the mother of all, of Swami Vivekananda, the disciple of Sri Ramakrishna and many other disciples, devotees and ordinary people. A Hindu or a Muslim anybody could be her son and she left her door open in the same manner for the Muslims as for the Hindus. The Indian ideal of wifehood also finds its actualisation in Saradamani who relentlessly served her husband and did all the household work. Saha provides a detailed account of the valuable aspects of her character that are cherished in the Indian tradition.

Apart from being a devoted wife and universal mother, Saradamani's other noteworthy character traits include being respectful to others, respectful to the motherland and forgiving to all creatures; in addition to these, her open-mindedness, purity of heart, love for learning, rational outlook, judicious temperament, and sobriety in attitude are worth mentioning. Her rational outlook is revealed by her belief that spirituality can be practised even without following rigid, religious norms. She herself had no formal education, but strongly advocated the need for imparting education to young boys and girls to broaden their outlook. Saradamani was no doubt an exemplary character and she is venerated by different communities. Rubai Saha's article brings to mind many more questions. How far is the ideal womanhood, exemplified by Saradamani, actually cherished today in the face of frequent crimes perpetrated against women relating to dowry deaths, domestic violence, child-marriage, trafficking and witch-branding, remains a question of great importance. Further, in the course of analysing Saradamani's character traits, Rubai provokes old debates as to eternality/universality *versus* contextuality/gender-race specificity of values.

Madhumita Chattopadhyay's article, "Swami Vivekananda's System of Practical Vedānta and its Integral Values," is self-explanatory. The author principally aims at explicating the inherent values of practical Vedānta. Instead of accepting the standard interpretation of Vedānta as the philosophy of a recluse, Vivekananda interprets it as a philosophy needed in everyday empirical life. Chattopadhyay takes into consideration Vivekananda's activity-oriented interpretation of Vedānta and his dislike for abstruse theorization just for the sake of intellectual gymnastics. The socialistic ideal also receives spiritualistic interpretation from Vivekananda. He suggests an ingenious way to combine Advaita Vedānta philosophy with socialism. Vivekananda vehemently opposes exploitation of the lower classes by the three upper classes. In his philosophy the resolution of the class conflict does not imply bringing down the upper classes; rather it means upliftment of the śūdras. Chattopadhyay explains how this philosophy rules out the possibility of any distinction between men and women or one race and another. What is moreover interesting is that the practical Vedānta kind of philosophy, as espoused by Vivekananda, leaves room for freedom as it is not deterministic in outlook. The practical Vedānta is not concerned with establishing equality from an external perspective; rather this philosophy teaches to go beyond externally imposed equality to a search for identity. Vivekananda believes in a gradual transformation of the individual from its lower individual form to its higher form of infinite existence-consciousness-bliss. He gives importance to the practice of sacrifice and speaks of sacrificing oneself for the benefit of others as a value. Through this sacrifice the highest evolution of mankind is possible. Practical Vedānta is catholic in outlook for it preaches the principle of acceptance according to which all religions only differ in suggesting different paths for reaching the same goal. Vivekananda also speaks of our faculty of feeling and he gives importance to feeling as well as reason. In the writings of Vivekananda we find much importance has been given to love. Knowledge is also considered to be a value. However, he was not against the modern science; rather he said, "Kindle their knowledge with the help of modern science." Some other virtues spoken of by Vivekananda are self-esteem, self-respect and self-confidence.

In the article entitled "Gandhian Economic Thought Revisited", Jhuma Chakraborty elaborates Gandhi's attitude towards man as an integral part of the cosmos. Gandhi believed in the principle of truth. In his opinion truth is not unrelated to *ahiṁsā*. The purpose of a man's life, who is potentially considered to be divine consists in going beyond the mechanistic structure of mind-body complex. In the view of Gandhi, for an individual, essentially as a member of a larger whole, labour, especially physical labour is important. The role of an individual as an economic being has been mainly discussed in this article. Gandhian thought on economics has an ethical orientation. Chakraborty shows that Gandhi's attitude is closer to Marx's vision of need-based economics. In fact by maintaining a distinction between material progress and real progress, Gandhi did introduce the concept of value in the realm of economics. That economics should be guided by ethical norms is obvious. Chakraborty uses Gandhi's ideal village community as an example to show how the economic policy must as well be guided by certain ethical norms. What is lacking in Gandhi's approach is the presence of any clear-cut directive about the method to be followed to reach the goal envisioned by him.

Gandhi's opposition to indiscriminate industrialization as leading to exploitation in some form or other shows his concern for overall justice. This should not carry the impression that Gandhi was an impractical person, for the author makes it quite clear that Gandhi is not arguing for the eradication of technology; rather he is arguing for the limited use of machinery. He was apprehensive of the destruction of village and village crafts because of too much reliance on Western technology. In his dream of an ideal village the individual enjoys *svarājya* or freedom. In Gandhi's picture of *svarājya* an individual belongs to a self-sufficient, egalitarian community, and is not overpowered by any external factors.

Decentralization is another ideal that Gandhi advocates. Gandhi's upholding the principle of *svadeśī* also is a value-paradigm for he believes that much of our poverty is due to the departure from *svadeśī* in the economic and industrial life. The philosophy of *khādī* as espoused by Gandhi is also another step towards regeneration of value in the domain of economy. Gandhian economics consistently denounces the modern system of production which goes on increasing human demands. Chakraborty clearly tries to establish that wanting more is in a sense depriving others or it can be linked with stealing what is not mine. The positive step suggested by Gandhi finds expression through his theory of trusteeship. According to one definition, man is a *homo economicus* indeed. But man is something more, and the values that encircle, sustain and nourish human beings must include the totality of his being. Another noteworthy point is that in the context of developing countries, like India, we find how important it has become to redefine the concept of economic development and to steer a clear path between the anti-development and the pro-development lobbyists. The Gandhian economic thought as we understand from Chakraborty's presentation makes us aware about the failure of economists to realize that the economy is merely one aspect of a whole ecological and social fabric. The Gandhian model of economics may shun as disvalue the fragmentary approach of those economists who are carried away only by their preference for an abstract quantitative model. Economists are bound to address and not to evade any value-related issues.

In the article, "Varṇa and Jāti," Indrani Sanyal engages herself in analysing one of the most obvious features of Indian society, viz. caste distinction. At times it becomes extremely difficult to provide any satisfactory answer to the question as to how we corroborate the ideals of equality and justice in the context of a caste-ridden Indian society. Generally, caste systems have been studied either from the angles of sociologists, anthropologists and historians through empirical investigation or from the angles of philosophers and ethicists by conceptual analysis. Strong differences of opinion persist among researchers regarding the actual characterization of the caste structure. They differ as to whether it is to be characterized in terms of hierarchy or in terms of the social stratification. There are some who characterize caste system as the sacralization of the social order. They believe that the ancient social institutions were the necessary sociological manifestations of the moral and philosophical presuppositions of Hinduism. The Vedic tradition is held responsible for all the problems relating to the caste system that we experience in recent time. The main thrust of the present article consists in showing that *varṇa* ideology and the stern empirical reality of more than thousand castes and sub-castes-ridden Indian society are not tied by any logical necessity. The reason for proposing or supporting any such perspective may be questioned. A vociferous counter-perspective is of course not ignored in this initiative. This article tries to focus upon the interpretation of the concept of *varṇa* after Sri Aurobindo by situating it in the larger context of civilization, development and society. While delineating the course of psychology of social development Sri Aurobindo advocated broadly five stages through which civilization proceeds. The present article discusses how *varṇa* which originally belonged into the symbolic stage and the typal stage got transformed into the conventional stage and took the shape of caste. The analysis and elaboration of *varṇa-dharma* and especially its inclusion in the research project on value needs to be clarified. To put it more straightforwardly, what makes performance of an action in compliance with one's *varṇa-dharma* a value? Further, worthy of consideration is whether each individual ought to follow one's *varṇa-dharma*. It is said:

> *sve-sve karmaṇy abhirataḥ saṁsiddhiṁ labhate naraḥ* ।
> — *Gītā*, 45.18
>
> One who performs his *svadharma* thrives . . ..
>
> *svabhāvaniyatam karma kurvan nāpnoti kilbiṣam* ।
> — *Gītā*, 47.18
>
> If one performs actions suitable to his type, he does not suffer from sin.

In India ethics is never confined to mere rationalization of certain conceptual models and theories. Morality is never considered as separated from human existence and life. Hence it has been felt it is necessary to consider the basic factors of morality in relation to the types of human nature. Moral type of an individual depends on the basic intrinsic nature of individuals. The *guṇa*s are supposed to represent potential subtle tendencies of things including beings and these *guṇa*s are constitutive of each *varṇa* type. Each individual according to his own capacity is supposed to sustain a society, and that is value, that is his *dharma*.

Anirban Ganguly in his article, "Values in Politics: An Exploration into Sri Aurobindo's Early Political Thought", explores some of the very basic values which are considered to constitute the core of values in politics. In this article he focuses upon some of the value-based stands and initiatives undertaken or upheld by Sri Aurobindo. Sri Aurobindo spent a very short period of his life in active politics but it would be wholly a partial assessment of his work and thought to consider him only as a *yogī*, a mystic and a spiritual thinker with a complete disregard for political thought and ideals. Sri

Aurobindo realized, in the context of colonized India, the importance of initiating mass based political actions through agitations and political movements. The concept of nation, as he understood, represents the mass of the population. Among the mass are the elitists and the proletariats and Sri Aurobindo could discern the potential force of the proletariats and their strength in making any political venture a success. Further, to Sri Aurobindo nation was not a loosely held conglomerate; rather it is a mighty Śakti, composed of the *śakti*s of all the millions of units. Sri Aurobindo was a great patriot and he looked at his country as a Mother. Thus patriotism assumes a new dimension in Aurobindo's philosophy. Sri Aurobindo is regarded as a nationalist leader and often his sort of nationalism has been described as spiritual nationalism. But his nationalism is not to be interpreted as religious nationalism guided by a narrow notion of religion. His nationalism depends on love and brotherhood. He introduced spiritual significance to the idea of internationalism. Sri Aurobindo spoke about freedom as an inherent right. The idea of *svarājya* that he preached is not directed towards spreading hatred for any organization or country. Freedom is not only something that is to be won, it is also something that is to be protected and maintained. To meet this demand he suggested selfless political workers should be prepared. Thus in Sri Aurobindo's political writing nationalism, patriotism and freedom are some of the values to which Anirban Ganguly draws our attention. However, questions may be raised as to whether nationalism, patriotism are to be considered as genuine values. There are arguments to maintain patriotism is morally permissible, but not morally required, nor morally valuable. How do we rate nationalism as a value in comparison to equality as a value? Is any and every form of nationalism morally permissible or justified? Why do nationalist claims need defence? The value of unconstrained creativity, the value of individual autonomy, the value of inter-ethnic co-operation often may appear to clash with nationalist claims. The Pṛthvī-Sūkta of the *Atharvaveda* speaks about the prevalence of different faiths in the world and wishes for their co-existence. The Pṛthvī-Sūkta says:

> Let this earth, where people of different faiths live peacefully like a family, give happiness to all of us.

Is this Pṛthvī-Sūkta anti-nationalistic?

If we turn to Sri Aurobindo we will find that he was a nationalist as well as an internationalist *par excellence*. Aparna Banerjee in her article, "The Ideal of Human Relations: Sri Aurobindo's Global Perspective", has dwelt on a very pertinent issue especially in the context of the emerging trends of globalization. Sri Aurobindo's *The Ideal of Human Unity* was definitely a call to go beyond nationalism to internationalism by overcoming cultural, geographical and economic boundaries. In the course of analysing Sri Aurobindo's vision of the "ideal of human unity, " Aparna Banerjee is reinstating the claim for internationalism. As with regard to an individual, the altruism is advocated to motivate an individual to go beyond himself and reach others, so internationalism may be projected as a strategy enabling a state to exceed itself. Sri Aurobindo strongly believes in a real identity between an individual and a state, though he acknowledges the nation soul to be more complex than the individual soul. Aparna Banerjee very meticulously develops Sri Aurobindo's suggestions for overcoming narrow national unity for a more evolved sort of international unity. No doubt the questions remain as to the nature of the universal standard of truth and the nature of universal social order. The ideal of political cosmopolitanism, or internationalism or whatever be the name by which it is addressed, Sri Aurobindo was in favour of accepting an organic unity and not a mere mechanical juxtaposition.

We are talking about values in the realm of economics, in the realm of politics, in the realm of society. Are values discrete and separate, to be stored into different watertight chambers? Shefali Moitra in her article, "Thoughts of Tagore on Man, Freedom and Value", delineates in the framework of Tagore's holistic world view man's urgency to comprehend the unity instead of looking for partial and discursive viewpoints. Rabindranath was not antagonistic to Western science for according to him science provides truth. But science projects without any moral ideals to guide those projects turn out to be objects of disdain as these may lead to violence and aggression. The Western culture designed on the model of European science, is empowered by economic and political forces. This culture makes false promises about freedom, and the Westerners are unfortunate to be deprived of the true taste of freedom. By freedom Tagore means leisure and creative space. Both are denied by Euro-science. Tagore, as observed by Moitra, was neither happy in projecting an uncritical attitude towards our tradition nor in offering a foundationalist interpretation of Indian history. Rabindranath also finds some value in the negative freedom created by science for in his opinion such freedom even if self-limiting is necessary for man's growth. Man proceeds from negative freedom to positive freedom. Tagore always gives primacy to human feeling, sentiments and human freedom. Moitra very rightly emphasizes Tagore's humanism as preaching a philosophy of man who is free from authoritative coercion of institutions, church and sects.

Tagore speaks of the virtue of purity of thought, feeling and will. But for Tagore the unifying principle is not the rational will present in all; rather the unifying principle would be love for all. For Tagore, love and joy are interchangeable. He accords supreme place to imagination for imagination facilitates the transition beyond the individual life. Moitra dwells on Tagore's concept of surplus. Man is transformed from creature to creator and this is possible only through love. The world can be sustained only by love. The onward journey is never ending. In his scheme Truth, Beauty and Goodness mingle together. Value is not restricted to the moral domain or aesthetic domain or religious domain. It exists in the merger of all three.

Beginning with the presupposition that love is a value, Arun Mahata and Aditi Dasgupta in the article, "Love and Sexuality in the Kurmi Culture", explore the viewpoint of the aboriginal Kurmi community residing in the western part of West Medinipur, Bihar, Orissa and Jharkhand. This they do through an analysis of the Kurmi folk songs. Love is indeed a value. But it is really difficult to define or delimit the range of love, or its beneficiaries as such. There are varieties of love that we experience as human beings. In this article the typical heterosexual love that takes place between a boy and a girl has been narrated hence it has been acknowledged by the authors that it is not a depiction of any transcendental love, but it is the depiction of love with sexuality where the human body plays an important role. The Kurmi culture views a sex-starved body as purposeless. The Kurmi society does not serve any injunction for looking at marital bond as ever lasting. The society is quite liberal in its viewpoint in keeping a provision for divorce and remarriage. Extra-marital relationships are not encouraged. The question of woman's freedom has also been discussed. The fate of women is not very encouraging in the house of her in-laws and also after divorce.

Love is a value indeed. Gandhi utilized love to uproot *hiṁsā*, Sri Aurobindo spoke about brotherhood which is an outcome of love. Practical Vedānta spoke about the role of love in human life, Sri Ramakrishna and Saradamani Devi preached and practised love throughout their life. Rabindranath gives pre-eminence to love. Love thus has varied dimensions. The interface of love and sexuality is also an important question. Is sexuality a value also? One may take sexuality to be a value because it involves sharing of energy. But others may condemn sexuality as a disvalue arguing that to give value to sexuality is to confuse desires of flesh with spiritual attainment. In many quarters there are debates and suspicion about taking sexuality as a value. In the Christian tradition it is believed that Jesus was not born as a result of sexual intercourse. "Had Adam not sinned, there would be no necessity for him to enter into carnal intercourse with Eve." Hence carnal relations originated as the result of Adam's transgression. Thus in this culture marriage by the law became honourable for the sake of procreation to the god, nonetheless in their essence they are the result of sin. "Love and Sexuality in the Kurmi Culture" clearly would reject this presupposition.The Kurmis have a much more liberal approach to love and sexuality.

"Exploring Ao Values and Ethics" by Sashinungla is a journey into the domain of values upheld by the Aos who are one of the fourteen major Nāgā tribes. The significant but not much discussed aspect of the life of the Aos people and their commitment towards values have been very carefully brought to our notice. Sashinungla analyses certain Aos concepts relating to values to bring out their inner essence. She shows how in the Aos culture and tradition a holistic approach to life and its goodness predominates. A man's liberation and dignity is always inclusive of the well-being and dignity of others including human beings, other living beings and the whole of creation. Sashinungla very meticulously brings out the organic approach to life and its values by the Aos. The author earnestly believes this Aos paradigm, if seriously pursued, would provide a very good alternative approach for tackling practical issues that crop up due to segregation, exclusiveness, imbalance and disharmony.

In this volume mainly emphasis has been laid on exploring Indian perspectives on values, cultures and related issues. In fact, majority of the thinkers and schools considered in the present volume are not deviating from the main stream of the Vedic and the Upaniṣadic tradition. In the classical Indian philosophical texts or literatures we come across various suggestive passages demarcating value from disvalue or *dharma* from *adharma*. In the article, "Rising Above Self-interest — The Prescribed Value", Ratna Dutta Sharma from the perspective of classical Indian philosophy tries to make sense of the notion of "rising above self interest." How to make sense of the notion of selflessness and what is the criterion for drawing a distinction between actions done out of self-interest and actions performed disinterestedly? It is not only in the classical Hindu Śāstra that we find reference to selflessness as a virtue, but in all other religious and ethical literatures as well. In the Śāstra we find some acts are enjoined for the benefit of doer the himself. Are we to draw a further line of distinction within actions done out of self-interest as between acts guided by motives for material gain and those that are guided by spiritual upliftment? If one acts for material gain one is said to act out of self-interest. But if one acts for the spiritual up-liftment can we say one is equally guided by self-interest? One is said to be motivated by self-interest if one acts for the benefit of one's ownself. Acting out of self-interestedness means acting out of one's own interests, including indirect interests. On the other hand, one is said to act rising above self-interest when one acts without any concern for oneself. To put it more straightforwardly, the pro-selfish philosophers would advocate actions performed out of narcissistic motivations, whereas the pro-selfless philosophers would advise not to desire anything for oneself and to promote selfless service. In Indian philosophy the highest ideal is liberation or *mokṣa*; of course even the *āstika* thinkers are not unanimous about the nature of the state of *mokṣa* or liberation, and which is said to be attainable, among other means, by selfless actions. When one strives for his liberation can he really be said to act rising above self-interest? The sceptic may retort that it is an instance where a selfless action produces the highest of selfish result. Datta Sharma poses similar such questions and reconstructs answers from the traditional Hindu viewpoint.

Atashee Chatterjee Sinha's starting point in her paper, "Communicating Moral Values to Adolescents," is the challenge towards values posed by the traditional social context of modern India. The author takes into account particularly industrialization, modernization and multi-culturalism as effecting great changes in the attitudes of younger generations towards values as such. How to re-instil values in the attitude of younger generations? The most practised way of transferring values by parents to their children is losing efficacy because of its problems. The practice of projecting role models does not viably work. The third approach, which she considers to be more effective, is the value-clarification approach consisting in helping young generations to think on values. She also refers to the ancient Indian *gurukula* system of imparting education. Chatterjee Sinha's emphasis is on evolving appropriate methods for communicating values. According to her, among core values to be communicated are truthfulness, honesty, respect for self and others, hard work, personal integrity, and community involvement. One of the oldest theories makes a claim for innate values. Recent scholars have also developed theories according to which human brains have in-built value system. Does this imply that the whole project for communicating values may turn out to be a futile attempt? The main thrust of the present article is to establish that even if one subscribes to the theory of innatism with regard to values, that does not lessen the importance of the programme for communicating values for values need to be regenerated, activated. It may be pointed out that through effective communication the sense of value attains maturity and fruition.

This introduces the research programme of the Value Group in Philosophy, Jadavpur University in the form of the volume, *Ethics and Culture: Some Indian Reflections.* No doubt this project has its very limitations some really unavoidable, and many significant, Indian perspectives could not be mentioned, considered or elaborated. Since our aim has been to delineate the Indian viewpoint on values and cultures in their completeness, our programme should not be equated with any move or practice prepared to sacrifice manifoldness at the altar of a forced unity. The objective of the present anthology does not consist either in truncating the difference across cultures or in eulogizing the difference. The analytical philosophical perspective with a catholic overview is what we seek to cultivate in *Ethics and Culture: Some Indian Reflections.* The dividing line between the main stream representing the Indian viewpoint, and the sub-altern stream, matters us only for raising more questions about the tenability of the great divide and also about the very motive to foster this divide. Our research would continue to focus upon the basic insights conveyed through the pan-Indian reflections on Ethics and Culture.

1

Sri Ramakrishna
The Embodiment of Pure Simplicity

Krishna Roy

WE all know that Sri Ramakrishna Paramahaṁsadeva is the repository of all values. Amidst all these values what specially attract me are his utter simplicity and purity. Not only his life but his thoughts and his messages are free from all sorts of complexities and impurities. He is truly an embodiment of simplicity and purity. Simplicity and purity are the virtues that we generally notice amongst the children and the children are universally loved because of their innocence and simplicity. Their unpretentious and spontaneous reactions immediately draw our affection and appreciation. That is a clear indication that all these admirable qualities are innate in human nature and all the complexities and impurities are the result of adverse, crooked socio-cultural milieu. It is not easy to preserve and cultivate such inborn simplicity and purity amidst the polluted socio-political circumstances. What we learn from Sri Ramakrishna's life and his gospel is that he remained steadfastly simple and pure all through his life even amidst the then conflicting socio-religious arena.

Theoretically the concept of value and the concept of virtue can be distinguished from one another. "Value" is that which is desirable and generally being pursued for its own sake.

"Virtue" refers to the faculties or qualities of an individual which are generally good and desirable as contrasted from the vices which are to be avoided. Since virtues are considered to be good, in the level of practice virtues are often treated as values. Truth, beauty and goodness are generally regarded as the *summum bonum* of human life; these are not only the highest values but are also the criteria by which we assess all human thoughts and actions. But besides these supreme values there are many other subsidiary values or virtues, which we cherish and appreciate; these are charity, chastity, cleanliness, courage, compassion, humility, patriotism, purity, self-effacement, simplicity, non-violence, righteousness and many more. Though in Sri Ramakrishna's life and activities we notice the manifestation of all these values — yet his simplicity and purity are most striking. Simplicity and purity often go together. Both simplicity and purity imply that they are unmixed and unadulterated. Without purity and egolessness, total simplicity, I think, becomes impossible. Whatever is simple is free from complexities and impurities and Sri Ramakrishna is the personification of such pure simplicity.

Sri Ramakrishna led a simple yet luminous spiritual life. Here I am reminded of Romain Rolland's description of Sri Ramakrishna:

> He was no hero of action like Gandhi, no genius of art or thought like Goethe or Tagore. He was a little village brahmin of Bengal, whose outer life was set in a limited frame without striking incidents, outside the political and social activities of his time. But his inner life embraced the whole multiplicity of men and gods. It was a part of the very source of energy, the Divine Śakti.[1]

Through this Śakti Sri Ramakrishna animated the modern India. For this difficult, significant and far-reaching task of

1. *The Life of Ramakrishna*, 1944, p. 14.

"animating" not only the then India but even the world in its entirety, Sri Ramakrishna did not choose any difficult and complicated method; rather he himself followed and inspired others to follow the sure and simple methods that everyone can comprehend and comply with. These are the methods of devotion and service: devotion to God and service to man. These simple ways are the keys towards bliss and spirituality, and Sri Ramakrishna is the sublime example of such spirituality.

Sri Ramakrishna was born in a pious and poor family of West Bengal and was brought up in the peaceful surroundings of nature. Here it will not be out of place to mention that most of the divine incarnations, excepting Śrī Rāmachandra and Lord Buddha, were born in poor and simple families. Śrī Kṛṣṇa was born in a prison, Lord Jesus in a stable and Prophet Mohammed in a humble situation. The hardship and poverty of their early life helped them to understand the misery of the common people and motivated them to eradicate such sufferings of the people by service and sacrifice. This has occurred in the case of Sri Ramakrishna also.

Ever since his early years, Sri Ramakrishna was thoroughly dissatisfied with the complicated process of formal education. He believed that such formal education was only necessary for the purpose of earning livelihood; he himself described it as "bread winning" education. Such bread earning education, which turns our attention towards sustaining our physical existence and gaining material prosperity, cannot be the primary goal of our life. It is undeniable that for the preservation of our existence and improvement of the quality of life some material and economic support is essential. But in addition to that goal of self-preservation we have another aim, which is development of the total self or *abhyudaya.* We must always remember that man is not merely a physical being; he has three levels of existence — physical, mental and spiritual

— and only by developing all these faculties we can uplift the total personality. Sri Ramakrishna was specially interested in developing the mental and spiritual faculties, for he was far more eager to bring about *niḥśreyasa* or salvation, which would liberate man from bondage by removing ignorance or *avidyā*.

Even without having any institutionalized education, Sri Ramakrishna certainly was a man of profound wisdom. All his discussions and dialogues manifest his strong common sense and deep knowledge. Sri Ramakrishna believed that too much emphasis on materialistic attitude would weaken our urge for eternal values and would alienate man from nature and society. The goal of true education is not to make man soulless and one-dimensional. The true aim of perfect education is to develop feeling for nature, and the sensitiveness of soul to human misery. We must cultivate the freedom of the mind, the magnanimity of the heart and the integrity of the individual. Sri Ramakrishna had the natural propensity for such perfect attitude towards learning and deeper spiritual wisdom and had the intuitive apprehension of truth and reality.

Sri Ramakrishna's natural acumen for spiritual knowledge gradually developed and manifested in all his thoughts and actions. All the basic teachings of the Indian scriptures, of the Vedas and the Upaniṣads, were revealed to him through direct apprehension and subsequently he explained all these complex philosophic and spiritual principles with the help of simple anecdotes and in simple language that could be easily understood and remembered by ordinary common people. The significance of Sri Ramakrishna lies not in formulating some novel religious ideals and doctrines but in conveying those highly philosophical and religious principles in such a simple way that has inspired all. Through all his discussions and dialogues, he used to convey the messages of the Vedas, Upaniṣads and of the *Bhagavad-Gītā* as well as that of even

Bible and Koran to his disciples and devotees.

As we go through the cultural history of India we notice that India has a long history of philosophy and religion. Generally we make a distinction between philosophy, which is primarily speculative, and religion, which is basically emotive; yet in the case of India we notice that some of the philosophical systems have close affinity with religion — often we cannot separate them from one another. Such trend of unifying religion with philosophy can be noticed even in the teachings of Sri Ramakrishna. He used to convey deep philosophical principles, propagated by the Vedāntins and other classical thinkers, through his advice and dialogues with disciples, which were often regarded as religious.

It is generally held that Sri Ramakrishna was influenced by the teachings of Vedānta philosophy, but it is equally true that he was also acquainted with other systems of understanding reality. There are, in the Hindu tradition, three major methods of approaching reality: they are Vedāntic, Tāntric and Mixed. The Vedāntic and the Tāntric ways are quite distinct from one another. But Sri Ramakrishna was acquainted with and influenced by both these trends. Both the followers of the Vedānta and the Tantra systems hold that the Ultimate Reality is *Sat-Cit-Ānanda* (Existence-Knowledge-Bliss) and man's final goal is to remember and realize his true identity with that Absolute or *Brahman.* But the ways of approximating that goal differs in these two systems. Whereas the Vedānta preaches the way of renunciation, the Tantra supports the way of enjoyment. The Tāntrics prescribe certain rites by which such enjoyment of the senses become spiritualized and get transformed into union with the Deity.

It is well known that even among the Vedāntins there are certain differences regarding the interpretations of certain key concepts. Śaṅkarācārya sin his interpretation of the *Brahma-Sūtra,* holds that the Ultimate Reality or *Brahman* is indeterminate and devoid of any quality. But if we look at this Absolute or *Brahman* from the empirical perspective He then appears as God or *Īśvara.* In his interpretation of *Brahma-Sūtras* Rāmānujācārya on the other hand regards that the Ultimate Reality is not devoid of qualities, as mentioned by Śaṅkarācārya, but is possessed of diverse qualities like matter and consciousness — *acit* and *cit.* Similar divergent views can be noticed even in the case of other Vedāntic concepts like the status of the world and of individual selves etc. Sri Ramakrishna was aware of all these conflicting views but was never perplexed by such differences of opinion. He always wanted to reconcile these different conflicting opinions and as such his views may be regarded as *Samanvayai Vedānta.* He accepted *Brahman* or the Absolute as the only reality but he also admitted that it had many forms and aspects. He regarded God or *Īśvara* as both *nirguṇa* and *saguṇa* (indeterminate and determinate); he who has realized God knows that God is both with form and without form. Here Sri Ramakrishna was explaining in simple language what was mentioned in the *Bṛhadāraṇyaka Upaniṣad,* i.e.

> *Brahman* has two forms — gross and subtle, mortal and immortal, limited and unlimited, defined and undefined.[2]

Sri Ramakrishna explained this truth with a simple example: *Brahman* or Absolute is like an unfathomable ocean. In such boundless ocean often we notice some visible ice blocks, formed by severe cold. Similarly, due to the earnest devotion of the worshipper the Infinite transforms itself and appears to the worshipper as God with form. But just as under the influence of the rising sun, the ice blocks melt into the ocean, similarly with the awakening of the true knowledge or *jñāna,*

2. *Bṛhadāraṇyaka Upaniṣad,* II.III.1.

the embodied God is conceived of as formless *Brahman*.

According to Sri Ramakrishna, impersonal, formless *Brahman* and the personal Goddess like Kālī or Śakti are not two distinct realities but are related to one another as substance and quality. Clarifying this metaphysical principle he stated:

> *Brahman* and Śakti are identical. If you accept the one, you must accept the other. It is like fire and its power to burn. If you see fire, you must recognize its power to burn also. You cannot think of fire without its power to burn, nor can you think of the power to burn without fire. You cannot conceive of the sun's rays without the sun, nor can you conceive of the sun without its rays.[3]

Hence, to Sri Ramakrishna *Brahman* is not different from the Goddess Kālī. *Brahman* Himself *is* Kālī. When He is inactive, He is called *Brahman* and when He is active — creating, preserving and destroying the world — we worship Him/ Her as Kālī. Analysing Sri Ramakrishna's position Brajendra Nath Seal states:

> In contemplating truth from the absolute (*nirupādhi*) point of view, he negated all conditions and modes (*upādhi*s) but from the relative or conceptual (*sopādhi*) point of view he worshipped Kālī, the divine Mother as well as other modes and adumbrations of the Deity. He worshipped the one in all and the all in one, and he saw no contradiction but only a fuller reality in this. So also he reconciled *sākāra* and *nirākāra upāsanā* (iconic and aniconic worship). For him there is nothing in the form of the Deity but God manifesting Himself. The antagonism between matter and spirit no longer existed for him.[4]

Sri Ramakrishna wanted to convey such deep ontological principle of identity with the help of simple examples which

---

3. *The Gospel of Sri Ramakrishna*, 1996, p. 134.
4. *Studies on Sri Ramakrishna*, 1988, pp. 4-5.

could be understood by all. He reminded us how we describe water differently in different languages, i.e. sometimes we call it *jala*, sometimes as *pānī*, sometimes as water but all these different terms refer to the same object. Similarly, we may describe the Ultimate Reality by different descriptions but they in no way change the nature of the Ultimate Reality. He always held that Ultimate Reality was one. *Brahman*, *ātman* and *Bhagavān* are only different descriptions of the same Reality. Those who follow the path of knowledge call him *Brahman*. To the *yogī*s He is *ātman* or *Paramātman* and to the devotees He is *Bhagavān*. The *Brahman* or *Paramātman* is present not only within us but He is also present in the external world. Some of the thinkers want to state that He Himself has become all these. But Sri Ramakrishna, like Ramprasad, would suggest that a true devotee of God wants to eat sugar, not to become sugar. With this simple example, Sri Ramakrishna wanted to clarify that so long as we do not attain total unification the duality between the worshipper and the worshipped could never be thoroughly eliminated.

Thus Sri Ramakrishna opined that just as there was one single Reality which could be described by different names, similarly there were different paths by which one could realize the Ultimate Reality. One is the way of knowledge, which is generally being pursued by the *jñānī*s or wise people; the other is the way of *yoga* which is generally being followed by *yogin*s and the third is the way of worship which is generally being followed by the devotees. Sri Ramakrishna emphasized that the way of worship or *bhakti* was the simplest and the surest way for the common people in the *Kali yuga*. To him God alone was "real"; everything else would have value and significance only in the background of God. In his characteristic way, he explained that any number of zeros put side by side have no value, but if number 1 precedes the zeros, they acquire value, so also everything in the world is like zero and God is the number 1, without which other objects have no significance or value.

One of the most far reaching and efficacious contributions of Sri Ramakrishna was his untiring effort to unify all religions. We know from the history of mankind that there are different religions in different civilizations and the conflicts and antagonism between these different religions are the causes of many wars and sufferings of the people. Most of the religious leaders wanted to develop and propagate their own respective religions. Probably there was no other religious leader who followed or practised a religion other than his own. Sri Ramakrishna is the only religious leader who believed, practised and preached that all religions were essentially one. The uniqueness of Sri Ramakrishna lies in that even being born and brought up in a conservative Hindu brāhmaṇa family, he himself practised other important religions like Islam and Christianity. In those days of orthodoxy and puritanism it was extremely courageous and revolutionary on his part to embrace other religions. Sri Ramakrishna was neither an eclectic or a person who selectively accepted different schools nor a syncretist, who was primarily interested in the amalgamation of different religions. The basic principle of Sri Ramakrishna was to realise that all the paths were leading towards the same goal. Different religions are the varied expressions of *the Religion*. There is one God and all the different religions are trying to realize this essential truth. He did not deny the value of different religions, nor did he decry the varied rites and customs suggested by different religions. His major aim was mainly to transcend those socio-religious, contingent rites and practices and to grasp the core of each religion, its deeper spiritual content. In order to comprehend fully a particular religion he himself became initiated in that religion and practised even the stipulated rites and customs. Since Islam and Christianity are the two most important religions besides Hinduism, with which Sri Ramakrishna was acquainted since birth, Sri Ramakrishna decided to have first-hand experiences of those two leading religions of the world. One after another he accepted these two religions, followed their stipulated customs and sincerely endeavoured to realize the deeper truth underlying those religions. Not only Islam and Christianity, Sri Ramakrishna wanted to understand the intricacies of the diverse Hindu traditions like Tantra, Śākta, Vaiṣṇava and Vedānta. Sri Ramakrishna accepted the divinity of Buddha and had great respect for the *tīrthaṁkaras*, though he was not formally initiated to their religion. While pursuing all these approaches, he had the basic aim of realising the essence of that religious trend. It is both interesting and illuminating to know that having followed these different ways he came to the conclusion that all these ways were leading towards the same goal — to realize the ultimate reality. The Hindus, Muslims and Christians are approaching the same destination by different roads. In an unambiguous, simple language he expressed his view thus:

> God can be realized through all paths. All religions are true. The important thing is to reach the roof. You can reach it by stone stairs or by bamboo steps or by a rope, you can also climb up by a bamboo pole.[5]

He clarified his view further by stating:

> Dogmatism is not good. It is not good to feel that my religion alone is true and other religions are false. The correct attitude is this: My religion is right, but I do not know whether other religions are right or wrong, true or false. I say this because one cannot know the true nature of God unless one realizes Him . . . Hindus, Mussalmans, Christians, Śāktas, Śaivas, Vaiṣṇavas, the Brahmajñānīs . . . all seek the same object. . . . A mother prepares dishes to suit the stomachs of her

5. *The Gospel*, op. cit., p. 111.

> children. . . . (similarly) God has made different religions to suit different aspirants, times and countries. All doctrines are only so many paths; but a path is by no means, God himself. Indeed, one can reach God if one follows any of the paths with whole-hearted devotion.[6]

Such underlying harmony between all the religions has been supported by some other thinkers but the uniqueness of Sri Ramakrishna lies in that he himself practised what he preached. Hence his message of the harmony of religions was expressed not merely in his words but also in his actions all through the life. Such unusual, unprejudiced acceptance of other religions could be possible only by someone who was thoroughly above all superficialities and superstitions, above all dogmatism and sectarianism. His catholicity further reveals his egolessness. Only by removing vanity and self-centredness one can accept other faith, other religion.

Sri Ramakrishna's pure simplicity is reflected in his total self-abnegation. Though he had lots of followers and disciples, he never claimed that he was the *guru* or the teacher himself. He always maintained that the ultimate authority was God only. He held:

> In every age God incarnates Himself as the *guru*, to teach humanity. *Satcidānanda* alone is the *guru*.[7]

Such utterances express his egolessness, humility and total surrender to the divinity. According to Sri Ramakrishna true simplicity demands that there should not be any discrepancy between our thought and speech or action. His life is the glorious example of such simplicity for he never pretended or hid anything, his words and actions used to reflect his purity of thought and belief. Moreover, we know that the simplicity of a child becomes evident as it does not make discrimination

---

6. *The Gospel*, op. cit., pp. 558-59.
7. Ibid., op. cit., p. 98.

between the rich and the poor, between the educated and the uneducated; similarly Sri Ramakrishna was equally generous and compassionate to all; he never made any discrimination between the privileged and the underprivileged. It has been aptly said about him:

> Without the least trace of any air of superiority about him, he would behave like a simple and innocent child and leave on the minds of his select audience the impress of a perfect picture of humility. He would lay no claim to originality and would ascribe the wisdom of his talks to his divine Mother, who, as he felt, was the moulder of his thoughts and expressions. . . . Writes one who saw him: "His spirit stood on a pedestal so high that those who approached him could only look up at it in incredulous astonishment. Men marvelled when they heard him, comprehending or mystified. His lucidity was as remarkable as his wisdom was unfathomable."[8]

Here I would like to point out that to some Sri Ramakrishna appears as a mystic. This view needs some elucidation. It is true that the concept of religion is conjoined with that of mysticism. As a quest for the Infinite, religion possesses certain mystical elements. Here I may recapitulate the comment made by Evelyn Underhill, the reputed exponent of mysticism:

> Almost any religious system which fosters unearthly love is potentially a nursery for mystics and Christianity, Islam, Brāhmanism and Buddhism each receives its most sublime interpretation at their hands.[9]

Consequently most of the great mystics are considered as "faithful sons of the great religions." Even if we transpose the statement and hold that most of the great religious persons

8. "Sri Ramakrishna and Spiritual Renaissance", in *The Cultural Heritage of India*, 1993, p. 675.

9. *Mysticism: A Study in the Nature and Development of Man's Spiritual Consciousness*, 1960, p. 96.

are faithful sons of mysticism then that may also be accepted as true. Accordingly Sri Ramakrishna being a great religious person can be regarded as a mystic. In fact most of the essential characteristics of mysticism can be found in Sri Ramakrishna. Here it is necessary to recount the basic characteristics of mysticism as expounded by Evelyn Underhill in her book entitled *Mysticism*:

> The development of mysticism is a continuous transcendence, having certain stages, for example, awakening or conversion, self-knowledge or purgation, illumination, surrender and union. The final goal of all spiritual endeavour is to attain union with the Ultimate Being.

In the gradual unfoldment of Sri Ramakrishna's spiritual life all these stages can be noticed. Yet it has to be admitted that there are certain aspects in which Sri Ramakrishna differs from a Buddhist or Sūfī mystic. A Buddhist mystic is primarily interested in attaining the state of *nirvāṇa* and a Sūfī mystic is craving for total absorption in God. Here we notice a different attitude in Sri Ramakrishna. Though Sri Ramakrishna was equally eager to realize his oneness with divinity, which he achieved in the stage of *samādhi*, he did not consider it to be the only objective of his life. Emancipation of his own self was never the primary motive of Sri Ramakrishna. He had many other aims like conveying his spiritual experience to others, to follow the path of spirituality, to serve mankind by alleviating their suffering and ignorance. Such objectives of Sri Ramakrishna become explicit with his famous advice to Swami Vivekananda. When Vivekananda wanted to remain in the state of *samādhi*, which gave him infinite bliss in unification, Sri Ramakrishna reminded him of his true mission. The true goal of Swami Vivekananda and his other disciples was not merely to achieve personal bliss and emancipation. They had to do many other things for the welfare of humanity.

They must transmit spiritual knowledge to men and seek to eradicate poverty, disease and ignorance of the people. Sri Ramakrishna emphasized that compassion, devotion and renunciation were the three equally important virtues to be pursued. This may be regarded as a distinctive feature of Sri Ramakrishna's religion. Whereas the other mystico-religious tendencies primarily imply the urge for union with the Ultimate Being, Sri Ramakrishna's goal was much broader. In spite of his impassioned craving to transcend worldly pleasures for realising oneness with the eternal Reality, he was eager to serve the suffering man as God. Some of the incidents of his life may appear as mystical as they were uncommon and beyond the level of the empirical. His experiences of *nirvikalpa samādhi*, having direct communication with Goddess Kālī, worshipping his wife Saradadevi as Goddess were such unusual trans-phenomenal experiences. But it must be remembered that in spite of such transcendental experiences, Sri Ramakrishna was totally transparent and pure; there was nothing hidden and complex in him. He used to give clear, lucid description of all his experiences and believed that such experiences were not unattainable for those who could pursue the goal with proper devotion and earnestness. In order to spread the messages of *dharma* and spirituality, Sri Ramakrishna wanted to express the ambiguous, ineffable, mystical principles in clear and simple language. We know that many philosophic and religious doctrines contain some amount of abstruse, mystical elements which make them vague, confusing and complicated. Sri Ramakrishna's lifelong effort was to disclose and convey that the subtle messages could be understood by everybody, privileged or underprivileged, intellectual and ordinary men at the same time. He always wanted to explain difficult philosophical and spiritual principles with the help of simple language, taking resort to simple anecdotes and simple metaphors. The relevance and significance of Sri Ramakrishna lies not in expounding some new religious principles or spiritual techniques; the importance and efficacy of Sri Ramakrishna lies in that he was the first one to disclose the messages of our Indian scriptures in such an easily understandable style. Here it is necessary to remember that though he used to convey his messages and advices in simple language, in simple style — yet he never diluted or simplified those rich and deep messages of the scriptures. He had the extraordinary capacity of conveying profound spiritual, philosophical and mystical doctrines in an unambiguous clear language that would touch the heart of the eager ones. Though straight and simple his messages were positive and powerful as they emerged from the spirit of his heart and were the results of direct intuitive apprehension. In this context I would like to recapitulate what Mahatma Gandhi wrote about him:

> Ramakrishna was a living embodiment of godliness. His sayings are not those of a mere learned man but they are pages from the Book of Life.[10]

Thus we notice that Sri Ramakrishna's *Book of Life*, simple as it may appear, is profound in wisdom, fathomless in spirituality and boundless in significance. The relevance of Sri Ramakrishna's life and message lies in giving us the simple but optimistic direction that not only sages and seers but even the ordinary common men or women like us can attain unification with divinity through purity of soul, devotion to God and service to mankind. By simple and gentle yet strong and subtle narrations he dispelled all doubts and queries and gave us the right direction for proper realization of divinity which, according to him, was the ultimate objective of human life. I would like to conclude this article with the most appropriate description of Sri Ramakrishan by Swami Nirvedananda:

---

10. *Sri Ramakrishna: The Great Prophet of Harmony*, 1986, p. 260.

Religion was the breath of his life, morality his backbone. In his perspective, realisation of God was the worthiest object of life, and devotion, purity, sincerity, selflessness, love and humanity constituted the real wealth of man, far superior in value and significance to anything of the external world. And he developed all these to a unique degree of perfection. In his life, one finds an unsurpassed record of God-intoxication, spotless purity and surging love for humanity. And then, with his mind broad as the sky, strong as adamant, and pure as a crystal, he plumbed the depths of spirituality, collected the treasures of the entire wisdom of the past, tested their worth, and reinvested them all with a fresh hallmark of truth. From his lips, the world hears the voice of the ancient prophets; in his life, it discovers the meaning of old lessons afresh.[11]

References

Gambhirananda, Swami, ed., *Bṛhadāraṇyaka Upaniṣad* in *Upaniṣad Granthāvali*, Prathama Bhāga, Kolkata: Udbodhana Kāryālaya, 7th impression, 1962.

Nikhilananda, Swami, *The Gospel of Sri Ramakrishna*, Chennai: Sri Ramakrishna Math, 1996.

Nirvedananda, Swami, "Sri Ramakrishna and Spiritual Renaissance", in *The Cultural Heritage of India*, Kolkata: Ramakrishna Mission Institute of Culture, vol. 4, 1993.

Rolland, Romain, *The Life of Ramakrishna*, Mayavati: Advaita Ashram, 1944.

Sri Ramakrishna: The Great Prophet of Harmony, Kolkata: Advaita Ashram, 1986.

Studies on Sri Ramakrishna, Kolkatta: Ramakrishna Mission Institute of Culture, 1988.

Underhill, Evelyn, *Mysticism: A Study in the Nature and Development of Man's Spiritual Consciousness*, London: Methuen & Co. Ltd., 1960.

---

11. *The Cultural Heritage*, vol. 4, p. 690.

2

Saradamani Devi
An Eternal Image of Traditional Indian Values

Rubai Saha

VALUES occupied an important place in the realm of ancient Indian social structure, which shaped her culture and tradition, as distinct from other civilizations of the ancient world. This tradition has proceeded down the ages but has undergone several pitfalls and lost its original significance with the passage of time. If we cast a glance at the happenings of the nineteenth-century Indian scenario, we shall realise that the waning traditional culture and value set-up was facing its revival under the Renaissance Movement[1] which had flourished in the-then India and enriched her in all spheres of life.

One such outstanding activity was the Ramakrishna-Vivekananda Movement, which received its impetus and

---

1. The Renaissance Movement which sprang up in India in the first half of the nineteenth century strove to eradicate the social evils which crept into society since the medieval period and announced the ushering of a new era under the guidance of many stalwarts like Iswar Chandra Vidyasagar, Raja Rammohun Roy, Keshab Chandra Sen, Swami Vivekananda, Debendranath Tagore, Rabindranath Tagore, Sri Aurobindo and many other leaders. It held its sway over the entire century and gradually gave birth to an enlightened nation.

constant inspiration from Sarada Devi, wife of Ramakrishna Paramahaṁsadeva, the great philosopher and priest of the Kālī Temple at Dakṣiṇeśvar and an ardent devotee of the deity Kālī. The great Hindu monk, Swami Vivekananda had been able to proceed to the West and spread his message about Hinduism in the World Congress of Religions at Chicago and finally establish the Ramakrishna Order only after receiving the consent of the Mother and her blessings showered on him incessantly yet silently.

Sarada Devi was an ordinary village girl of Bengal, being the eldest child of her parents who were poor but honest and religious. Right from her tender age, we notice the manifestation of traditional values in her character. She was married to Ramakrishna Deva at the age of five only and as she grew up she depicted all the exquisite qualities of an ideal Indian woman and eventually emerged as the Universal Mother, who was the Mother to all people, and all living beings.

Here we need to review our ancient history and try to discover for ourselves as to what qualities are essential to be present in a woman in order to be regarded as "ideal," upholding the age-old traditional values in her character.

Traditional Picture of an Indian Woman

In India, a girl grows up into a woman with the ideal image of the "mother." This concept has been instilled in the minds of an Indian through the teachings of the Vedas — the oldest literature of the world — which proclaim the dignity of women in being "Mothers" of the human race. The mother is held to be the incarnation of God on earth in every Indian family.[2] Only her love towards her children is the most selfless. She undertakes all the responsibilities in the family and has to

2. *Women of India,* 2006, pp. 18-19.

suffer the most. She stands out to be the embodiment of purity (mental as well as physical), selflessness, untiring service, kindness, affection, endurance, forbearance and contentment[3] and here she has no parallel. We find in Sarada Devi a coherent assimilation of all these virtues which have raised her to a noble stature.

There lies a stark difference between the thoughts and values of the Orient and those of the Occident. In India, a woman is deified as the Mother and her essence lies in Motherhood. On the contrary, a Western woman is adored as the wife who is the pivot in the family. The tradition of India lays emphasis on moral strength, which is acquired through penance and renunciation. The Western culture insists on exhibiting strength by dint of work and work alone.[4]

Women in the West were much more educated than their counterparts in the East. It has resulted in broadening their outlook towards the world, in extending their hands to redeem the poor and the distressed. Yet, they remain the same, committed to their religious beliefs.[5] But the triumph of Indian women over their Western counterparts (in regard to familial peace and solidarity) rests on their chastity and dedication to their husbands.[6] In India, the institution of marriage is sanctified by religion; it is not a mere means of satisfying sensuous impulses.[7]

Turning our attention to Sarada Ma, we find her, in her maiden days, assisting her parents in every household work — cooking food for the family, picking cotton from the fields

---

3. *Bhāratīya Nārī*, 2007, p. 1.
4. Ibid., p. 26.
5. *Indian Women and Western Women*, 2005, pp. 33-34.
6. *Bhāratīya Nārī O Pāścātya Nārī*, p. 39.
7. Ibid., p. 40.

to prepare sacred threads[8] which are needed to earn their living, collecting fodder for domestic animals, separating husk from the paddy, taking care of her younger brothers at the same time and even teaching and feeding them. Her concern for the distressed was remarkably noticed in an incident where the little girl used her tiny hands to fan the hot food served to the hunger-stricken villagers afflicted by the famine who were being fed by her generous father. We find her absolutely dedicated to all kinds of household duties just like any other woman of a rural family.

Little Sarada, at the age of five, was given in marriage to Sri Ramakrishna, a young priest in Dakṣiṇeśvar who was twenty-four years old then. She stayed at her father's house at Jayrambati (in Bankura district of Bengal) while her husband stayed at Dakṣiṇeśvar. She was brought to the house of her in-laws in Kamarpukur (in Hooghly district) when Sri Ramakrishna used to visit there.

Only after twelve years of her marriage did she have the opportunity to stay with her husband and know him thoroughly whose state of God-intoxication was misinterpreted as a case of insanity by gullible rural folk. Traversing a long journey on foot with her father from the village, she arrived in Dakṣiṇeśvar with high fever. She was cordially received by her husband and taken care of, till she recovered from illness. Thereafter, she went to stay with her mother-in-law in the music tower[9] of the temple and bore the

8. It is a thread, which is prepared from cotton. It is a religious custom among Hindu brahmaṇa (upper-caste) men to wear this thread after being initiated by the religious ceremony known as *upanayana* and he is believed to be spiritually born after completing his formal education and acquiring knowledge of the Absolute.

9. This is known in Bengali as *Nahabat*, it is a place situated →

responsibility of all household work on her own shoulders.

Picture of a True, Devoted Wife

It is remarkable to note that Sarada Devi arrived in Dakṣiṇeśvar to serve her husband since she was under the impression that her sympathetic care and attention would help him to recover from illness if, at all, he was sick. When Sri Ramakrishna asked her apprehending that she might have come to drag him down to worldly life, Mother's reply was astounding. She assured him open-heartedly that she had come only to assist and accompany him in his journey towards spiritual quest, which relieved him as well as pleased him. Sarada depicted in herself the true image of an ideal traditional woman, devoted to her husband in word and deed alike, and sharing equal responsibility in building up a harmonious bond between each other which rested on mutual respect and co-operation.

While Sri Ramakrishna was attended to by his followers and devotees most of the time throughout the day, Sarada was confined in the meagre-spaced uninhabitable music tower all the time for which she did never express any word of complaint or disappointment. She engaged herself in serving her husband and mother-in-law, looking after all sorts of comfort of his disciples, cooking varied items according to each of their tastes, and also tackling every hassle of the family. It was possible for her only whose love and care for everyone was utterly selfless and demanded nothing in return.

Being a Hindu girl, she was married in early years of her life. But she did not enjoy the privilege of leading a conjugal life, bearing her own children. In addition, she had to face many familial troubles caused by her brothers and their family.

→ beside the roof of a house from where Indian musical instruments like the *śehnāī* used to be played.

But noticeably, she stood calm amidst all crises and solved the problems judiciously.

Sri Ramakrishna was considerate towards his wife and trained her in many worldly matters. He advised her to return to his village at Kamarpukur after his demise and sustain herself by growing vegetables in the land. After his passing away, Mother had earnestly followed his advice and lived most humbly, wearing worn-out clothes and consuming most simple food. She did never allow anyone to learn about her distress nor did she stretch her hand to anybody for help.[10] Her self-restraint and painstaking patience strikes us even today as it did at that time to her devotees who came to know about her misery much later.

Mother of All — Kind and Affectionate

Once Sri Girish Chandra Ghosh, the renowned playwright and actor asked Mother about who she really was. To this she replied, "I am 'Mother' in the true sense of the term."[11] Her attitude and behaviour towards others aptly coincided with her declaration. To her, all men are her most beloved children and she did not discriminate among them. Amjad, the notorious Muslim-dacoit was as dear to her as was Sarat Maharaj (Swami Saradananda), a direct disciple of Sri Ramakrishna and attendant of the Mother. Her motherly affection was best reflected when she served food to Amjad with her own hands with loving care and rebuked the lady who was serving him with disrespect.[12] Moreover, she did not at all hesitate to clean the place after people had their food there as she felt that all men are her most loving children even though they might belong to different castes or creeds.

10. *Śatarūpe Sāradā,* 1985, p. 520.

11. *Śrīmā Sāradā Devi,* Baiśākh 1408, p. 170.

12. Ibid., p. 289.

All apparent differences dissolved before Mother's eyes. Her statement, "I am the Mother of the virtuous and also of the sinner,"[13] was best depicted in her behaviour. She replied "Amjad is my son as much as my 'Sarat' is."[14] Her generosity was such that all sorts of misdeeds committed by her children were forgiven at once when they surrendered themselves at her feet. She was Mother to all her sons in order to relieve them from burden and she prayed to God for their good.

Even animals, birds and petty insects like ants were not deprived from being her children. She was the Mother to them too. A monk used to tease the cats in her country place. Her caring soul had place for them too. Before leaving the village, she once requested that monk to preserve food for them, lest they would go in search of food to neighbours' houses and be beaten up.[15] In another instance, she responded to the call of a calf addressing it as "my son"[16] and untie its knot, and again feed a pet bird with her own hands.[17]

Other Good Qualities of Sarada

Mother was an upholder of eternal humanitarian values, which is the sound foundation of an ideal social atmosphere. She taught us the lesson of paying due respect to those who deserve it.[18] She instructed her nieces to bow down before an aged

---

13. *Śrī Śrī Mā Śatavarṣa Jayantī Saṅkhyā,* Baiśākh, 1361, p. 261.
14. Ibid., p. 289.
15. Ibid., p. 281.
16. Ibid., p. 292.
17. *Śatarūpe Sāradā,* p. 494.
18. Society was divided in ancient India into four *varṇa*s or classes — brāhmaṇa, kṣatriya, vaiśya and śūdra. The brāhmaṇas were regarded as superior to all the three classes and demanded respect from them and not the other way round.

"Kāyastha"[19] devotee and a doctor and to offer regards to them.[20] She maintained that reverence should be duly paid to those who are worthy of having it. This advice can be best illustrated through another instance from her life where she instructs a lady to keep the broom in its proper place gently after use as it will be required in future again.[21] The most ordinary things in our daily life deserve proper care and demand their due worth in serving our needs.

She used to attend to all kinds of prayers of her devotees and tried to solve their multifarious problems in different ways. She realized the mundane pains of ordinary people and offered her blessings on them to ease their suffering for which she even ignored her own pleasure and comfort. She prayed to God for her sons. But once, a female devotee, wife of a doctor asked for her blessings so that her husband could earn well. Surprisingly, we notice her being wonderstruck at this request and declined such a prayer[22] where increase in a doctor's income would mean rise in suffering of ordinary people.

Men, at large, commit mischief but if there is none to forgive them, they would never realize their faults and rectify them. Sarada was compassionate in this respect. Once Swami Vivekananda had dismissed a young servant from work owing to theft. The poor fellow came to Mother and surrendered himself. Mother's heart was moved by pity at his miserable condition. She forgave him at once and allowed him to resume his work.[23] Such was her generosity, but where protest was

19. *Śatarūpe Sāradā*, p. 429. Kāyastha is a caste belonging to Hindu Bengali tradition who are said to be inferior to the brāhmaṇas. Thus it is not usual for them to be respected by people belonging to the brāhmaṇa class.

20. Ibid., pp. 494-95.

21. *Śrīmā Sāradā Devī*, Baiśākh 1408, p. 301.

22. Ibid., p. 287.

23. *Eternal Mother*, 2004, p. 172.

needed, she did so too.

Her nature was soft in general but stern when required. She flew into rage at a drunkard's misbehaviour towards his wife and child. When she spoke out scorning him vehemently, the drunkard regained his senses and feeling ashamed, left the place at once silently. Her tender heart wept at the suffering of the Indian subjects in the hands of the unruly British rulers. Learning that British police had compelled an expectant woman to walk a long way to the police custody, she became furious and wondered, was there no person courageous enough to save her?[24] She even stated that such tyrannical foreign rule would end soon.

Devotion of a wife towards her husband is needed but it is not at all desired that the wife should obey him blindly. Mother asserted herself to be the Universal Mother and even dared not to follow Sri Ramakrishna's words in certain cases. One day when she was about to serve food to her husband, Sri Ramakrishna, a lady came up to her, took the plate from her and placing it before the Master went away at once. The Master was disappointed at this and reminded our Mother not to send his food in the hands of a woman who had a dark, past life. Most humbly, Mother replied that she herself would bring food for him as usual but if anyone addresses her as "Mother," she is unable to turn down her request.[25] What a revolutionary statement she made in those days! Her doors were open to women of social disrepute as well, and once she felt glad to find a lady repentant for her evil past. Sarada accepted her wholeheartedly and initiated her.[26] She taught us the lesson of hating sin, and not the sinner. Another day, a group of people came walking all the way from a distant

---

24. *Śatarūpe Sāradā,* 1985, p. 314.

25. Ibid., p. 314.

26. Ibid., p. 316.

village, Ghatal, situated in Midnapore district to visit Mother at her residence in Calcutta. When they arrived in the late evening, it was time for her to take rest. Hence her attendant informed the visitors of her inability to meet then. When Mother came to know about their arrival, she at once instructed her attendant to bring them upstairs to her.[27] She explained that their hearts are pure and their intention sincere though their feet and clothes were not clean. This was her attitude. Her sweet affection had place for the downtrodden and despised section of the society. Most noticeably, she had no apathy towards the Britishers in general and regarded them too as her sons.[28] As a result, she did not approve the idea of boycotting foreign products.[29]

She may not have borne her own children but remarkably her figure stands out as the most dear mother to all people. Aged Sarada was found to be going in search of milk in the village for preparing tea for her son Girish[30] and fetching vegetables to cook food.[31] She washed their clothes, utensils and other usables. At the request of a young devotee, she removed her veil and fed him with her own hands.[32]

She was efficient in managing household affairs and did not like the misuse of anything. The cows in her house were fed with the skin of the vegetables peeled off. One day, a morsel of fish somehow dropped on the milk, which was going to be consumed by the Master. Following her advice, it was preserved for young boys instead of being thrown away. She used her

---

27. *Eternal Mother*, 2004, p. 170.
28. Ibid., p. 170, *Śrīmā Sāradā Devī*, Baiśākh, 1408, p. 301.
29. *Śrīmā Sāradā Devī*, Baiśākh, 1408, p. 300.
30. Ibid., p. 300.
31. Ibid., p. 293.
32. Ibid., p. 291.

clothes till they could be worn, to the last day. Today's consumerist class should take note of this quality and try to adopt it.

She rendered tireless service to ailing people also. Once, she prepared herbal medicines for a lady who was suffering from a severe skin disease and asked her to apply it on the affected area.[33] Another poor, helpless widow had a sore in her ear, which had turned fatal. Preparing medicines, she applied it on her with her own hands. Later on, Mother arranged for her treatment in a health camp though she breathed her last, turning all effort useless.[34]

Being married to Sri Ramakrishna, she was intimately entangled in world-life situations, but at heart, she was absolutely detached and led an austere life of renunciation. To her, relation between husband and wife is sanctified by religion and is inseparable. It is an eternal bond. Concentrating on the thoughts of the Lord, dedicating everything at His feet and meditating on Him is the only solution to all familial turbulences. She felt that the company of a husband is the most secure shelter to his wife, no matter what the circumstance is. And modesty is the ornament of every woman. It upgrades her stature in the society. She followed the practice of covering her head with her *sāṛī* even in front of her male disciples and devotees as a token of courtesy.[35]

The age in which she lived was gradually witnessing the rays of renaissance. The once-dormant Indian society was steadily reviving her glorious past with the advent of Western culture and education. But it still contained the germs of superstitious beliefs and dogma, which lay beneath the surface. In this age of reform, Mother's life stood as an example. She

33. *Śatarūpe Sāradā*, 1985, p. 567.

34. Ibid., p. 498.

35. Ibid., p. 498.

upheld the triumph of rational thinking, love of knowledge and progressive bent of mind over the prevalence of blind faiths, which still crept in the society. Perhaps, the most striking characteristic of Mother's nature was her belief in the status of all men being equal irrespective of caste or religion and her mind was free from the evils of untouchability and discrimination.

It was a point of time when men still cherished the belief that crossing the oceans to reach the West will make a man lose his position in the society. But, our Mother was significantly bereft of such narrow thoughts. Swami Vivekananda, then known as Narendranath Dutta was granted the permission of travelling to the West crossing the oceans to spread the Vedāntic message of Hinduism as preached by his preceptor Sri Ramakrishna, by Mother alone. With her blessings, he proceeded to attend the World Congress of Religions at Chicago and returned victorious.

Sarada Devi met Miss Margaret Nobel (later known as Sister Nivedita) in the late nineteenth century when the latter came to India to serve "her" under the inspiration of her master Swami Vivekananda. Their first meeting was noteworthy. Both stared at each other for some time. Inner warm feelings evaded the apparent differences of their language and culture. And most astonishingly, Mother, being a Hindu brāhmaṇa widow did take her lunch with Margaret Nobel[36] and her companions. Later, she agreed to sit before a male British photographer for her snaps to be taken at the earnest request of her daughters — Sister Nivedita and Mrs. Oley Bull.

That she had no prejudice regarding caste was evident from the fact that she accepted fruits and vegetables gladly from a Muslim devotee[37] and even shared her meal in the

36. *Śatarūpe Sāradā*, p. 533.

37. *Śrīmā Sāradā Devī*, Baiśākh, 1408, p. 288.

house of a low-caste without the least hesitation. A man belonging to the class of śūdra was known to be one of the corpse-bearers of her paternal uncle[38] and this was possible only due to her broad outlook.

Mother had a profound interest for learning. In her childhood, she had attended school for a short period. Later, Sri Ramakrishna's niece Lakshmi-di used to teach her. In her old age, she taught her own nieces. When Sister Nivedita inaugurated a school to promote education for the girls, she blessed her from the core of her heart and instilled the spirit of learning among the pupils and other devotees.[39] She insisted that young girls and boys should keep their senses alert so as to be aware of the incidents going on in the surroundings wherever they happen to be present.

One notable characteristic of her nature is her sense of rational insight, which marked her as a progressive woman in the late nineteenth century. She was religious in the truest sense but did not at all indulge in dogmatism. That is the reason for her approving women's education in order to be self-sufficient. She was a staunch opposer of child marriage, which was a very common practice in those days. It was possible for her only to advise a woman to educate her girl child first instead of getting her married at a very young age.[40] When that woman felt worried for her daughter remaining unmarried even after attaining the age of puberty. Widows, at that period had to lead a miserable life following austere methods of penance. On the occasion of *ekādaśī*,[41] they were

38. *Śatarūpe Sāradā*, 1985, p. 429.

39. Ibid., p. 430.

40. Ibid., p. 430.

41. *Ekādaśī* refers to the eleventh day in each fortnight. In that age, *brahmaṇa* widows had to undergo many hardships and follow penance on these days as a mark of their chastity and devotion, to the soul of their departed husbands.

forbidden to have any food and even water. It was Mother only who advised a young widow to quench her thirst with water as that little girl fell tired of thirst and hunger.[42] Ma Sarada maintained that it is of no use to make our soul starve or die of thirst following rigid, social norms. It is rather advisable to act according to the dictates of one's conscience in the name of the Lord.

Moreover, she was of the opinion that her disciples must have some food before worshipping God otherwise their concentration will be disrupted.[43] She was also against the convention that celibates should wear white robes and accept vegetarian food only which, according to her help to make their minds turn older than usual.[44] Even when malaria was rampant in the city, she arranged for boiled rice[45] for Sri Ramakrishna in order to fight against the epidemic. Mother felt the need of studying English for the celibates so that they are able to converse with the Britishers and also be aware of the recent on-going events in the country.

Once upon being asked about what should be the conduct of the disciples she answered that the preceptor's advice should be obeyed strictly in spiritual matters, but in case of domestic affairs, it is practicable for them to consult their own reasoning faculty and select the proper path. Her progressive mentality could easily be assessed when she declared that even if one utters any unpleasant truth to his preceptor, that will not involve him in any sin.

---

42. *Śatarūpe Sāradā,* 1985, p. 432.

43. Ibid., p. 531.

44. Ibid., p. 530.

45. Rice made directly from paddy (*Atap Chal*) was considered as an auspicious food which Master used to consume. But (*Siddha Chal*) rice made from boiled paddy was usually not taken by him as it was not regarded as so much pure as the former.

She was very sober in her behaviour. After the demise of her husband Ramakrishna Deva, she cried out aloud only once and thereafter withdrew herself and became silent. When she was about to wear widow's dress, it appeared to her that Sri Ramakrishna in person appeared in front of her only to remind her that his soul has only shifted from one room (world) to another along with his physical departure. These words made Sarada Devi wear a red-bordered *sāṛī* with gold bangles on her arms, which could not be imagined of in those days from a Hindu brāhmaṇa widow.

On one occasion of a *pūjā* in her ancestral place Jayrambati, she distributed *prasāda* to everyone assembled there except a lady. When asked about the reason she replied that unless the lady who was a Brāhmo by faith, asks for the *prasāda* herself, she cannot offer her without the latter's consent.[46] Mother gave due respect to the belief of every individual belonging to a different faith and it was only the vivid application of the doctrine, "As many views, so many paths"[47] propagated by her husband Ramakrishna Deva.

Respectful to Motherland

Those were the days when India wore fetters of bondage under the British regime. The youth were renouncing their homes in the name of the Motherland, to rescue her from the pangs of foreign rule. Mother had profound devotion for India which she once expressed by taking the dust of Jayrambati and touching it on her head said, "Mother and motherland are superior to even heaven."[48] In this context, we notice that

---

46. *Śatarūpe Sāradā*, 1985, p. 537.
47. Sri Ramakrishna's famous dictum was, *Yata mata, tata patha* which means "there are different paths corresponding to different views regarding the way to reach the Absolute."
48. *Śatarūpe Sāradā*, 1985, p. 498.

Mother felt pain at the suffering of the native Indians at the hands of the foreign rulers. The news of suicidal deaths committed by Indian women owing to scarcity of food and clothing shocked her. She regarded that patriotic zeal should be manifested through constructive work like weaving clothes on Indian soil instead of mere agitation with the slogan *Vande Mātaram.*[49] She even wished to have a spinning wheel herself. Many a revolutionary came to seek her blessings before joining the freedom struggle. Two of them later joined the Ramakrishna Order, but could not help evading the vigilance of the rulers. Mother's words, "Live like a leaf at the mercy of the wind . . ." brought peace and confidence in their minds.[50] On another occasion, when Lord Carmichael declared in a speech in 1916 that Ramakrishna Mission should stop sheltering "those mean-minded, cruel revolutionaries" who are a threat to the nation, Mother, after coming to know of it boldly replied that the Maṭh has been established by Sri Ramakrishna's disciples in his name who have renounced their homes to dedicate their lives for the noble cause of serving their land of birth, and that they could never perform any heinous act.[51] Her message was communicated to the Governor-General which made him apologise and withdraw his previous statement.

Sarada Devi stands out to be an outstanding figure of universal Motherhood, equally affectionate to the virtuous as well as the vicious, even down to the lower creatures. All have a secure refuge at her feet. Her open-minded outlook could easily be assessed from her attitude being free from all kinds of bigotry and prejudice — welcoming people from all classes of society and all corners of the world warm-heartedly and even daring to ignore the restrictions of the society and

49. *Eternal Mother*, 2004, p. 171.

50. Ibid.

51. Ibid., p. 173.

even her husband in certain cases without the least hesitation. Being herself deprived of formal education in those days, she was a great patron of learning, especially for girls, for building up their confidence. She was not against the British as a nation but protested against their tyranny as rulers over the Indian subjects. She was also an upholder of assigning due respect to every being and everything which they are worthy of.

Perhaps the most significant point in her character was to overlook the limitations inherent in men and consider them all as her own "children." She upheld the virtue of equality among all her children and in this respect, she ranked superior even to Sri Ramakrishna. A few days before her departure from the mortal frame, she announced her last all-embracing message to mankind with the following words:

> If you want peace, do not find fault with others. Find it in yourself. Try to make the world your own. None is alien, my child, the world is yours.[52]

References

Amalaprana, Pravrajika, *Eternal Mother*, Kolkata: Sri Sarada Math, Dakṣiṇeśvar, 2004.

Gambhirananda, Swami, *Śrī Mā Sāradā Devī*, Kolikata: Udbodhan Karyalaya, Baishakh 1408.

Lokeshwarananda Swami, *Śatarūpe Sāradā*, Kolikata: Ramakrishna Mission Institute of Culture, 1985.

Śrī Śrī Mā Śatavarṣa Jayantī Saṁkhyā, Kolikata: Udbodhan Karyalaya, 2003.

Vivekananda, Swami, *Bhāratīya Nārī*, Kolikata: Udbodhan Karyalaya, 33rd rpt., 2007.

Vivekananda, Swami, *Our Women*, Mayavati, Kolkata: Advaita Ashram, 20th impression, 2005.

Vivekananda, Swami, *Women of India*, Chennai: Sri Ramakrishna Math, 2006.

52. *Śatarūpe Sāradā*, p. 499.

3

Thoughts of Tagore on Man, Freedom and Value

Shefali Moitra

TAGORE was never a moralist in the real sense of the term. He did not propound moral philosophies as Aristotle, Kant or Rawls did. When Gandhi greeted him with the epithet *Gurudeva* (the great teacher), it was not solely for his moral teachings; it was for his general prescription for a full life. Conventionally understood, ethics or moral philosophy is a subject too restricted in its scope to serve Tagore's value-scheme. The question of values and their application was central to his philosophy. The idea of compartmentalizing the discussion on values into separate sections relating to truth, beauty and good seemed artificial and capable only of giving a truncated account. Tagore was interested in outlining a philosophy of life based on the two central themes: freedom and creativity. As a result we receive an integrated system in which the metaphysics of the self and its development takes man from a lower stage to a higher stage of fulfilment. In this journey from non-freedom to freedom man widens the domain of his relationship to the universe. Scientific cultures with their emphasis on objectivity and reason have a valued place in the search for ever-expanding unifications. Ethical values along with socio-political commitments also have an important place. Science and ethics are merely stepping stones; the highest value, however, is given to the creativity of the artist.

Tagore maintained that one could become a true artist only after acquiring certain sensibilities. Unity with the universe cannot be established through any discursive practice, a practice proceeding by argument and reason, or by merely preaching certain doctrines. The unity has to be felt within one's consciousness. In the Indian tradition there are these two acknowledged paths to the realization of the unity in the universe. One is the path of argumentation, followed by the *muni*s, the sages, and the other is the path of poetry, where the unity is something that is felt. This latter is the path of the *ṛṣi*s, the seers. While the *muni*s follow the path of reason, the *ṛṣi*s follow the path of emotion. Tagore was drawn to the second option. Niharranjan Ray observes that Tagore did not

> feel any interest in the ontology and psychology . . . of the Upanishads nor in the problems of textual interpretations; but the attitude of the sages to life and death, to peace and bliss, . . . these would have very great impression on a poet's sensibility.[1]

His philosophy is resistant to investigation by the methodological tools commonly used by the great Indian philosophical systems. He remarks, "we cannot attain the supreme soul by successive additions of knowledge. . . ."[2] Truth has to be apprehended through direct intuition. Tagore was never interested in the traditional epistemological and metaphysical discourses; texts like *Vedāntaparibhāṣā* or *Bhāṣāpariccheda* never attracted him. What appealed to him most was the poetry of the Upaniṣads. Creative emotion is of special

1. Niharranjan Ray, "Rabindranath Tagore and the Indian Tradition", in *Rabindranath Tagore: A Centenary Volume (1861-1961)*, New Delhi: Sahitya Akademi, 1961, p. 228.
2. Rabindranath Tagore, *Sādhanā*, The Macmillan Pocket Tagore Edition, 1979 (first published in 1913), Delhi, p. 31.

importance. His philosophy has a mystic flair grounded in a dualistic metaphysics akin to the Vaiṣṇava metaphysics.

The dominant trend in Indian universities today is to confine the study of Indian philosophy to logic, epistemology, metaphysics and ethics. In other words it is the discursive tradition that dominates the institutionalized study of philosophy. The Sūfī and Bhakti traditions of India, based on the philosophy of love, are thought to be appropriate for departments of literature, not hardcore philosophy. No doubt the teaching of philosophy can be handled in a much more efficient manner if one remains confined to definitions and counter definitions. Domains of experience that relate to emotions seem resistant to precise definitions, and are difficult to handle in a context of classroom teaching; especially where the teaching is monitored by various quantified assessment-procedures. Tagore was aware of this problem. First, we shall have to set our priorities. If our aim is to produce efficient students then the existing focus of philosophy may continue. But if our aim is to seek the truth then our approach to philosophy has to change. Tagore reminds us that:

> Living things have far-reaching relationships with their surroundings, some of which are invisible and go deep down into the soil. In our zeal for definition we may lop off branches and roots of a tree to turn it into a log, which is easier to roll about from classroom to classroom, and therefore suitable for a text-book.[3]

While the discursive tradition of Indian philosophy has been very influential in academic institutions, the common man is hardly aware of the logical sophistications of traditional texts. Tagore thought India had nurtured a long tradition of co-

3. Rabindranath Tagore, "What is Art?", in *Personality*, Macmillan Pocket Tagore Edition, 1980, Kolkata, p. 7 (first published 1917).

existence and constant mutual interdependence among the common rural labouring masses. According to Ray, Tagore believed India had a continuous homogeneous agricultural tradition sustained by Sūfism, Kabīrism, Vaiṣṇavism as well as the traditions of the Auls and the Bauls.[4] All these comments regarding multi-culturalism and mutual interdependence were made by Tagore before India gained Independence. Tagore passed away in 1941. He was aware of the fact that the tradition of love was not the only tradition followed in rural India; there was also the propensity of following lifeless rituals in the name of religion, without caring to pause and ponder upon the relevance of these deeds. In 1923, Tagore wrote:

> The India which keeps her religion shackled in chains of dead custom that refuse to be responsible to reason or to conscience, is *maya*.[5]

Unfortunately, the dead customs of religion continue to enslave the people of India; many of these customs are being upheld in the name of tradition. No doubt, being rooted to a tradition is very important. Tradition gives one a sense of identity, a sense of rootedness, and a sense of belonging. The two key words in the above quote are "reason" and "conscience." Tagore emphasizes the need "to be responsible to reason or to conscience." He thought that the absence of reason and/or conscience led to the conflicts between caste, class, and race. These ills are still dogging our society. Dogmatism, however, is not the sole cause of our cultural decadence.

Tagore also referred to the misuse of power as a cause of India's cultural decadence. He thought that chauvinism, parochialism and misuse of power were at the root of our

4. Niharranjan Ray, op. cit., p. 231.
5. Rabindranath Tagore, "The Way to Unity" (first published in 1923), in *The English Writings of Rabindranath Tagore* (henceforth *EWRT*), vol. 3, ed. Sisir Kumar Das, New Delhi: Sahitya Akademi, 1996, p. 466.

decay. These are to be recognized as evils. The lesson that he learned from our tradition was that only those elements should be perpetuated which can build a bridge between the past and the future of our country, and between India and the rest of the world. Tagore had always been an ardent student of Indian history, and of world history. While gleaning inspiration from history he was selective in his approach. In his article, "A Vision of India's History", originally written in Bangla in 1912, revised and translated by him in 1923, Tagore writes:

> It would be wrong for us, when we judge the historical career of India, to put all the stress upon the accumulated heap of refuse, gross and grotesque, that has not yet been assimilated in one consistent cultural body.[6]

Much of our history was relevant to an earlier time and place but has no significance for modern India. Having just stepped into the twenty-first century the same question still persists: "what are the values that have relevance to modern India?" Tagore valued the traditional ideals that bounded the people of India to one another and to the world. He was not interested in that part of history which was exclusionary in spirit.

Tagore was not willing to accept the Western concept of progress. He felt that in the West progress was quantified in terms of economic affluence. This has remained the yardstick of progress even today. It is the market mantra that works. All our priorities are being determined by the logic of demand and supply. Tagore observed that with the rise of the standard of living human beings were getting more and more selfish, more inhospitable. He thought property begets envy, and people get more self-centred. Tagore remarks:

---

6. Rabindranath Tagore, "A Vision of India's History" (first published in 1923), in *EWRT* vol. 3, p. 457.

> With what is called material progress, property has become intensely individualistic, the method of gaining it has become a matter of science and not of social ethics. It breaks social bonds; it drains the life sap of the community. Its unscrupulousness plays havoc all over the world, generating forces that can coax or coerce peoples to deeds of injustice and wholesale horror.[7]

These observations were made in 1924. They seem to have gained in their pertinence in the present age of globalization. The breaking of social bonds is a major contemporary problem. The so-called material progress referred to above has been attributed to the progress of science. Tagore advocated a limited use of science, confined to man's welfare and not for plundering nature. He had great respect for science, for him science is truth; it gives us freedom in the realm of matter.[8] He welcomed Western science; at the same time he wanted science projects to be guided by moral ideals. For him a world of science minus moral norms is a world of violence and aggression, "fit for the world of tigers."[9]

To live a good life man must learn to minimize his needs. It was not correct to think that the West had acquired freedom with the help of science and technology. Mankind is yet to attain freedom. Tagore speaks of America and says:

> The idea of freedom, which the people in this country have, is the imaginary freedom of a fly shut up in a glass case whose walls are invisible.[10]

---

7. Rabindranath Tagore, "City and Village"(first published in 1924), *EWRT* vol. 3, p. 511.
8. Rabindranath Tagore, "Judgeinent" (first published in 1925), *EWRT* vol. 3, p. 557.
9. Ibid.
10. Rabindranath Tagore, "American Experience" (first published in 1927), *EWRT* vol. 3, p. 593.

While in America Tagore felt that there was a total lack of freedom there. He would perhaps say the same thing about contemporary India. He points out, "leisure and space are the most precious gifts for us; for we are creators. Our real freedom is in the world of our own creation . . .."[11] Western culture is designed on the European science model. Science has gained in power to an extent that it claims control over all our activities. We gladly succumb to this dictatorship since it makes us powerful. The power that is derived from science is merely external. Science produces good constructionists out of men. Tagore distinguishes construction from creation. Construction is always use-oriented, whereas creation has no utilitarian aim; it is an expression of love and joy. To be a good constructionist one needs certain skills and needs to be clever. Science can provide us with superior skills. Tagore does not prescribe the replacement of construction by creation; he only wants to remind us that the former has a limited role to play in our lives. Utility must be allowed only a subordinate position in our lives. The remaining expanse of space must be occupied by creation. For creation we need leisure and space. When Tagore refers to the "total lack of freedom" or "imaginary freedom" in America he is referring to the lack of creative space. He says, "modern civilization has become shudra in its character."[12] "Shudra" is not being used as a caste name. This is a symbolic expression of a man who is merely useful and not recognized for anything above that. "The word shudra denotes a classification which includes all named machines who have lost the decency of humanity, be their works manual

11. Ibid., p. 594.

12. Rabindranath Tagore, "Construction *versus* Creation", in *Lectures and Addresses by Rabindranath Tagore*, Selected from the speeches of Tagore by Anthony X. Soares (first published in 1928), Kolkata: Macmillan and Company Ltd., 1970, p. 70.

or intellectual."[13] All forms of usefulness are being quantified and valued in terms of their market price by our modern civilization. The loss of decency of humanity was at the heart of the crisis that calls for a discussion of value.

Aggressive competition is the corollary of a commercial culture. Competition enters not only in the field of commodities; cultures also compete for capturing supremacy over markets. Presently the globe is being dominated by the blue-jeans and Coca Cola culture. When a culture is threatened by the possibility of being dominated it becomes defensively insular and assertive. All forms of insularity lead to separation and suspicion. Tagore felt that separation and suspicion were signs of weakness. The more a culture opens up to cross-fertilization with other cultures the stronger is its identity. All processes of homogenization lead to dogmatism and non-freedom. The modern cities are monstrosities. Tagore refers to them as poison-centres that create opportunities not ideals.[14] He says:

> Wherever in the world, this modern civilization is spreading its dominion, the life principle of society, which is the principle of personal relationship, is injured at the root.[15]

For him poverty is not the main problem, the problem of unhappiness is the great problem. Happiness can be gained through inner resources. M.N. Roy sharply reacted to Tagore's attitude towards poverty. Tagore's article, "City and Village," was sternly criticized by Roy in his article titled "The Philosophy of Poverty."[16] This criticism seems misplaced since

---

13. Rabindranath Tagore, "Construction *versus* Creation", p. 70.
14. Rabindranath Tagore, *City and Village*, p. 514.
15. Ibid.
16. See editor's note, *EWRT*, vol. 3, p. 975.

Tagore never spoke of poverty as a preferred way of life. He has often referred to poverty as a curse. He is simply in favour of moderation and is cautioning us against seeing trade and commerce as ends-in-themselves. In the age of globalization we are witnessing the primacy of the market forces, and noticing how moral values are riding on the back of economic values. Tagore believed that the inner contradiction of this way of life will be self-destructive. He said:

> Political and commercial ambition is the ambition of cannibalism, and through its years of accumulation it must get ready for its carnival of suicide.[17]

Almost a hundred years after this observation the world community has begun to see the writing on the wall. The commercial trend of civilization, however, is likely to continue for some time longer. Its longevity will be ensured through making certain internal adjustments. "The world has enough for our needs but not for our greed" is a commonly heard expression today. In a similar vein, Tagore asked, "But were we born for this, to extend our proprietary rights over this world and make of it a marketable commodity?"[18] He says the progress of civilization must not be assessed by the wealth and power it has developed, "but by how much it has evolved and given expression to, by its laws and institutions, the love of humanity."[19]

Tagore had faith in the Indian people. He thought they had this inner power within themselves, though in a masked form to give expression to the love of humanity. In order to

---

17. Rabindranath Tagore "At the Cross Roads"(first published in 1918), in *EWRT*, vol. 3, p. 381.
18. Rabindranath Tagore, *Sādhanā*, The Macmillan Pocket Tagore Edition, 1979 (first published in 1913), Delhi, p. 89.
19. Ibid., p. 92.

discover their strength they must critically look back to their tradition and find out what is living and what is dead. Till date this critical exercise has not taken place, we have not put our scriptures to critical, historical and scientific tests. Tagore is pained by our uncritical attitude to our own tradition and he attributes this to "our greed for immediate political result."[20] This observation sounds contemporary indeed. In recent years there has been a tendency to refer to a "golden past," meaning the Vedic era. Subsequent foreign influences have been seen as pollutants to our pure crystalline Vedic culture. Tagore does not offer such a foundationalist reading of Indian history and culture. He observes:

> The evolving Hindu social ideal has never been present to us as a whole, so that we have only a vague conception of what the Hindu has achieved in the past, or can attempt in the future.[21]

In spite of this it is true that "our greed for immediate political result" has led to the tendency of projecting a golden era "of what the Hindu has achieved in the past."

Tagore has always been conscious of our discursive tradition and our poetic tradition in philosophy, as mentioned earlier. Niharranjan Ray makes an interesting observation when he says:

> While men like Bankimchandra, Tilak, Gandhi and Aurobindo went to the *Gita* for their ideological sustenance and emotional and intellectual inspiration, Tagore sought out the Upanishads and the Buddha and Buddhism for his.[22]

---

20. Rabindranath Tagore, "The Way to Unity", in *EWRT* (first published in 1923), vol. 3, p. 468.
21. Ibid.
22. Niharranjan Ray, op. cit., p. 229.

Tagore found a transnational global appeal in the Upaniṣads. At the end of his article, "A Vision of India's History," Tagore quotes from the *Śvetāśvataropaniṣad* (4.1) to explain India's national cultural ideology of peace. He translates the Upaniṣadic *śloka* as follows:

> He who is One, who is above all colour distinctions, who dispenses the inherent needs of men of all colours, who comprehends all things from their beginning to the end, let Him unite us to one another with the wisdom which is the wisdom of goodness.[23]

The catholicity expressed in this prayer is unmistakable. Any distinction that distances one individual from another is a human construct, and is to be recognized as such. These distinctions have to be sublimated. This insight of Tagore is based on his metaphysical thesis of ontological monism. The universe is one; all forms of substantive separation and "othering" are detrimental to human growth and flourishing. The Upaniṣadic prayer asks for unity through the wisdom of goodness, other forms of unity will not do. A unity through fear or any form of unholy alliance is to be despised. The prayer for unity does not imply a glossing over of differences. It is to be noted that the prayer speaks of "the inherent needs of men of all colours." Tagore spoke of a creative type of unity without uniformity. He remarked, "the mistake that we make is in thinking that man's channel of greatness is only one."[24] The state tries to build a kind of unity through uniformity. Thus a kind of efficiency is built that thrives on

---

23. Rabindranath Tagore, "A Vision of India's History", in *EWRT*, vol. 3, p. 458.

24. Rabindranath Tagore, "Nationalism in India", in *Nationalism*, Macmillan Pocket Tagore Edition, 1950, Delhi, p. 65 (these lectures were delivered in Tokyo and then in the U.S.A. in 1917).

impersonality. At some point of history it may be prudent to build efficient political machineries but they cannot be ends-in-themselves.

Many believe that India's problem of diversity can only be solved by a strong political administration. Tagore has always been critical about politics. He felt that political power further enslaves human beings. He remarks, "power grows bloated on the blood of its victims only to perish of surfeit."[25] The enhancement of India's position in the world, among other nations surely depends on a form of empowerment. This could not be an empowerment gained through a power-over-power relation. What Tagore had in mind was some kind of non-hierarchical power to be shared by all. The power-sharing notion is clearly reflected in Tagore's Bangla song, *amra sabai rājā* (we are all kings). The difference between the hierarchical and non-hierarchical power structures could be signified by the two words, *śakti* (power) and *kṣamatā* (strength). Tagore says:

> It is the power of self-sacrifice, the moral faculty of sympathy and co-operation which is the guiding spirit of social vitality. Its function is to maintain a beneficent relation of harmony with its surroundings.[26]

Power is not meant for concentration but for distribution. This is also true in the case of power of wealth and knowledge. Tagore writes:

> Cities have their functions of maintaining wealth and knowledge in concentrated forms of opulence, but this also should not be for their own sake; they should be centres of

25. "Thoughts from Rabindranath Tagore", *EWRT* (first published in 1921), vol. 3, p. 32.
26. Rabindranath Tagore, "To the Nation"(first published in 1917) in *EWRT*, vol. 3, p. 861.

> irrigation; they should gather in order to distribute.[27]

Arguably, the sharing of power and its decentralization fits well with the ideals of democracy. We have of course seen that even democracy may succumb to corruption. Instead of sharing power with the people a democratically elected government can become an instrument serving vested interests. Tagore made scathing remarks about the way democracy was being practised in his time. What he said, in 1924, has proven to be true again and again in different parts of the world where democracy has been embraced. He felt that democracy cannot flourish in a country where greed is admired. He says, "democracy becomes like an elephant whose one purpose in life is to give joy rides to the clever and the rich."[28]

The omnipresence of politics has been the defining feature of Western culture. Right from the time of Plato and Aristotle the West has accepted the primacy of the political. In his *NicomacheanEthics* Aristotle describes politics as the "master science." The post-modernists also call our attention to the omnipresence of politics in all theory-constructions. Post-modernism is said to have initiated a political turn in philosophy. Tagore believed that the ideal of the social man is to be unselfish, whereas politics involved power and selfishness. India, according to Tagore, has always had a social identity independent of her political identity. In his opinion the distancing of the political and the social has been a blessing in disguise. Ray has commented on this stance taken by Tagore. Ray observes:

> Indian history and culture, in his [Tagore's] opinion, was not state-centred but centred round the society as constituted

---

27. Rabindranath Tagore, "City and Village", p. 517.
28. Ibid., p. 513.

> in groups of varying size. His objective was, therefore, *swadeshi samaj,* that is, a self-governing social community and not merely *swadeshi rashtra,* which by and large meant a political sovereign state. Since this was his objective, his main preoccupation was with the problems of social cohesion and co-operation, social integrity and social self-reliance.[29]

A *swadeśī rāṣṭra* or politically sovereign state was what India's freedom struggle was all about. Tagore was all for independence from British rule; he despised all forms of bondage. What he did not support was an identity-politics based on exclusion. Identity-politics leads to a kind of national selfishness and pride resulting in apathy and contempt for the "other."[30] Tagore firmly believed that man's personal identity is dynamic. Any form of identity-politics has to maintain that there is a static core. He remarks:

> In human beings differences are not like the physical barriers of mountains, fixed for ever — they are fluid with life's flow, they are changing their courses and their shapes and volume.[31]

Tagore felt that the Indian freedom fighters had a tendency of overlooking the dynamic nature of human identity. He remarks that the nationalists of India seem to be of the opinion that the task of constructing our social and spiritual ideals has already been done, thousands of years ago — as if the social system has been perfected for all time to come.[32] This led to national selfishness and pride. What followed was an identity-politics that excluded the "other." Tagore observed that

29. Niharranjan Ray, op. cit., p. 226.
30. Rabindranath Tagore, "Nationalism in India", p. 63.
31. Ibid., p. 70.
32. Ibid., pp. 73-74.

geographical boundaries have become imaginary; this is more so in the age of globalization, so also is his observation that "all the different races of men have come close together" due to the facilities of communication. He realized that the world was becoming one through scientific facilities.[33] These facilities give us the means to bridge the gaps between races with phenomenal speed. The increase of proximity, however, may lead to contempt or it may lead to friendship. It is not known "whether the different groups of peoples shall go on fighting with one another or find out some true basis of reconciliation and mutual help. . . ."[34] Tagore was optimistic, he thought the path of conflict would be self-limiting. He had realized that "the moment is arriving when you must also find a basis of unity which is not political."[35] He was of course hinting at the need for a spiritual unity.

What we are witnessing in the present form of globalization is the shrinking of the powers of the State with a proportionate increase in the powers of the market. Political unity is being replaced by some form of market unity. States are expected to make necessary structural adjustments for the free flow of capital. The State machinery is at least a tangible form of power that can be criticized and confronted. Today's market forces, dominated by multinational capital, are much more intangible and irresponsible. Multinational companies also have a tendency to oscillate towards a polarization of power. The basic philosophy of this unified (read polarized) market is competition. It follows the philosophy of survival of the fittest. Tagore felt that competition breeds cruelty and makes the atmosphere thick with lies and deception. His observations have been proved to be true. Today's economic

33. Rabindranath Tagore, "Nationalism in India", pp. 59-60.

34. Ibid., p. 60.

35. Ibid., p. 59.

power is being buttressed by political maneuverings and military force. Tagore refers to a time in India's history when the production of commodities was brought under the law of social adjustments.[36] He advocates the necessity for regulating our needs. However, this regulation should not go to the extent of extreme repression. What he saw in the economic world was that "our appetites follow no other restrictions but those of supply and demand which can be artificially fostered . . ."[37] growth through a utilitarian philosophy of life cannot be sustained. So what we need is a vision for a paradigm shift. Tagore is giving us an alternative. He says, "therefore man will have to exert all his power of love and clarity of vision to make another great moral adjustment."[38] This shift will require a change in the individual's mental make-up along with a commensurate change in his surroundings. He says, "no nation looking for a mere political or commercial basis of unity will find such a solution sufficient."[39] What is required is a spiritual unity of all human beings. Such a unity will lead to the empowerment of men of the world. For this individuals will have to regain their inner strength. Through the worship of science individuals have denied their inner resources, and have taken the easier option of surrendering to organizations. Tagore says:

> Man is reducing himself to his minimum in order to be able to make amplest room for his organisations. He is deriding his human sentiments into shame because they are apt to stand in the way of his machines.[40]

---

36. Rabindranath Tagore, "Nationalism in India", p. 71.
37. Ibid., p. 72.
38. Ibid., p. 61.
39. Ibid., p. 64.
40. Ibid., p. 77.

Tagore wants to reinstate the primacy of human feelings and sentiments, and he also wants to emphasize the importance of human freedom in his proposed paradigm. Man must regain self-reliance.

By emphasizing the importance of self-reliance Tagore is supporting the nurturing of certain virtues. He feels that "what is necessary is purity in thought, feeling and will, and the rest will follow."[41] Institutions are an integral part of social life, but institutions on their own cannot ensure moral practice, even when institutions are based on the principles of justice. What I have in mind is Rawls' theory of justice. Rawls begins his thesis by first looking at the problem of how the basic structure of a well-ordered society can be made just. He gives us a procedure for formulating the principles for the basic structure of a just society. Once we arrive at these principles social institutions can be structured accordingly. Tagore warns us that it is pointless to replace one system by another so long as the participants in the system have not overcome their greed, vanity, jealousy and idolatry of the baser passions. Man's inner strength, his mental make-up, his psychology need to be groomed and developed. Without the proper mental orientation values cannot be achieved. Individuals who have not overcome their greed will in time corrupt the institutions they belong to. Such corruption at a local-level institution will in time contaminate global institutions as well. An attempt to stem the rot by introducing strict principles and policing will be ineffective. Tagore says:

> We have forgotten this simple truth that all systems produce evil sooner or later when the psychology which is at the root of them is wrong. . . . Because we are trained to confound good system with moral goodness itself, every ruined system makes us distrustful of moral law.[42]

---

41. Rabindranath Tagore, "To the Nation", p. 862.
42. Rabindranath Tagore, "To The Nation", p. 861.

Tagore's humanism preaches a philosophy of man free from institutions, church, sects and a personal god. His is a religion that continuously accepts and rejects, thinks and doubts, progresses, changes and evolves. It is for the sake of our growth that we must turn towards the unity of man. All other forms of unity are fragile and centres of covert power. Tagore dreamt of a world that is not fragmented by narrow domestic walls. This, however, is far from the idea of a global village held together by commerce and the internet. The external walls can only break when the internal and internalized mind-blocks are removed. This will involve a long-drawn painful process.

In spite of our incomplete acquaintance with our tradition there is no reason to be diffident. Tagore felt, "some one must show the East to the West, and convince the West that the East has her contribution to make to the history of civilization."[43] This should not be interpreted as a form of nationalistic chauvinism. Tagore was unhesitantly willing to borrow Western know-how on any subject of relevance. His logic was very clear. He said:

> We shall know for certain that just as it is futile mendicancy to covet the wealth of others in place of our own, so also to keep ourselves segregated and starved by refusing the gift which is the common heritage of man because it is brought to us by a foreign messenger, only makes for utter destitution.[44]

An emphasis on man's inner strength may seem romantic and apolitical. Tagore is aware of this criticism and, therefore, remarks:

> I know that it must take time before we can adjust our minds to a condition which is not only new, but almost exactly the opposite of the old.[45]

---

43. "Nationalism in India", p. 66.
44. "A Vision of India's History", p. 456.
45. "The Way to Unity", p. 469.

His religion of peace and love requires a preparedness and strength. Education, he thought, was a prerequisite for freeing the mind. He, however, felt that the moral ideal of unity and love must grow from within a culture. The idea of being a global citizen without any roots in any tradition or culture did not appeal to him. Each tradition gives rise to a specific temperament which is unique to that tradition.[46] He believed that a mind that had gained the profound knowledge of its own tradition "is ready to accept and assimilate the cultures that come from foreign countries."[47] Tagore felt that our system of education is "absurdly un-Indian."[48] He would like the facilities of the lore of the Hindu and Muslim to be included in our culture studies.

The India that Tagore knew was in chains for several centuries. Today, India as a free country is competing for a position of regional leadership, and in many ways she is perpetuating the goals of globalization as a philosophy and praxis of the future. In the present context of aggressive market forces Tagore's prediction that the age of prudence has come to an end, and the age of morality is about to emerge, may seem romantic. Market forces seem to be gaining in authority and for some years to come they are going to be further strengthened. Tagore felt that any social transformation can be beneficial to man only when it is accompanied by a philosophy of man. He was utterly opposed to superficial social changes, strategic adjustments and pragmatic approaches to social problems. Short-term ad hoc arrangements could at times delay the process of degeneration but such moves cannot give a lasting solution. For a permanent solution to India's problem a change in people's mind-set must take place.

---

46. "Nationalism in Japan" in *Nationalism*, p. 32.
47. "The Way to Unity", p. 467.
48. Ibid., p. 467.

Among other things man's inner strength grows through the control of desires and the sublimation of greed. In this context Tagore repeatedly refers to the teachings of the Buddha who paid much attention to the development of character. A total denial of the desires of our sense organs was never recommended by him. The world offers abundant beauty that has to be savoured through our sensuality. For this the virtues of moderation and control need to be cultivated. Tagore believed that Buddha developed the practical side of the teachings of the Upaniṣads. Buddha preached the Upaniṣadic message when he said:

> With everything, whether it is above or below, remote or near, visible or invisible, thou shalt preserve a relation of unlimited love without any animosity or without a desire to kill.[49]

This teaching beautifully brings out Tagore's kind of humanism.

Tagore is obviously referring to man's inner world of personality. Man for him is not merely a physical being or a political being. There is a divinity dwelling in man; it manifests itself through creativity and freedom. The contemporary mind may not be willing to accept the concept of divinity. Tagore, however, uses the notion of divinity in a secular sense of the term; he is merely referring to man's inner potential — his inner world of personality. It would be wrong to associate the realization of divinity with some kind of transcendence of our mundane existence. Divinity is not to be achieved by denying nature. This option of defying the laws of nature is not available to Tagore's scheme of things. Tagore tells us:

> Only by discovering the law and following it, do we become great, do we realize the universal; while, so long as our

49. *Sādhanā*, p. 15.

> individual desires are at conflict with the universal law, we suffer pain and are futile.[50]

Divinity is not a central immutable core in man that burns like an un-flickering flame. Such an interpretation would fit in well with the *Gītā* image of man but not with Tagore's view. In his essay, "The World of Personality," Tagore says:

> They enter the region of the dark who are solely occupied with the knowledge of the finite, and they into a still greater darkness who are solely occupied with the knowledge of the infinite.[51]

Human existence is a mixture of both the finite and the infinite. Both aspects are equally real and they are both equally important. Man has a distinct personality with a will of his own. Similarly, nature has her laws. Man cannot wish away these laws, he has to honour them.

> Things are what they are, and we have to know them if we would deal with them, and knowledge of them is possible because our wish is not their law.[52]

Knowledge of the finite gives us knowledge of facts. Factual knowledge helps us protect ourselves in this world. But the knowledge of facts cannot be an end-in-itself; in addition we must acquire the knowledge of truth. A search for the links of causality leads us to the laws of nature. Tagore says, "law is the first step towards freedom, and beauty is the complete liberation which stands on the pedestal of law."[53] Nature has these two aspects, the aspect of law and the aspect of freedom.

---

50. *Sādhanā*, p. 50.
51. Rabindranath Tagore, "The World of Personality", in *Personality,* Macmillan Pocket Tagore Edition (first published 1917), 1980, Delhi, p. 56.
52. *Sādhanā*, p. 50.
53. *Sādhanā*, p. 82.

Science gives us the knowledge of laws, and creativity acquaints us with freedom. By obeying the laws of nature we gain in strength. The evolution of man that Tagore refers to, time and again, is a transition "from the law to love, from discipline to liberation, from the moral plane to the spiritual."[54] Our knowledge begins by concentrating on physical nature. "We wish to enjoy our food and drink, we hanker after bodily pleasure and comfort."[55] The satiety of these wants is not always conducive to our well-being. While keeping within the physical realm we turn to a more holistic approach and look at the unity of the parts. Gradually our sensitivities are further widened and we look beyond the location of our physical body. The social body then comes into focus. Knowledge takes us beyond the immediate self-centred concern with pleasures and licences, and we learn to consider the welfare of a society as a whole. When we are looking at the physical body as a whole, or we are looking at the social body as a whole, we are still confined to the realm of selfhood which is independent. With the progress of knowledge we pass from the independent self to the unified self, the harmonious self. Tagore refers to the latter as the soul. For the unified self, or the soul, utility has a subordinate role. Relatedness is a central concept in Tagore's philosophy. He holds that just as there is relatedness throughout our bodily organization, similarly, there is an uninterrupted relation throughout the world.

Both the self and the soul enjoy freedom, of course, of different kinds. The self is conscious of its separateness. It enjoys a freedom that allows it to be detached. This is a kind of licence that Tagore calls negative freedom; it is a kind of self-will. He says, "our self-will has freedom up to a certain

---

54. Ibid., p. 88.

55. Ibid., p. 68.

extent. . . . For we are finite on our negative side."[56] Positive freedom or the freedom of the soul leads to harmony and love, it is infinite in nature. Man has been asserting his freedom to be detached in multiple ways. He has been continuously creating symbols that are meant to give shape to his dreams. These symbols have taken the form of empires, of institutions and of theories. In the process man has made mistakes, he has suffered for his deeds. As long as man remains confined to this detached mode of freedom his surroundings seem to be in a state of continuous flux. Man has been given the freedom to be detached from his settings. Anarchy is permitted in the domain of the will. Extreme anarchy and detachment are self-defeating. At some point man will have to search for some principle of integration and harmony. Tagore holds that a lasting integration can only be achieved through the relation of love. Love both integrates and retains the dignity of freedom. When man becomes conscious of his soul, of a personality that is unified within as well as with the surroundings he gains a sense of positive freedom.

The soul gives an individual the sense of oneness; it is the unifying principle. Tagore speaks of two sides of the soul. One is the moral side, and the other is the spiritual side. When the moral power is cultivated to its highest end then the motive-power of action no longer remains; desires and actions are then guided by joy. The moral side of the soul must be cultivated along with the spiritual side. A truncated development of the moral would lead to a kind of narrowness in our attitude, resulting in a regimented practice of moral prescriptions. This is what he calls the "intolerant arrogance of goodness."[57] By simply focussing on the spiritual side of the soul another kind of imbalance is created. Tagore refers

---

56. *Sādhanā*, p. 69.

57. "The World of Personality", p. 69.

to this as the "intemperance of imagination."[58] He says when the two sides of the soul work in union only then can we realize the teachings of the Buddha and appreciate the essence of the *yoga* of action mentioned in the *Gītā*. He has of course a novel way of interpreting these messages.

It is interesting to note how smoothly Tagore seems to glide from a discussion of morals (a discussion of good) to a discussion of spirituality (a discussion of unity) and from there on to creative imagination. He says:

> The teaching of Buddha is to cultivate this moral power to the highest-extent, to know that our field of activities is not bound to the plane of our narrow self. This is the vision of the heavenly kingdom of Christ. When we attain to that universal life, which is the moral life, we become freed from bonds of pleasure and pain, and the place vacated by our self becomes filled with an unspeakable joy which springs from measureless love.[59]

From this citation it is abundantly clear how moral power leads to freedom by taking us beyond the motivating force of pleasure and pain. Desires cannot be the probative force for moral action, nor does reason act as the motivating factor for moral actions. Any mention of a universal life, free from the bonds of pleasure and pain, is likely to bring to mind Kant's moral philosophy where the categorical imperative moves us beyond the domain of desire. Tagore walks far away from the trajectory of reason. Reason is an apt tool for science, since science is concerned with the element of sameness. Kant prescribed the same imperative for all rational beings, since, for him, all human beings were primarily rational beings. In this manner Kant achieved an ethic of universality. Tagore does not associate morality with universal prescriptions. He

58. Ibid.

59. *Sādhanā*, pp. 47-48.

does speak of a universal life. This life would be compatible with Kant's notion of a "kingdom of ends." The unifying principle of such a kingdom is not a rational will present in all. For Tagore the unifying principle would be love for all. This is made possible when we realize that "our field of activity is not bound to the plane of our narrow self," as quoted above.

Love is the perfection of consciousness. Tagore uses the words "love" and "joy" interchangeably; he says: "this joy, whose other name is love, ..."[60] He also believes that love begets justice. In order to love humanity one has to be imaginative enough to appreciate the uniqueness of the "other," and have the generosity to embrace that uniqueness. For Tagore imagination is the most distinctive faculty possessed by humans. This distances him from the Greco-Roman tradition, which considers rationality to be the defining feature of man. Tagore respects the value of being rational but he is not willing to give it the highest position. Nor does he approve of giving reason the role of a regulative principle. He holds: man is imperfect; he can only be perfected with the help of imagination. "Our imagination makes us intensely conscious of a life we must live which transcends the individual life. . . ."[61] Perfection is not to be achieved by becoming more and more rational as Aristotle, Kant or Rawls would want us to believe. Tagore said science is concerned with reason because science is concerned with facts, that is, with the literal. He reminds us:

> In the first place we must keep in mind the fact that man is never literal in the expression of his ideas, except in matters most trivial. . . . The men who are cursed with the gift of the literal mind are the unfortunate ones . . ..[62]

---

60. *Sādhanā*, p. 86.

61. Rabindranath Tagore, *The Religion of Man*, Unwin Books, 1975 (first published 1931), p. 33.

62. *Sādhanā*, p. 59.

It is true that we believe our mind to be like a mirror that pictures the world faithfully. Science does try to capture the world as it is without the intervention of imagination. When Tagore says, "science sets up an impersonal and unalterable standard of space and time" he sounds so contemporary, as if he is depicting the positivistic model of objectivity and detachment. Undeniably the findings of science help us, it has its use and attractions, but the world does not belong to impersonal science; the world belongs to personality. Man's personality creates new relationships with the world. Tagore says, "of course, there is a law of the game."[63] Many games can be played within the rubric of the same laws. The aim of the unification of science taken up by the positivists, and earlier by Plato is not a project that can be accepted by an individual who is a personality in Tagore's sense. Unity and plurality go together. Tagore says, "for the nature of Reality is the variedness of its unity."[64] Man goes wrong in his adoption of scientific findings when he gives science an omniscient and omnipotent status. Science gives us the capacity of mastering geography. Undoubtedly, this is a source of power. It is through this power that we attempt to reach out to people. But our attempt to gain power through this avenue is bound to be superficial. There is another kind of empowerment that we gain through creatively uniting with the world. This latter form of unification is much wider and much deeper.

Connectivity with remote corners of the globe and even with outer space has increased manifold with the advance of science. Technical communication has been upgraded. Nevertheless communication through a scientific vocabulary can only fulfil our purposes of trade and commerce. The soul

---

63. "The World of Personality", p. 53.

64. Ibid., p. 54.

does not flourish on the produce of trade and commerce; it needs more to fulfil its requirements. The distinction made by Tagore between the self and the soul needs to be kept in mind. The soul aspires for an expression through freedom, love, and through joy. Science may seek to "construct" many apparatus for this purpose. Such constructions, however, will not suffice, the soul desires creative expression. A mode of communication, that is qualitatively different from the mode available to science, is necessary. Tagore points out that the citizens of a European science culture "forget that science and law are not a perfect medium for human communication."[65] He further explains his point by using an example from literature. He draws a parallel between the role of grammar in poetic compositions and the role of natural laws in man's various creative pursuits. Poetry cannot be composed without syntax, yet poetry is not equivalent to syntax, it is much more than that. Similarly, man cannot do without science but, at the same time, man needs much more than science; he needs creative space.

That something more that is involved in creativity is the living presence of the poet, the creator. The poet's contribution to a poem, over and above the grammar, is something that cannot be codified or computed. The presence of this extra element can be comprehended, but it cannot be defined. This is why in the very beginning we referred to the fact that Tagore believes that living things have far-reaching relationships to their surroundings; all of which cannot be defined. Communication through intellect is bound to be partial. For a fuller communication we need both imagination and sympathy.

Even during Tagore's time any reference to values, other than the intellect and material wealth, were looked down upon

---

65. "Construction *versus* Creation", p. 75.

as some kind of queer mysticism. He was aware of this dismissive attitude. During his second trip to Tokyo he spoke in detail about the dangers of mimicking the West, which has a science and commerce-centric culture, at the cost of foregoing all that is valuable in Japanese culture. Globalization has the tendency of trying to homogenize world culture. An attempt is made to valorize one culture over others, and subsequently impose that culture as the master model to be followed by all others. There are several corollaries to this process, found in realms other than culture. The valuing of one culture implies the devaluing of other cultures. The other cultures then constitute the periphery and the valued cultures constitute the centre. Thus a core and periphery is produced, not only in terms of culture but also in terms of acceptability and power. So there arises a polarization of power. Since all values are assessed from the perspective of the core, and values not admitted by the core are excluded a closure is instituted. The master culture then does not admit the entry of alternatives. A "closure" also signifies a static condition, meaning thereby that once and for all a decision has been taken regarding which position is to be accepted and which one rejected.

We have already seen from Tagore's approval of the Upaniṣadic prayer that the inherent needs of people of all colours must be respected. Any form of centrism would therefore be unacceptable to him. As mentioned above he is in favour of the decentralization of power, not in the concentration of power. He is aware of the fact that a balance has not yet been struck between the races of the world. At the same time, he also thinks that this balance cannot be achieved through external forces. What is lacking in the relationship of races is a harmony, a balance of beauty and goodness.[66] The problem is that we are being guided by formal

66. "Construction *versus* Creation", p. 61.

laws and regulations. This is so true. We could just take a look at how Kant arrives at his notion of a moral law, the categorical imperative. For this we are required to consult pure reason and pure reason alone. Any thought of joy, of creativity, of beauty, is to be scrupulously avoided while engaging with the categorical imperative. They act as pollutants in the pure exercise of arriving at a moral law — a law meant for all. Similar is the case with Rawls. The procedure for arriving at the principle of justice is by invoking a veil of ignorance. This figurative veil is meant to keep aside all individual differences at the time of discussing what the basic principles of justice should be. Tagore observes:

> The vital harmony is lacking to-day in unity of man, for the formalness of law and regulation has displaced the living ideal of personality from human affairs, and science has taken the office of religion in man's greatest creative work, his civilization.[67]

Tagore talks of religion in a very non-conventional sense. For him "religion can only have its significance in this phenomenal world comprehended by our human self. . . ."[68]

Tagore's repeated reference to man's personality, to his soul, to his creative identity may seem out of place in the contemporary world. He was acutely aware of this possible reaction. He knew he would be excluded from the consideration of all respectable persons; there was always the risk of being labelled an idealist. He never denied being a poet and an idealist.[69] Whatever be the stance taken by Tagore; be it one of a poet or one of an idealist, the problem he is

67. Ibid., p. 62.

68. *"The Religion of Man,"* p. 127.

69. Rabindranath Tagore, "Nationalism in Japan", in *Nationalism*, p. 56.

trying to grapple with has immense contemporary relevance. How do we ensure that the needs of people of all colours are looked after? How can we be global citizens and retain our personality too?

Mainstream ethical systems in the West solve the problem by selecting a representative individual as a prototype of a category of individuals and laws are tailored to the needs of that prototype. So the founding of laws is founded on the principle of homogenization and not on differences. The problem is how to cater to "the inherent needs" of individuals and yet hold them together. Tagore holds that ontologically the universe is one and it is united. At the same time each individual is distinct. Distinction and separation are generally considered to be two sides of the same coin and, therefore, relations are all external, as in the case of contractual relations. This is where Tagore differs from the commonly held view. For him distinctions can be honoured within an integral relation, which is unitary in nature. He succeeds in doing this through his concept of dynamism and freedom.

Once interpersonal relationships are regimented by rigid moral laws and institutions, they cease to be dynamic; they lose their vitality and become mechanical. These institutions fail to facilitate human development. Tagore accepts dynamism in every sphere of the universe. The dynamism is displayed in man's creation. Man constantly rearranges the meanings of things. He says:

> We create not only art and social organizations, but our inner nature and outer surroundings, the truth of which depends upon their harmony with the law of the universal mind.[70]

---

70. "The World of Personality", p. 55.

Human creations may be devastating or they may sustain growth. Their success depends on their capacity to maintain a harmony, harmony being "the law of the universal mind." Tagore says, "the world is a movement, and this movement must not be retarded in any of its parts by a break of cadence."[71] He often refers to the cadence, the music, the dance, the rhythm of the world. For him the originator of this cosmic rhythm is the universal mind, the Creator; Whom he often refers to as God. Tagore was an ardent believer in a Creator of this universe. Man and animal are creatures. As philosophers what we find amazing is the way in which Tagore takes traditional notions of the Creator of the universe, the Creator's design, the self as immortal, the notion of going from darkness to light, as well as concepts like unveiling reality, and he transforms them into a philosophy of his very own. He successfully avoids the essentialist doctrine, the doctrine that there is a fixed inexpressible Absolute. He does not believe that Truth can be conceived through consciousness alone by denying/undermining/transcending all that is not pure consciousness. I believe Tagore's system could stand without this reference to God. All that is needed is a dynamic cosmic principle of harmony to which man is to resonate through his creative deeds. He says:

> Let us seek the religion of this and other people not in their gods but in Man, who dreamed of his own infinity and majestically worked for all time, defying danger and death.[72]

Instead of conceiving of the Creator as pure consciousness Tagore characterizes the creator as pure will. However, this pure will should not be equated with the Kantian will which is purely rational. Had the will been purely rational then

71. "Construction *versus* Creation", p. 61.

72. *"The Religion of Man,"* p. 37.

creation would be subsumed under reason/cognition. Tagore never speaks of the Creator of the universe in isolation, side by side he also speaks of man as creator. In *The Religion of Man* Tagore speaks of the humanity of God and the Divinity of Man. He says:

> Our creations are mere variations upon God's great theme of the universe. . . . Our freedom as a creator finds its highest joy in contributing its own voice to the concert of the world-music.[73]

Thus it is clear that our creation is not a copy or imitation of God's creation. That would be sheer slavery and a travesty of freedom. We are merely to follow the law of the universal mind. The law prescribes the creation of unity through love and harmony. How this is to be done is left to the imagination of the creator. For the expression of this idea of "unity through love and harmony" may require the reformulation of the form. "Forms must always move and change."[74] The wisdom of goodness is not to be actualized through some form of categorical imperative, or through a mode of procedural justice. Creativity is the essence of man. Man is primarily a willing being. His creative will is not guided by reason; the will is guided by emotion, more specifically by the emotion of love. Tagore says: ". . . the freedom of personality has its fulfilment, not in itself, but in other personality, and this is love."[75] This wisdom can only come gradually through the sequential stages of development leading finally to the unity of consciousness. We shall discuss these stages one by one.

---

73. "The World of Personality", p. 55.
74. Ibid., p. 60.
75. Rabindranath Tagore, "The Second Birth", in *Personality*, p. 96.

Tagore had a deep faith in cosmic unity produced by the Creator; at the same time he says that if we want to assert ourselves as individual creators we must first succeed in asserting ourselves as separate, discrete individuals. The creation of the Creator is no doubt unified, but that is not what we are searching for. Tagore does not talk of merely merging into a pre-given unity by simply unveiling the golden disk. No, Man's aim is to create a new unity or else how is he to assert his existence as a creative being? Man's autonomy as a creator develops gradually. Initially men have the freedom, but since they are untutored, and undisciplined the path to creative unity is full of obstacles for them. It is something towards which man has to strive.[76] In *The Religion of Man* Tagore refers to life's story of evolution as a three-stage drama. He also speaks of the continuity of the adventure. To come to an absolute satisfactory conclusion is to come to the end of all things. Difficulties are created, answers are offered, and new obstacles are posed, and the adventure continues.

Evolution of life begins with the introduction of a simple living cell. This was the first triumph over the inert. It must be remembered, however, that when life came out it did not bring any new material into existence. After the advent of life numerous cell units were grouped together into self-sustaining spheres of co-operation. These groups were not mere collections; they displayed an intimate unity which fought to maintain its integrity. This field of life's onward march is a life of ruthless competition. The inception of life simply evolved a value in the existing material. The material world is a world of quantity, its resources are limited. So is its value limited. As the world evolves newer values emerge. Gradually the world displays a value that is not limited within the bounds

---

76. *"The Religion of Man,"* p. 33.

of space and time. "Therefore when the world takes its shape it always transcends its shape; it carelessly runs out of itself to say that its meaning is more than what it can contain."[77]

With the advent of Man evolution entered a new phase; mind and consciousness evolved, but again no new materials were brought into existence. Tagore says that the physiological process in the progress of life's evolution reached its finality in man. Due to man's carelessness he has lost a considerable amount of physiological efficiency. Life has its own rhythm, an excessive use of instruments leads to an un-rhythmic existence. Evolutionary progress at the physical plane has its limitations. Such progress tends to train subjects into specialists; this in turn leads to a compartmentalized existence. Bodily skills keep individuals tied to habits and facilitate standardized productions. For centuries the bee repeats its hive. This does not mean that the bee or the bird has no freedom. Tagore compares the freedom in the physical realm to the circumscribed freedom in a cage. The freedom outside the cage is not an unbridled freedom. The laws of nature still remain operative; in addition a new space is created for self-expression. Self-expression is rule-guided too. It is like the poem being guided by grammar. The poet has the liberty of creating new rules. Man's freedom allows him to continuously create anew. The motive force behind new creation is not a feeling of imperfection, but a feeling of being incomplete. Tagore says, "he is aware that he is not imperfect, but incomplete. He knows that in himself some meaning has yet to be realized."[78]

The first step of evolution, the emergence of life, marked the struggle of spirit of life against inert matter. The second

---

77. "The World of Personality", p. 60.

78. *"The Religion of Man,"* p. 36.

step of evolution, the emergence of the element of mind, marked the struggle of the spirit of life against the circumscription of physical efficiency. Mind has its meaning in freedom. Mind enables man to give up the necessity of specialization and allows him to dream. The origin of man marks a shift in the original creation-drama, the spirit of life recedes into the background and the spirit of man comes to the forefront. Man's creative personality brings about this change in the third act of the drama. No longer is God seen as the only Creator, Man also emerges as a creator. In *The Religion of Man* Tagore writes:

> And from now onwards Man's attempts are directed fully to capture the government and make his own Code of Legislation prevail without a break.[79]

In the realm of the physical and the mental man is related to nature, he has to follow the rules of nature, "but in his self he is free. . . ."[80] In the realm of the self God comes to man as a guest and has to wait till he is invited.[81] This is the region where utter anarchy is permitted. This self has to attain its ultimate meaning which is the soul. The ultimate meaning is attained "not through the compulsion of God's power but through love."[82] The concept of love has a central position; it appears like a leitmotif in Tagore's explanation of values.

An important point to be noted is that with the change of direction in our evolution man is possessed with a Spirit, which has its enormous capital with a surplus far in excess of the requirements of the biological animal in man. Tagore refers to "surplus" as a form of boundlessness, an abundance or

---

79. *"The Religion of Man,"* p. 26.

80. Sādhanā, p. 34.

81. Ibid.

82. Ibid., p. 35.

superfluity. Surplus is a form of energy, a restlessness that seeks expression in varied forms. Man's surplus is dominated by his imagination. "Man has a fund of emotional energy which is not all occupied with his self-preservation. This surplus seeks its outlet in the creation of Art, for man's civilization is built upon his surplus."[83] There are two aspects of Man's activity: one is the activity of his living body, guided by the laws of nature, and the other is the activity of his will. The former aims at self-preservation and the latter aims at self-expression. These two parallel lines of energy tend to meet and mingle.[84] Through surplus Man is transformed from a creature to a creator. He is no ordinary creator, he realizes himself in the perspective of the infinite. As a mark of this superior and final status Tagore uses the capital "M" while writing "Man."

The third stage of evolution is characterized by three cardinal principles — *surplus, creativity* and *unity*. These three are intimately related with one another. Surplus arouses man to be creative and creativity proceeds in a unified manner. All three need constant nurturing or else the individual will slip back to a lower stage of evolution. For Tagore evolution does not mean a linear process where the earlier stages are negated or transcended. Union is followed by separation and vice versa. Tagore says:

> That is why our self has to go through endless renewals. . . . Separateness is the finitude where it finds its barriers to come back again and again to its infinite source.[85]

In the third stage man retains his physical body, his mental faculties and his soul. Each level needs a specific kind of normative prescription. He says:

---

83. "What is Art", p. 81.

84. Ibid., p. 85.

85. *Sādhanā*, p. 72.

> The emancipation of our physical nature is in attaining health, of our social being in attaining goodness, and of our self in attaining love.[86]

By love, Tagore means the Buddhist notion of extinction of selfishness; this is also a state of infinite joy.[87] Needless to say health, goodness, and love mutually enrich one another, and one cannot be had by neglecting the other.

Tagore perceives the existence of unity in each stage of evolution. He asks what the truth of the world is. His answer is, "the truth is not the mass of materials, but their universal relatedness." Personality comprehends and transcends the details of facts, knowledge, feeling, wish and will, as well as the individual's memory, hope, love, activities and all his belongings. The transcendence takes place through a unity; the sublimation is a product of love. The "I" realizes its extension and infinity when it realizes the existence of the other. This unification through crossing of boundaries produces joy.

In the first stage of evolution when units of single cells united through interrelationships there were inexplicable gaps. Tagore says:

> We can never know concretely what this relation means. There are gaps between the units, but they do not stop the binding force that permeates the whole.[88]

A mystery shrouds the unification of parts even in the very first stage of evolution. Tagore remarks:

> Curiously enough, there are men who lose that feeling of mystery, which is at the root of all our delights, when they

---

86. *Sādhanā*, p. 69.

87. Ibid.

88. *"The Religion of Man,"* p. 28.

> discover the uniformity of law among the diversity of nature.[89]

In the second stage of evolution, physical evolution takes place. In this stage unity is achieved through efficiency in a perfect communication with the physical world. Such a unity, according to Tagore, is gained through a "tame and timid rule of faultless regularity."[90] The discovery of regularity gives man a sense of security. The second stage is the stage in which man discovers the laws of nature. The discovery of laws allows individuals to escape from the tyranny of facts. But laws are also tyrannical. Neither facts nor laws leave any room for creativity. By finding the hidden reason of all the caprices of nature, we do not reach the end.[91] Tagore tells us that the unity of law is not self-conscious. No, it is not, but how does that matter? He holds that in the outer world of activity nature has one aspect, but in the inner world it has an altogether different aspect. On this point there is a difference of opinion between the scientist and Tagore. The scientist assures us that nature has only one meaning, "the purpose of a flower is nothing but what is outwardly manifested."[92] All the inner meanings that Man attributes to nature are gratuitous and imaginary. This interpretation of the world of nature is not acceptable to Tagore. He believes that a flower comes with two introductions — one is functional and the other is its identity as a thing of joy. He says:

> That the flower has got its being in the unbroken chain of causation is true beyond doubt; but that is an outer truth. The inner truth is: *Verily from the everlasting joy do all objects have their birth.*[93]

89. *Sādhanā*, p. 81.
90. "The Religion of Man", p. 23.
91. *Sādhanā*, p. 81.
92. Ibid., p. 83.
93. *Sādhanā*, p. 84.

Objects have their birth in joy is an Upaniṣadic idea. The two contrary aspects of nature, necessity and joy can only be comprehended when man reaches the final stage of evolution.

In the third stage of evolution with the emergence of the spirit Man realizes unity in his personality. The spirit of love institutes this unity. The spirit of love resides in the realm of the surplus. Love emancipates our consciousness from the illusory bond of separateness of self. Tagore says, "I become more in my union with others . . . when different personalities combine in love."[94] Love is consummated through harmony, the harmony between freedom and freedom.[95] Such a union is only possible through a freedom of consciousness.

Tagore's understanding of consciousness needs to be understood against the backdrop of this evolutionary drama. Further, his notion of consciousness can only be understood in the context of his philosophy as a whole. Consciousness cannot be understood independently of the body, nor can it be understood independently of society. "All our poetry, philosophy, science, art, and religion are serving to extend the scope of our consciousness towards higher and larger spheres."[96] The scope of Man's consciousness is the measure of his Reality according to Tagore. The unity of consciousness engenders holism. Like all holisms Tagore's holism too is not amenable to analytic explanation.

The three characteristics of the third stage of evolution mentioned above were surplus, creativity and unity. Creativity is the essence of Tagore's philosophy. To remain creative one has to attain a unity of consciousness. The process involves several levels of unity leading to the final stage of creative

---

94. "The Second Birth" p. 83.

95. *Sādhanā*, p. 72.

96. Ibid., p. 16.

unity — unity with the natural surroundings, unity with society, and finally unity with the universe. The creative surplus, which is dormant in every man, has to be cultivated into an expressive medium so that the individual is connected with the universe through a unique harmonious bond of love. Leisure and space are necessary prerequisites for creativity. An efficient world always running after material success lacks this space. Spiritual unity is of utmost importance for Tagore; it is essential for the growth of humanity. By contrast, political unity *per se* is of little significance. Tagore maintains that creation is programmed for a culmination in unity between the finite and the infinite without loss of identity of either partner. God therefore has to wait for man's will to seek harmony with his own. This again is a central tenet of Vaiṣṇavism.[97] Tagore says:

> . . . our God must win his entrance, . . . His armed force, the laws of nature, stand outside its gate, and only beauty, the messenger of his love, finds admission within its precincts.[98]

Through the exposition of the three stages of evolution it should be clear how the notion of value gradually unfolds itself and how all values are ultimately subsumed under the value of love. Love in turn is a relationship, which has to be sustained through creative communication. Tagore says:

> Want of love is a degree of callousness; for love is the perfection of consciousness. We do not love because we do not comprehend, or rather we do not comprehend because we do not love.[99]

Man repeatedly tri es to recreate Nature and to outlive his own nature. Though man is located in the world, he has the

---

97. "The Second Birth", p. 102.
98. *Sādhanā*, pp. 34-35.
99. Ibid., p. 88.

imagination and the surplus to relocate himself. Man dislocates himself in order to relocate himself in a creative relation of unity. The desire to relocate arises out of Man's acknowledgement of his surplus. Thus surplus, creativity and unity work in tandem. There is one single regulative principle that regulates man's creation as well as that of God and that is the principle of harmony, without harmony there will be destruction; in case of the universe there will be *mahāpralaya*, the final destruction. The regulative principles are not rigid formal principles, as mentioned earlier. Tagore writes: "for revealment of idea, form is absolutely necessary. But the idea which is infinite cannot be expressed in forms which are absolutely finite."[100] That is why forms need repeated reformulations.

Tagore does not suggest that all and sundry are creative, imaginative and loving. These are states one has to aspire for, and work towards; man must keep aspiring for and cultivating the creative spirit. This is the only way in which he can establish his dignity of being.[101] Surplus provides the motivation, it inspires us to make a series of new beginnings, this also means a series of deaths; every day is a death, every moment. The concept of the *natun, naba, nabīn* (the new) appears in Tagore's songs (in Bengali) as a refrain to remind us that "Essentially man is not a slave either of himself or of the world; but he is a lover."[102]

Only through love is it possible to accept man as something more than a machine, something more than a śūdra. Love is a unique relation, and an apparently contrary one. In this relation both dependence and independence are respected. "It is the

---

100. "The World of Personality", p. 60.

101. *"The Religion of Man,"* p. 37.

102. *Sādhanā*, p. 13.

high function of love to welcome all limitations and to transcend them."[103] How the two modes of independence and dependence can be combined in a single relation defies logical explanation. Too much dependence could be suffocating, because it leads to a state of pure passivity. One partner is then always at the receiving end. A clinging relation impedes growth. The relation of dependence calls for respect, humility and acceptance. These are all virtues by themselves; they lead to a kind of bonding, but if the relation is one of dependence alone it leads to retardation. No space is provided for the development of personality. The development of personality requires the warmth and security of proximity as well as the independence of self-expression. There can be no pre-given quantitative and qualitative prescription for ideal proximity or ideal independence. All parties involved in a relationship must contribute to the relationship in order to enrich it. Caution must be taken to make sure that a relationship does not fall into customary-practice or dead habit. An ideal instance of the relation of love exists between God and Man when "He gives us from his own fulness and we also give him from our abundance. And in this there is true joy not only for us, but for God also."[104] The world can only be sustained by love among equals. This is the message we get when we find Man is given the same creator-status as God. There is beauty in this universe that does never insult our freedom. We are free to ignore this beauty. The love of beauty cannot be a compulsion. "It is a call to us, but not a command."[105]

Tagore's philosophy may be categorized as a form of process philosophy. The onward journey of man is never-

---

103. *Sādhanā*, p. 95.

104. "The Second Birth", p. 102.

105. *Sādhanā*, p. 96.

ending. For harmony is to be achieved through a relation of creative unity with the universe. The relation has also to be nurtured through creativity; there is never a static moment of completion. Harmony is to be established entirely by human efforts. The grace of God has no role in this journey. The synchronization of Man's creation with that of God is comparable to a *jugalabandī* as found in Indian classical music. It is like a turn-by-turn ball game. One musician plays a complicated piece to be copied by the other, in a manner of acceptance and appreciation. The second player plays an equally complicated piece to be appreciated and reproduced in the same way by the first player. In this way there is an appreciation and counter-appreciation of tunes without any sense of victory. A *jugalabandī* is meant to bring forth artistic participation resulting in the sharing of creative joy. By reproducing a tune a moment of identification and bonding is experienced. This is followed by an innovative moment through which autonomy is experienced. Autonomy and identification are the two dimensions of a single relation. Thus autonomy is directed not with the purpose of subjugating the other but with the purpose of embracing the other. Autonomy is prized as a value both in oneself and in others. That is why an embrace is not meant to smother the other. In Tagore's system both the value of love and the value of autonomy are upheld; the value of the autonomy of the individual is respected and, at the same time, love for all is also given primary importance. To be a lover one must overcome selfishness. One must also have the courage, the strength to pursue the goal of being creative and respecting the creativity of others. In the process that emerges through man's onward journey Truth, Beauty and Good mix and mingle in an inextricable manner. So in the final analysis value is not solely associated with morality or with aesthetics or with religion.

The values that are associated with each dimension of life have to be gained in unison. It is not that each set of values are gained separately and then somehow they are put together. A unity and harmony of values need to be realized.

References

Ray, Niharranjan, "Rabindranath an Artist in Life", in *Rabindranath Tagore: A Centenary Volume (1861-1961)*, New Delhi: Sahitya Akademi, 1961.

Tagore, Rabindranath, "American Experience", in Sisir Kumar Das (ed.), *The English Writings of Rabindranath Tagore (EWRT)*, vol. 3, New Delhi: Sahitya Akademi, 1996.

———, "At the Cross-Roads", in *EWRT*, vol. 3.

———, "A Vision of India's History", in *EWRT*, vol. 3.

———, "City and Village", in *EWRT*, vol. 3.

———, "Creative Unity", in *EWRT*, vol. 2. 1996.

———, "Construction *versus* Creation", in *EWRT*, vol. 3.

———, "Judgment", in *EWRT*, vol. 3.

———, "Nationalism", in *EWRT*, vol. 2

———, "Personality", in *EWRT*, vol. 2.

———, "Sādhanā," in *EWRT*, vol. 2.

———, "The Religion of Man", in *EWRT*, vol. 3.

———, "The Way to Unity", in *EWRT*, vol. 3.

———, "Thoughts from Tagore", in *EWRT*, vol. 3.

———, "To the Nation", in *EWRT*, vol. 3.

4

Swami Vivekananda's System of Practical Vedānta and its integral Values

Madhumita Chattopadhyay

THE concept of "value" in Vivekananda literature is very complex. It carries with it a vision of well-articulated world-view which takes note of the social, moral, cultural aspects of the individual. In the *International Encyclopaedia of Ethics*, value has been defined as "what makes actions, character traits and objects good or bad." Values are of great significance in the life of the individual, since without them human life would turn out to be "a bland and textureless existence without differentiation." The contribution of Swami Vivekananda in the world religion is to highlight the essence of Hindu religion to the Western people — to focus on the true spirit of our philosophical teachings. The philosophical position which he upholds is the Vedānta system, but he gives it a new form which he designates as "Practical Vedānta." The objective of the present paper is to explore the values that underlie such practical Vedānta system. The paper will consist of two parts. In the first part we will discuss the nature of Practical Vedānta as formulated by Swami Vivekananda and in the second part we will try to delineate the values upheld by this system.

The epithet that Swami Vivekananda attaches to Vedānta is "practical." Before proceeding to discuss what Swamiji wanted to highlight by adding this attribute, let us take a look at what the term "Vedānta" really signifies. Of the six orthodox systems of Indian philosophy, Vedānta is the most popular one. Derived from the two words *veda* and *anta* the word "Vedānta" conveys two senses depending on two separate meanings of the term *anta*. *Veda* means knowledge and *anta* can mean either (i) end, conclusion or (ii) essence, core or inside. Accepted in the first sense the term Vedānta means "culmination of knowledge" and taken in the second sense the alternative meaning will be "the essence of the Vedas." The word "Vedānta" is, generally, accepted in the latter sense and stands for the Upaniṣads. In this sense, texts like the Upaniṣads, the *Gītā* and the commentaries on the *Brahma-Sūtra* are taken to constitute what we understand as the Vedānta philosophy. Accordingly any philosophy which accepts the fundamental principles of the Upaniṣadic thoughts, is considered as Vedānta. The Upaniṣadic principles, however, have been interpreted in different ways. In accordance with such different interpretations we have different systems of the Vedānta philosophy like the Advaita Vedānta of Śaṅkara, the Viśiṣṭādvaita of Rāmānuja, the dualism of Madhva, the Dvaitādvaita system of Nimbārka, etc. Starting from the time of Śaṅkara till the middle of the eighteenth century there had been at least twelve different sub-sects of Vedānta system depending on the differences in the interpretation of the *Brahma-Sūtra*. Swami Vivekananda in his philosophy acknowledged the merits of all the different Vedāntic schools like the Dvaita, Viśiṣṭādvaita, Advaita and Dvaitādvaita, but regarded the Advaita Vedānta system of Śaṅkara as the definitive formulation of Vedānta philosophy and "That Thou art" as the Supreme Principle and all the other schools of Vedānta as steps toward that Advaita system.

Though Swami Vivekananda had great admiration for Śaṅkara's Advaita Vedānta system, he saw its defect to lie in the thought that the whole of the Upaniṣads taught a single message, viz. that truth consists in monism or advaitism alone and nothing else. Any passage bearing the dualist idea was twisted and its meaning was interpreted differently to fit in with the Advaitic tune. This approach was not accepted as satisfactory by Swami Vivekananda. He did not believe in the fragmentation of the Vedānta philosophy into different systems or schools. On the contrary, he thought that Vedānta is indeed Vedānta and it may be Advaitist or Dvaitist. The Advaitists cannot reject Dvaitism as un-Vedāntic. Accordingly while speaking on the Vedānta philosophy, Swami Vivekananda did not bring in the notions of non-duality, qualified non-duality or duality-non-duality. He put stress on the comprehensiveness, all-embracing character of Vedānta. This all-comprehensive character of religion was shown to him by his Master Sri Ramakrishnadeva who not only preached the idea that all the different religions are different expressways to the same Godhead but also exhibited the sameness of all religions through his own experience. To be brief, the Vedānta of Swami Vivekananda was that variety of monism which was exhibited in the lifestyle of Sri Ramakrishnadeva and which was absolutely necessary for the-then scenario of Indian society. While commenting on Swamiji's Vedānta, Sister Nivedita observes:

> His doctrine was no academic system of metaphysics, of purely historic and linguistic interest, but the heart's faith of a living people, who have struggled continuously for its realization, in life and in death, for twenty-five centuries. Books had been to him not the source and foundation of knowledge, but a mere commentary on, and explanation of, a life whose brightness would without them have dazzled him, and left him incapable of analysing it. It had been this

> same life of Ramakrishna Paramahaṁsa that had forced upon him the conviction that the theory of Advaita, as propounded by Śaṅkarācārya — the theory that all is one and there is no second — was ultimately the only truth.[1]

Thus Vedānta has not been restricted to the monistic views alone but has taken on a new form in his hand. This new form has been designated differently by different interpreters - some regard it as Neo-Vedānta, but Swami Vivekananda himself described it as "Practical Vedānta."

The *Concise Oxford Dictionary* points out the meaning of the term "practical" as "inclined or suited to action rather than speculation" and also "feasible." Used in the context of knowledge, as opposed to theoretical, the word "practical" means applied, empirical, pragmatic, and work-a-day. "Practical" as an adjective contains the sense of pragmatic, matter-of-fact, down-to-earth, hard-headed, realistic, utilitarian, and expedient. Swami Vivekananda accepted the term in these senses and expressed his thoughts and ideas accordingly. In fact turning Vedānta from a theoretical, spiritual doctrine to a doctrine applicable to all spheres of practical mundane life, is the contribution of Swami Vivekananda. He did not view Vedānta as a sort of intellectual gymnastic but as contributing to the betterment of the individual, to whatever station of duty he may be in. The Vedāntic scriptures suggest that liberation can be attained only by the monks or the *saṁnyāsins*, that is, by those who practise the fourfold scheme of *sādhanā*. Accordingly the recluses or the monks were regarded to be primarily eligible for the study of the Vedānta and the householders were only secondarily eligible. But Upaniṣadic passages discussing the doctrine of the *Brahman* or Absolute carry the suggestion that the meditation on the Absolute can be done by any person at any stage of life. This

1. *The Master as I Saw Him*, p. 192.

aspect of the Upaniṣadic thought impressed Swami Vivekananda and he was led to think that any action performed at any vocation of life is an action of the *Brahman*. This is the first and foremost aspect of his Practical Vedānta. The goal of this Vedānta had been envisaged by Swamiji as follows:

> What we want is progress, development, realization. No theories ever made men higher. No amount of books can help us to become purer. The only power is in realization, and that lies in ourselves and comes from thinking. Let men think. A clod of earth never thinks; but it remains only a lump of earth. The glory of man is that he is a thinking being. It is the nature of man to think and therein he differs from animals. I believe in reason and follow reason having seen enough of the evils of authority, for I was born in a country where they have gone to the extreme of authority.[2]

Thus emphasis on reason alone and not on any authority constitutes the Vedāntic teaching, the basis of ethics of such a system.

The chief aim of Vivekananda's Vedāntic philosophy has been to carry the messages of Vedānta out to the practical life of man. He sincerely believes that the worth of any theory whatsoever lies in its practical applicability. "If it be absolutely impracticable no theory is of any value whatever, except as intellectual gymnastics."[3] Accordingly throughout his lectures on Practical Vedānta, he tried to show the worth of Vedānta philosophy, specially the Advaita Vedānta philosophy, in every sphere of life emphasizing the fact that for it, it is not needed to lead the life of a recluse or retire into the forests, but can be

---

2. *Complete Works of Swami Vivekananda* (henceforth *CWSV*), vol. 4, p. 336.

3. *CWSV*, vol. 2, p. 291.

realized in every aspect of ordinary empirical life. Let us quote Swamiji:

> In various Upaniṣads we find that this Vedānta philosophy is not the outcome of meditation in the forests only, but that the very best parts of it were thought out and expressed by brains which were busiest in the everyday affairs of life.[4]

He cites the example of *Bhagavad-Gītā,* where to teach Arjuna the essence of the Vedānta philosophy Lord Śrī Kṛṣṇa has chosen the battlefield. Every page of *Gītā* speaks of intense activity. So Vivekananda remarks:

> This is the secret of work, to attain which is the goal of the Vedānta. Inactivity, as we understand it in the sense of passivity, certainly cannot be the goal.[5]

This activity-oriented interpretation necessarily shifts the direction of Vedānta philosophy from the spiritual plane to the practical one. It was so far believed that the proper understanding of the Vedāntic views helped man proceed towards liberation. That is, the application of the Vedānta was restricted to the spiritual sphere, to the attainment of liberation and that through the realization of the nature of the Absolute; and it had no application to the other spheres. But it was Vivekananda who convinced people that the Vedāntic teaching can be applied to all the spheres of life, to the educational institutions, to the judge's office, to the fisherman's bastion, to the huts of the poor. And by such application the quality of life of the respective persons can be improved. When the individual realizes the Vedāntic principle of *so 'ham,* every action that he performs will be considered by him as the action of the Absolute and so it will be performed with much care and affection than ordinarily done and as a

4. *CWSV,* vol. 4, p. 292.
5. Ibid.

consequence the result will be much better. While commenting on the "practical" aspect of Vedānta, Vivekananda remarks:

> What I think as practical is to me the only practicality in the world. If I am a shopkeeper, I think shop-keeping the only practical pursuit in the world. If I am a thief, I think stealing is the best means of being practical; others are not practical. You see how we all use this word practical for things we like and can do. Therefore, I will ask you to understand that Vedānta, though it is intensely practical, is always so in the sense of the ideal. It does not preach an impossible ideal, however high it be, and it is high enough for an ideal. In one word, this ideal is that you are divine, "Thou art That." This is the essence of Vedānta.[6]

Belief in this practicality will bring in self-confidence in the mind of the individual in such a way that whatever act he performs, will be of the highest order:

> Believe, therefore, in yourselves, and if you want material wealth work it out; it will come to you. If you want to be intellectual, work it out on the intellectual plane and intellectual giants you shall be. And if you want to attain to freedom, work it out on the spiritual plane and free you shall be and shall enter into *nirvāṇa*, the Eternal Bliss.[7]

Thus in Vivekananda's thinking the merit of the Practical Vedānta lies in freeing the Vedāntic teachings from the forests and the mountain caves and applying it to every sphere of empirical life. Practical Vedānta is not a mere intellectual discipline where we are to apply our intellect. The non-intellectual emotional aspect of the individual receives recognition in the Practical Vedānta for it has been assigned some function in an individual's life. No amount of intellect can help us to reach God. We have to feel the presence of the

---

6. *CWSV*, vol. 2, p. 294.
7. Ibid., vol. 1, p. 427.

Absolute in us and then we can work for others. In his conversation with his disciple Sarat Chandra Chakraborty he raises the question, what is the utility of reading the texts of the Vedānta? We have to apply the truths of absolute monism in the practical life. Swamiji believes that it is his task as distinguished from the Advaitin Śaṅkara to carry and apply the truths of Advaitism to every corner of the society:

> What is the use of merely reading the Vedānta? We must prove the truth of pure advaitism in practical life. Śaṅkara left this Advaita philosophy in the hills and forests while I have come to bring it out of those places and scatter it broadcast before the workaday world and society. The lion-roar of Advaita must resound in every hearth and home, in meadows and groves, over hills and plains.[8]

In a lecture delivered in New York on "The Real and the Apparent Man" Swamiji hopes to spread the thoughts of the Upaniṣads throughout the world in such a way that everyone can realize in his own self the truth "Thou art That":

> Instead of living in monasteries, instead of being the exclusive possessions of sects and of a few of the learned, they will all be sown broadcast over the whole world, so that they may become the common property of the saint and the sinner, of men and women and children, of the learned and the ignorant. They will then permeate the atmosphere of the world, and the very air that we breathe will say with every one of its pulsations "Thou art That."[9]

But why is Swamiji so much insistent on applying the Vedānta doctrines to the practical empirical life? The answer may be found in the values underlying this doctrine. The value that is focused here is *greatness of heart* exhibited through love, sympathy, catholicity of outlook, respect for each other, and

8. *CWSV*, vol. 7, p. 162.
9. Ibid., vol. 4, p. 288.

all these improve the relation between man and man and thus work for the betterment of society. The consequence of such a doctrine will be that it will hinder the degradation of mankind and will work for the upliftment of their status. "Man should not be degraded to worldly slavery, but should be raised up to God."[10] The old concept of exclusiveness on the basis of castes is rejected and casteism is given a new interpretation so that it is no longer looked upon as something detrimental to the progress of the society but is helpful for the establishment of an equalitarian social order.

It may be noted here that Swami Vivekananda valued socialism as it is conceived in the West, because it contained the possibility of being understood in terms of monistic humanism which is the only way for the salvation of human beings. Though in one of his letters addressed to Mary Hale he justified his preference for socialism by saying: "I am a socialist not because I think it is a perfect system, but half a loaf is better than no bread,"[11] he did not consider the socialism as was present at his time, to be a perfect system. It is less than perfect, and has to be made perfect by blending it with the Advaitic ideal. He conceived of an ideal socialistic society as one in which the knowledge of the priest period, the culture of the military, the distributive spirit of the commercial and the ideal of equality of the labourer will be kept in tact, minus their evils. His notion of socialism has been very much different from the notion of socialism that has been put forward by Karl Marx and his contemporaries. From the Marxist point of view the essence of socialism lies first in the state ownership and then in social ownership of property. The French Socialists also emphasized the need only for the socialization of private

10. *CWSV*, vol. 4, p. 299.

11. Ibid., vol. 6, p. 382 quoted by Amiya Kr Mazumdar, *Understanding Vivekananda*, p. 88.

property. However, in the ultimate analysis, that society must be the owner of all property has been the common standpoint of French Socialism and Marxism. Both schools feel that private ownership of property gives rise to discrimination among classes in the society and thereby the social harmony is lost. Swami Vivekananda did not comment on the ownership of property — the question of politics and economics were not discussed by him in detail; he concentrated chiefly on social harmony. He felt that so long as there is discrimination among the masses on the basis of caste, culture or attainment of knowledge, society cannot make progress. So, on the basis of his spiritual understanding of the Vedānta, he argued for equality among the different classes in society. He declares:

> None can be Vedāntists and at the same time admit of privilege to anyone, either mental, physical or spiritual, absolutely no privilege for anyone.[12]

Herein lies the essence of his socialistic thinking. In respect of the realization of the ideal, the Reality, he finds that there can be no inequality among individuals, in respect of caste, class, sex — everyone is not only eligible for the attainment of the highest ideal, there is presence of the ideal in all.

The same power potentially is in every man, only the extent to which that power is manifested varies from one individual to another. So, there cannot be any discrimination among people. The knowledge of the Absolute is embedded in every soul, even in the ignorant, though it may not be manifested. So, there cannot be any inherent distinction between the learned and the ignorant, all difference is due to external factors like opportunity, environment, etc. So, given the adequate opportunity, the latent power will be manifested in

---

12. *CWSV*, vol. 1, p. 423.

the same manner. The same is true in respect of other differences on the basis of wealth, strength, intellect and even on spirituality. Not only in the context of individuals, even in the level of nations there can be no question of superiority and inferiority. Vivekananda urged his people and the people of the world as a whole to work for the abolition of all privileges. The work of the Advaita, according to him, is to break down all these privileges; though he is aware that it is the hardest work of all. The Advaita view encourages us to look upon our fellow being with kindness and compassion. The wise sees the one God in all beings and develops the quality of equal mindedness towards all. So, it is through the spiritual upliftment that all kinds of discrimination, inequality and repression can be removed and we can build-up a liberated, free society open to all. In other words, the change will come from within the individual himself. Swami Vivekananda strongly believed that this will be possible only if the younger generation can identify themselves with the progress of the society and consider their endeavour as part of a larger and all-extensive religious revival. The only way to get rid of all sorts of social and other evils is through reviving the latent spirituality of the individual mind in the way as has been advised in the Vedānta. If we realize the celebrated dictum of the Advaita philosophy, *tat tvam asi* (That Thou Art) we can find out the essence of socialism. Since the individual soul is basically identical with the Universal Soul, there cannot be any difference between one individual and the other. Even the most ignorant can be the messenger of God just as the most intelligent one. Since every man is potentially divine it follows that the same Power, the same Consciousness lies in everyone of us. Hence to think that one class is in a better privilege position than the other is not justified. In other words, according to Vivekananda, the socialistic outlook should not have to be imposed from outside — it is already there — we have only to bring it to focus.

Thus seen, Swami Vivekananda's outlook on socialism is spiritualistic in essence, and not based on any materialistic claims. He embarked upon the model of Practical Vedānta to bring about an upliftment in religion and not to mobilize economic changes. His advice has been to deluge India with spiritual ideas before flooding her with socialistic and political ideas. He advised in this way for he could very well feel the pulse of Indian people. In India religious life occupies the focal position, so to say, it is the keynote of the whole music of national life. Accordingly if anyone plans to give up religion and replace it with politics or anything else for the betterment of society, the result will be very grave. So, anything that has to be done in Indian context is to be done with the help of religion.

Swami Vivekananda was pained by the different forms of inequality that are existent in Indian society. He noticed with unerring insight that the so-called upper three classes of society, namely the brāhmaṇas, the kṣatriyas or the warriors and the traders all derived their fortune and position through the exploitation of the lower class, that is the class of the śūdras, the downtrodden. But with his prophetic vision, Swami Vivekananda observed that this will not continue for ever — a change has to come and that will be definitely through the upliftment of the lower class:

> Human society is in turn governed by the four castes — the priests, the soldiers, the traders and the labourers . . . the first three have had their day. Now is the time for the last — they must have it — none can resist it.[13]

What is novel in his observation is that the śūdras or the lower

13. *Letters of Swami Vivekananda*, pp. 317-18.

class will rise up, not losing their identity but retaining their śūdrahood. The cultivator, the fisherman, the clay potter will become more efficient in their profession. The people of the upper class will have to express sympathy for the so-called lower and downtrodden people and at the same time feel themselves as belonging to the same body as that of the śūdras. Through such process of give and take the barrier between the three classes will gradually disappear. So, in Vivekananda's insight the only way to remove the Indian problem of class division is by spreading education among the masses so that the position of the lower class can be raised up to the level of the upper class. To quote him:

> The ideal at one end is the brāhmaṇa and the ideal at the other end is the caṇḍāla, and the whole work is to raise the caṇḍāla up to the brāhmaṇa. Slowly and slowly you find more and more privileges granted to them.[14]

Thus the resolution of class conflict does not demand the bringing down of the higher but the arousal of the lower up to the level of the higher. This is the characteristic of Vivekananda's socialism which is based not on historical determinism, but on education, love, and other qualities of the mind.

Practical Vedānta also encourages the removal of the discrimination on the basis of sex and welcomes upgradation of the position of women in the society. In the age when the women were considered as burden to the family and to the society and were denied any status of their own, Swamiji attempted to fight for their upliftment in an Advaitic way. Swamiji identified disrespect for the women to be the cause of the degeneration of the society. To quote Swamiji:

---

14. *CWSV,* vol. 3, p. 220.

> The principal reason why your race has so much degenerated is that you have no respect for these living images of Śakti.[15]

So to disprove this he put forward arguments from the standpoint of practical Vedānta. Since the Absolute *Brahman* is present in every individual being, irrespective of whether he is a male or a female, we have to open the possibility of providing equal opportunity to all, especially by giving them scope for proper education. Education will not only improve the position of the women but it will enhance the society as a whole. His argument is that in the highest reality of the *Para-Brahman*, there is no distinction of sex. We notice this only in the relative plane. And the more the mind becomes introspective, the more that idea of difference vanishes. Ultimately, when the mind is wholly merged in the homogeneous and undifferentiated *Brahman*, such ideas as this is a man or that a woman do not remain at all. Therefore, though outwardly there may be difference between men and women, in their real nature there is none, and there can be no difference between them in respect of apprehending the *Brahman*. If a man can be a knower of *Brahman*, why cannot a woman attain the same knowledge? And Swami Vivekananda hoped that if even one amongst the women became knower of *Brahman*, then by the radiance of her personality thousands of women would be inspired and awakened to truth and that will lead to the great well-being of the country and society at large. Thus Practical Vedānta preaches the socialist ideal in its optimum. In the first of the series of lectures on "Practical Vedānta," Swami Vivekananda points out that there is neither man nor woman or child nor difference of race or sex, nor anything that stands as a bar to the realization of the ideal, because Vedānta shows that it is realized already, it is already

15. *CWSV*, vol. 7, p. 215.

there.[16] So the socialistic outlook should not have to be imposed from outside. It is already there, we have only to bring it to focus.

The doctrine of Practical Vedānta also paves the way for socialistic ethics. The celebrated dictum "That art thou" enables the individual to realize that the individual soul is basically identical with the Universal Soul, and hence there cannot be any difference between one individual and another. In society we come across inequalities of various types. The teaching of the Advaita is to break down all privileges. The solution of our problem of division among masses on the basis of caste can be found not in bringing down the higher but by raising the lower up to the level of the higher:

> The ideal at one end is the brāhmaṇa and the ideal at the other end is the caṇḍāla, and the whole work is to raise the caṇḍāla up to the brāhmaṇa. Slowly and slowly you find more and more privileges granted to them.[17]

The bedrock of this socialism is freedom and not historical determinism. Although Vivekananda's goal was achievement of a kind of classless society, he did not encourage class struggle. His philosophy was a philosophy of love, a philosophy of sacrifice.

The Advaita Vedānta teaches us that the same divine nature is present in all — in the lowest worm as well as in the highest human being. But the Absolute or *Brahman* is not manifested in the same way among all. There is hierarchy of being. The worm is the lower form, and man is the higher form of manifestation of the Divine. Accordingly the advice, "love everyone as your own self" gets a new significance in the Vedāntic teaching. It follows that in injuring others I am

---

16. *CWSV*, vol. 4, p. 295.
17. Ibid., vol. 3, p. 220.

injuring myself, in loving others I am loving myself. When I realize myself among all beings in this way, I am able to transcend the shortcomings like hatred, jealousy, etc. which are associated with the narrow individualistic sense of the ego.

Vivekananda believes in a gradual spiritual transformation of the individual — from its lower individual form to the infinite Existence-Consciousness-Bliss. As such he does not accept the Darwinian interpretation of "evolution" in terms of "struggle for existence," and "survival of the fittest" as applicable in all spheres. Though it may be true at the lower level, at the level of animal kingdom; at a higher level, i.e. the level of human kingdom, where there is manifestation of rationality, there is reversal of this law. In the human level, which he designates as rational human kingdom, there cannot be any progress through harming the interest of others. History teaches us that the greatest evolution of mankind is attained through sacrifice — one who sacrifices one's own self for the benefit of others, is considered to be the greatest among mankind:

> The highest evolution of man is effected through sacrifice alone. A man is great among his fellows in proportion as he can sacrifice for the sake of others, while in the lower strata of the animal kingdom, that animal is the strongest which can kill the greatest number of animals.[18]

Thus it is not competition among individuals that explains evolution and progress in the human level. It is rather the potential divinity of man that determines the course of progress. The progress of man is not from error to truth but from truth to truth, from lesser truth to greater truth. In the final stage of spiritual evolution and progress, man realizes

18. *CWSV*, vol. 7, p. 154.

himself as *Brahman* as Universal Consciousness. But the individual is not thereby lost, he rather finds himself integrated with the Universal Spirit and Universal Consciousness; he attains a richer life and is not swallowed up by an all-engulfing Absolute. So this all-encompassing love brings a new meaning to his life. Integrated with the Absolute, the Universal Spirit, the individual realizes his true self. To quote from the lectures on Practical Vedānta:

> But the Vedāntic idea is not the destruction of the individual, but its real preservation. We cannot prove the individual by any other means but by referring to the universal, by proving that this individual is really the universal. If we think of the individual as separate from everything else in the universe, it cannot stand a minute. Such a thing never existed.[19]

In this process of transgression, education and culture, concentration and meditation play important roles. Swami Vivekananda in his writings points out that:

> Whatever may happen in the lower strata of Nature's evolution, in the higher strata, at any rate, it is not true that it is only by constantly struggling against obstacles that one has to go beyond them. Rather it is observed that there the obstacles give way and a greater manifestation of the soul takes place through education and culture, through concentration and meditation, and above all, through sacrifices.[20]

Thus what has been highlighted is that the real process of evolution from the lower to the higher form of existence in the human plane can be achieved not through struggle for existence, but through feeling for others, through sacrifices. There is a struggle in human being; but that struggle is not for the preservation of the gross body. On the human plane of

19. *CWSV*, vol. 4, p. 333.
20. Ibid., vol. 7, p. 152.

existence it is for gaining mastery over the mind or for the attainment of a state of balance. Thus Vivekananda interprets the Vedāntic concept of evolution as greater and greater manifestation of the infinite Self within, to a socialistic outlook where one can attain one's highest form through sacrifice for others, through love for others.

Another aspect of the gospel of Practical Vedānta consists in its catholicity of views, which is expressed in terms of the Principle of Acceptance. The trouble that the whole world is facing today is due to the fact that each believer in a particular religion upholds his own religion to the supreme position and thereby turns down the views of others, the beliefs of others as wrong. To resolve such a conflict the only alternative is to admit pluralism and that also in a non-hierarchical manner. This idea we find in the doctrine of Practical Vedānta. In fact, it is the spirit of the Ramakrishna movement. Ramakrishnadeva in his discourses preached the idea and exhibited through his life the truth that all religions are means to realize the same Godhead. Influenced by this spirit Swami Vivekananda established through this Vedāntic logic that all are manifestations of the divine being. God is in everything, God is everything, and so there is no question of any hierarchy among religious beliefs. Forms of worship other than one's own, including the worship of God through ceremonials are not to be regarded as erroneous. His request is:

> Do not disturb the faith of any of those who through ignorance have attached themselves to lower forms of worship.[21]

From the Advaitic standpoint all the religious beliefs are ways to help man to get higher and higher — all are struggling to attain to the whole. According to the Advaita philosophy God

21. *CWSV*, vol. 2, p. 141.

is the sum total — everything else is a part of it. So there can be no antagonism among the different sects of people. "We should see others with eyes of love, with sympathy, knowing that they are going along the same path that we have trodden."[22] Thus the Practical Vedānta system of Vivekananda not only highlights on tolerance of beliefs, but accepts all other religions of the world as different paths leading to the same God. In his address "The Way to the Realization of Universal Religion" Vivekananda says:

> I accept all the religions as true that were in the past, and worship them all; I worship God with every one of them, in whatever form they worship Him. . . . I shall go to the mosque of the Mohammedan; I shall enter the Christ's church and kneel before the crucifix; I shall enter the Buddhist temple, here I shall take refuge in Buddha and its law. I shall go into the forest and sit down in meditation with the Hindu who is trying to see the Light which enlightens the heart of everyone.[23]

This announcement is not an outburst of intellectual liberalism but is an expression of his Vedāntic realization. This catholicity of the religious mind has its root in his Practical Vedāntic faith in the oneness of the universe, in the idea of the inescapable one which led him to respect the many. This respect for the pluralism is not found in old classical Vedānta, but is the contribution of his new Practical Vedānta.

Swami Vivekananda believed that Vedānta alone has the capacity to be recognized as "the universal religion of man." In his address at the final session of the Parliament of Religions Swami Vivekananda appealed very briefly for a spirit of universality in religion. To quote him:

---

22. *CWSV*, vol. 4, p. 327.

23. Ibid., vol. 2, p. 374.

> The Christian is not to become a Hindu or a Buddhist, nor a Buddhist to become a Christian. But each must assimilate the spirit of others and yet preserve his individuality and grow according to his own law of growth.[24]

For such a belief we cannot accuse him of any form of cultural chauvinism, since by this he does not mean to say that a Christian or a Muslim has to renounce his faith to be a Vedāntin. He needs to give only a Vedāntic dimension to his faith. The same is true for a Hindu too. The Vedānta, as understood by Vivekananda, does not believe in the exclusive sanctity of any scriptural text. It only values a free mind, unconstrained by any fixed doctrine, a free mindset on the pilgrimage to the One who is residing in the very soul of all. The mission of the Vedānta is to knock at every door and raise the divinity that is already there but hidden within every soul. Thus to believe in practical Vedānta does not imply any conversion from one religion to another — rather it is an appeal for a new spiritual outlook which does not touch one's religion.[25] Thus tolerance of others' opinions is another important value of Vivekananda's system. In fact, here we find a non-hierarchical form of humanitarian approach to the global problem, no doctrine is in competition with others.

For the betterment of society, along with the value of tolerance, Swami Vivekananda insisted on combining the faculty of feeling with that of reason or intellect. In the original teaching of Śaṅkara we saw an emphasis on the intellectual faculty whereas in Lord Buddha we have found the focus is on the element of compassion. Swamiji in his different speeches insisted on greatness of heart which he found lacking in the philosophy of Śaṅkarācārya, but was exhibited through the life and teachings of Lord Buddha. He said:

---

24. *CWSV*, vol. 1, p. 24.
25. R.K. Dasgupta, *Swami Vivekananda's Neo-Vedānta*, p. 37.

> In Śaṅkarācarya we saw tremendous intellectual power, throwing the searching light of reason upon everything.[26]

But what is required is "the bright sun of intellect joined with the heart of Buddha, the wonderful infinite heart of love and mercy."[27] The reason why Swamiji stressed so much on greatness of heart, had been explained by him in a lecture delivered in London on 27 October 1896:

> It is through the heart that come the inspirations of life. I would a hundred times rather have a little heart and no brain, than be all brains and no heart . . . he who has no heart and only brains dies of dryness.[28]

The element of compassion or *karuṇā* or mercy is the essence of Buddha's moral teachings. Swamiji accepts Buddha's notion of *karuṇā* and finds that doing good to others is the only genuinely good work. Yet he is a Vedāntin, since his God is *Saccidānanda*. Thus in a way Vivekananda's practical Vedānta is a blend of Śaṅkara's metaphysics with Buddha's ethics. This synthesis makes his Vedāntic socialism a philosophy of life.

This philosophy of life is also expressed through Swami Vivekananda's insistence on *love* which also is another form of highlighting the "heart" rather than the "brain." In his opinion, as compared to love, all the usual methods of attainment of liberation like books and learning, Yoga and meditation, are dust, — love alone gives the supernatural powers. This love is a powerful weapon that can transform the nature of the universe entirely. Love is a going out of one's narrow self. It is expansive, inclusive and thirsting for identity with the object of love. It knows no bargaining. Love is always the giver and never the taker. This love also knows

---

26. *CWSV*, vol. 1, p. 25.
27. Ibid.
28. Ibid., vol. 2, p. 145.

no fear. The most glorious feature of love is that it is the highest idea. It changes our outlook towards others. To the lover the beloved is the most beautiful being that ever existed. This is because the lover sees her own ideal, latent in her mind, to be on the man. The beloved is, as it were, what she had so long aspired, thought of and upon that suggestion she throws her own ideal. But that this ideal has been superimposed on the beloved is totally lost sight of; rather the ideal is thought to be there in reality and is made the object of her worship. Thus looked at, by love the external world becomes only the world of suggestions — all that we see are projected out of our own minds. The lover passes beyond all rewards and punishments, beyond fears and doubts, beyond scientific or any other demonstration. He has developed in him by the power of love a uniting/binding force which ties up one individual with the other — one man with another, one man with another woman, one woman with another man, animals with animals, drawing the whole universe, as it were towards one centre. The manifestation of love is from the lowest atom to the highest being: omnipotent, all pervading is the love. One who has incurred this love in him rises above all selfish blemishes and expands his mentality. This transmutation goes on till matter ceases to be itself. Love is also associated with freedom. One who is under pressure, afraid of others cannot love. Only one who is free can love. When we really begin to love the world, then we understand what is meant by brotherhood or mankind, and not before. Out of love we can come out of our selfish egoistic spirit and feel for others. This is a logical extension of the Advaitic teaching.

This love not only enhances the value of an individual's own existence but leads to the service of mankind. Once one realizes the truth of the doctrine that the Self is in everything, the logical consequence that follows is to feel the living God in every being:

> The only God to worship is the human soul in the human body. Of course, all animals are temples too, but man is the highest, the Taj Mahal of temples. If I cannot worship in that, no other temple will be of any advantage.[29]

So one is to serve them in the spirit of worship and not help them or be kind to them as people ordinarily think and believe. Service to man becomes then service to God.

In Swamiji's system, knowledge itself has been considered as a value. In fact knowledge is considered as a primary or mother value which leads to social upliftment by widening the horizon of our thinking mind. This knowledge does not mean ordinary knowledge like the knowledge of tables, chairs, etc. It has a transcendental reference but at the same time it encompasses other disciplines like history, geography, literature, culture, religion, science, mathematics, etc. So, he recommends the extension of learning, imparting education among the masses through modern scientific methods. He advises his disciple:

> Therefore I say, set yourselves to the task of spreading education among the masses. Kindle their knowledge with the help of modern science. Teach them history, geography, science, literature and along with these the profound truths of religion. In exchange for that teaching, the poverty of the teachers will also disappear. By mutual exchange both parties will become friendly to each other.[30]

Such knowledge will help the people to know their own culture, their own surroundings which will make them good citizens and thereby the country will prosper. Thus, there is a

29. *CWSV*, vol. 3, p. 281.

30. Ibid., vol. 7, p. 149.

fundamental difference in the attitude towards teaching of Vivekananda from that of the Upaniṣads. The knowledge that the Upaniṣadic texts speak of is mainly spiritualistic in character. The Upaniṣadic philosophy is a philosophy of consciousness in terms of which every form of the cosmic manifestation can be explained. It is a philosophy of ultimate existence, knowledge, truth. It is a value philosophy of eternal consciousness and eternal life, a life of knowledge, freedom, bliss, immortality and truth. It is a transcendence from sensory/sensuous realm to spiritual values. In short, the Upaniṣads highlight the value of spiritual attainment of ultimate value of Truth, Existence and Bliss by the individual. Swami Vivekananda acknowledging the necessities of these values in the individual's life changed the direction of development from the individual to the social. For him the objective is not merely the individual's perfection but the improvement/ betterment of the society as a whole. In short, his emphasis was on an altruistic goal. This has been an important aspect of his Practical Vedānta.

This Practical Vedānta also helped Swamiji to argue for female education and thereby their upliftment. To be very brief, the Vedānta that we find in Vivekananda is humanitarian in nature rather than intellectual. He was in favour of retaining the truths of the Vedānta, which are very much Indian in nature but at the same time wanted to bring in some modifications to make it suitable for the changing society:

> It is true that all the ancient Vedic laws will not have a go, but if we introduce additions and alterations in them to suit the needs of the time, codify them, and hold them up as a new model to society, why will they not pass current.[31]

Another important value that has been emphasized by Swamiji

---

31. *CWSV*, vol. 7, p. 150.

through his Practical Vedānta is self-esteem, self-respect, self-confidence. The Vedānta teaches men to have faith in themselves first. To think of oneself as weak, as inferior is a means to make one's bondage a bit tight. From the beginningless past, several people in our country have been taught to think that they belong to a lower class, they are not permitted to perform many jobs; Swamiji considers this to be the greatest error. In the light of the essence of Vedānta he inspires us to believe that since the Divine is in all of us, each one of us is capable of doing everything. To consider oneself as inferior is to disrespect oneself, which is a great lie. Whosoever thinks he is weak, is wrong. Whosoever thinks he is impure is wrong. He not only commits a wrong to himself, but does so to the whole world. He is degrading the spirit of the Vedānta and thereby is "throwing a bad thought into the world." The Vedānta teaches man to have faith in himself first. There is no need to search for any personal God outside of himself — God is within him. So the man who has no faith in himself, who does not believe in himself, is an atheist. When man is able to give up this atheistic attitude and has the strong belief in the identity of the Supreme Self within him, man will have extra confidence in the work he performs. And obviously his actions will be a better performance. Swami Vivekananda assures us that then:

> All your actions will be magnified, transformed, deified, by the very power of the thought.[32]

This Vedāntic ideal of oneness of all has another important moral bearing. The moment it brings self-respect in one it asks for showing respect to others. Since all of us have the same ideal, same reality and all are treading towards the same goal, no one is to be looked down with contempt. It is no

32. *CWSV*, vol. 4, p. 302.

doubt true that there is difference among individuals in respect of skill, strength or intelligence. But that difference is not one of a great kind. As Swamiji reminds us:

> All differences in this world are of degree and not of kind, because oneness is the secret of everything.[33]

The difference between weakness and strength is one of degree; the difference between virtue and vice is one of degree; similarly the difference between life and death is also one of degree. Since all differences are of degrees only, we do not have any right to condemn others. What we can is extend our hands of help to them so that they can overcome their drawback and come forward.

To have faith in oneself has a great significant role in one's life. If we go through the stories of the lives of the great men of the world we will see that they had the confidence that they are born to be great and this confidence made them great. So, faith in one's own self will diminish the evils and miseries from which the individual suffers. But this faith is not to be looked upon as a selfish faith. In fact, it is the faith in the Absolute Spirit, which underlies every being. The moment one realizes this Spirit in oneself, one realizes the spirit to be present in all and at the same time one realizes that there is no difference between oneself and others. Thus the difference between man and man exists so long as there is absence of faith in oneself. So faith in oneself has a twofold advantage — on the one hand it brings in self-confidence in the individual and enables him to realize his ideal and on the other, it removes the difference between man and man and brings in a sense of equality among different individuals. Accordingly, love for oneself becomes love for others, love for all. It is a universal love — a feeling for others. And once this broad outlook arises

33. *CWSV*, vol. 4, p. 299.

in man, the whole world would be better for him. Thus the Practical Vedānta enables man to shun off his narrow selfish egoistic outlook, to develop confidence/faith in himself and others, and thereby improve the interpersonal relationship which ultimately results in the betterment of the whole world. In other words, Practical Vedānta is to be admitted not simply for its spiritualism, but because of the values it upholds. Though Practical Vedānta is founded on a spiritual belief, belief in the Absolute as immanent in every individual being, the values upheld therein are free from all sorts of spiritualistic, religious flavour. These values are universal in essence, applicable to all, irrespective of religion, sex, caste or anything and they have bearing on the society as a whole.

References

Dasgupta, R.K., *Swami Vivekananda's Neo-Vedānta,* Kolkata: The Asiatic Society, 1999.

———, *Swami Vivekananda's Vedāntic Socialism,* Kolkata: Ramakrishna Mission Institute of Culture, 1995.

Mazumdar, Amiya Kumar, *Understanding Vivekananda,* Kolkata: Sanskrit Pustak Bhandar, 1972.

Shastri, Dinesh Chandra Bhattacharyya, *Vivekanander Vedantacinta* (in Bengali), Kolkata: Ramakrishna Mission Institute of Culture, 3rd edn. 2000.

Sister Nivedita, *The Master as I Saw Him,* Kolkata: Udbodhan, 2001.

Sister Nivedita, *Notes of Some Wanderings with Swami Vivekananda,* Kolkata: Udbodhan, 1978.

Swami Vivekananda, *The Complete Works of Swami Vivekananda* (*CWSV*), Kolkata: Advaita Ashrama, 6th impression, 2008.

Swami Vivekananda, *Letters of Swami Vivekananda,* Kolkata: Advaita Ashrama, 16th impression, 2007.

5

Gandhian Economic Thought Revisited

Jhuma Chakraborty

GANDHI was not a conscious theoretician. His entire life symbolizes a relentless search for Truth. Truth and non-violence are the two pillars on which his entire philosophy of life rests. Gandhi's approach was holistic. In his constant endeavour to fight against injustice and untruth he could not compartmentalize the ethical, social, political and economic issues. As he writes in this context:

> The whole gamut of man's activities today constitute an indivisible whole. You cannot divide social, economic, political and purely religious works into watertight compartments. To see the universal and all-pervading spirit of Truth face to face, one must be able to love the meanest creature as oneself. And a man who aspires that cannot afford to keep out any field of life. That is why my devotion to Truth has drawn me into the field of political viewpoint.[1]

It becomes obvious from the above quotation that it will be a difficult task to focus only on the economic proposals put forward by Gandhi, yet I shall try my level best to extrapolate the economic programmes from the entire set of ideas that are closely interwoven together. It must be noted in this

1. *Harijan*, 24.12.1938, p. 393

context that the economic proposals of Gandhi was a part of a larger scheme of *svarāja.* The term *svarāja* had a deep meaning for Gandhi. The term was not used in the ordinary sense of political independence. *Svarāja* for Gandhi was a holistic concept with four important dimensions, political, social, economic and spiritual. *Pūrṇa svarāja* for Gandhi meant complete freedom from any kind of exploitation. Gandhi strongly believed that *pūrṇa svarāja* should be our ultimate goal, where the individual and social interests merge together. The economic theory will be an important aspect of the larger programme.

In this article my focus will be on the economic aspect of Gandhian philosophy, and in that context I will try to determine the relevance of his ideas in the modern scenario. In discussing this part, I will not only confine myself to an exegetical account of Gandhian ideas,[2] but will try to reinterpret Gandhi when required, at times consulting the expert opinions of the critiques and commentators. Again it is indeed unfair to attempt to judge the relevance of his proposals without considering the context in which they were made. So a brief study of the historical context has been made.

My article has three sections: In the first section I will discuss some of the presuppositions of the Gandhian economic theory.[3] The discussion of these presuppositions is a prerequisite to a proper understanding of his views. In the second section I will briefly outline the context, that played the most vital role in giving birth to Gandhian economic views, as has been already mentioned. In the third section I will be focussing mainly on the economic aspect of the Gandhian

---

2. As expressed in his numerous letters, speeches and other writings.

3. Though there is no proper theory, for our convenience I will refer to his ideas as a theory.

thought and try to understand the relevance of his model in the modern scenario.

Fundamental Presuppositions

COSMOCENTRIC VIEW

Unlike almost all major traditions of the Western thought which proposes an anthropocentric view of nature and assigns a supreme position to human beings, Gandhi followed the Indian tradition in subscribing to the cosmo-centric view where cosmos is a well co-ordinated whole whose various parts are all linked in a system of *yajña*,[4] or interdependence and mutual service. The entire universe is governed by its own laws and the different laws stand in a complex relationship with the rest.

Human beings according to Gandhi are an integral part of this cosmos and are tied to it by deepest bonds. For Gandhi the cosmos is not like a pyramid with the material world at its base and the human beings at its apex, but it consists of a series of ever widening circles encompassing the material world, the sentient world, the human kind and all other aspects. Since the cosmic spirit that is present in the universe is not transcended but immanent in nature, the natural or the material world with all its dimensions is not only natural but also divine in nature with a purpose.

Gandhi believed that the human beings have involuntarily inherited debts towards the entire creation that are too vast to be repaid. Even a whole lifetime is insufficient to attempt to pay back to one's parents, let alone all others. In addition to that most of the creditors are unspecifiable because they are either dead or unknown, and it is no use to try to repay these debts. Gandhi maintains that the best thing for a human

4. A kind of sacrifice.

being to do is to "recognize the conditions of his/her existence," and continue in the ongoing universal system of interdependence by discharging his/her duties and contributing to the collective well-being. Since human beings are necessarily interdependent, every human action is both self-regarding and other-regarding, he can never degrade or brutalize others without doing the same harm to his own self.

Though Gandhi did not explicitly develop any ecological theory one cannot overlook the non-anthropocentric perspective of Gandhi according to which the human species is treated as an integral part of the cosmos contributing to it's well-being and not enjoying a higher status.

Truth and Non-Violence

The entire Gandhian philosophy, his social political economic and religious thoughts as expressed in his numerous speeches, letters and writings have an ethical orientation developed around two fundamental principles. In fact, it would be more appropriate to consider them as two aspects of only one fundamental principle, the principle of Truth. Throughout his life he has never compromised with this principle. His entire philosophy, his social, political, economic views be it *sarvodaya* or *svarāja* or the theory of trusteeship follow from his view of truth, the supreme principle which is inseparably related to *ahiṁsā* (non-violence). In Gandhi's words:

> Truth and non-violence are not two unrelated concepts, they are the two sides of the same coin . . . "non-violence is embedded in truth and vice versa."[5]

Gandhi firmly believed that truth could never be achieved through violence since violence constitutes violation of truth, the law of the unity of life. In this context Gandhi argues:

---

5. *Harijan*, 13.07.1947, p. 232.

> Non-violence is the law of our species as violence is the law of the brute. The spirit lies dormant in the brute and he knows no law but that of physical might. The dignity of man requires obedience to a higher law — to the strength of the spirit.[6]

We all know that Gandhi was basically a man of action and not simply a dreamer. In all his life he tried to realize the truth, through non-violence. His pragmatism helped him to cope with the changing situations and accordingly he never hesitated to change his previous views on many occasions but as far as the relation between truth and *ahiṁsā* is concerned he remained consistent throughout his life. Gandhi reiterates:

> Where there is *ahiṁsā*, there is truth and truth is God. How He manifests Himself I cannot say. All I know is that He is all-pervading and where He is, all is well. There is therefore one law for all. Whenever in the world truth and non-violence reign supreme, there is peace and bliss.[7]

In his childhood Gandhi like everyone else grew up with the idea that God is supreme and since he valued truth from his early years, he gradually realized that he wanted to worship God in the form of truth only. In 1925 in a talk with the Christian missionaries in Darjeeling, he explicitly declared that truth and God are convertible, meaning thereby that truth can enjoy the position of God and vice versa. But some time later Gandhi went a step further and said that though he can reject the concept of God, he can never even think of sacrificing the concept of truth:

> Devotion to this truth is the sole justification for our existence. All our activities should be centred on Truth. . . . Truth should be the very breath of our life.[8]

---

6. *Harijan*, 29.09.1946, p. 232.
7. Ibid.
8. *Yeravda Mandir*, p. 1.

A number of questions will arise in this connection that can be summarized as follows:

1. What is the exact nature of Gandhian truth?
2. How this truth can be known by human beings, whose knowledge is limited? In other words how this truth can be realized by ordinary human beings?
3. What is its exact relationship with non-violence?

There are many such pertinent questions, but for our present purpose I am not going to address these questions, simply because these issues are not relevant for our present purpose.

The holistic approach of Gandhi did not allow him to look at truth in some remote corner of the world far away from human civilization. Since truth or God is an omnipresent indivisible reality, it can be sought everywhere, in every dimension of nature, in every field of activity. Non-violence is a holistic action that springs from truth, the wholeness of life. Life has to be governed not by the selfish fragmented self but by the completeness within the inner self of the individual that is in harmony with this beautiful unlimited nature. Violence is an attempt to break this unity.

Gandhi maintains that so long as the consciousness is imprisoned in this body mind frame, truth will appear differently to different individuals. An individual in such a situation has no alternative but to act according to the dictum of truth at a given moment and to keep moving or shifting his position with a different understanding of truth at another moment. As long as the absolute truth is not realized, the relative truth must be the guiding star of one's actions. Gandhi knew that this view of truth paves the way for the possibility of constant conflict among individuals but this conflict is apparent according to Gandhi because at the deeper level there is an inner harmony, the different views being the parts of one indivisible whole. A sincere selfless pursuit of relative truth will ultimately merge with absolute truth.

As far as non-violence is concerned a few important things must be mentioned in this context. It must be noted that non-violence is not a passive state; it is rather a state of an active engagement in every field of activity due to the dynamic and creative force of love that is inherent in it. The practice of non-violence prompts an individual to participate in collective life, whether religious, social, political or economic, not for any individual gain but in the spirit of *niṣkāma karma*. Thus the individual aim and the social aim converge into each other being simultaneous and synchronous. Gandhi's entire social, political and economic philosophy follows from his premise of truth and non-violence representing a synthesis of means and ends, finite and infinite, individual good and social good.

The Purpose of Man's Life

According to Gandhian paradigm man is constituted of both matter and spirit. Matter is responsible for making him fragmented, selfish, and provokes him towards ceaseless violence. The spirit in him gives him the glimpse of the holistic world-view and inspires him to rise above passions. The tension and conflict between light and darkness, between evil and good is a constant phenomenon in human nature but Gandhi is confident that man has an inherent potentiality to overcome his mundane selfish existence and transcend this limited self. Gandhi has clearly declared that:

> The essential difference between man and brute is that the former can respond to the call of the spirit in him, can rise superior to the passions that he owns in common with the brute and therefore, superior to selfishness and violence,

> which belong to the brute nature and not to the immortal spirit of man.[9]

Thus Gandhi considers man to be potentially divine who has the capability to go beyond the mechanistic structure of mind-body complex and can realize the wholeness lying dormant within him. Although initially he is the prisoner of the sensual psychological self, he can ultimately free himself from the shackles of the lower existence to become rooted in the Truth, the pure sinless state. To quote Gandhi in this context:

> I believe it to be possible for every human being to attain that blessed and indescribable sinless state in which he feels within himself the presence of God to the exclusion of everything else.[10]

Gandhi strongly feels that the purpose of man's life is self-realization. Gandhi argues that since man is not essentially material the endless pursuit of materialism cannot be the ultimate goal of his life:

> He (man) is born day after day not to explore avenues for amassing riches and to explore different means of livelihood, on the contrary man is born in order to utilize every atom of his energy for the purpose of knowing his Maker."[11]

Gandhi reiterates that,

> The purpose of life is undoubtedly to know oneself.[12]

Gandhi has remained consistent regarding the path that must

---

9. M.K. Gandhi, *India of My Dreams*, comp. Prabhu, p. 27. also in *Amrita Bazar Patrika*, 2.08.1934.
10. *Complete Works of Mahatma Gandhi* (*CWMG*) vol. 21, 1966, p. 440 also in *Young India*, 17.11.1921.
11. *The Hindu*, 18.10.1927, also in *CWMG*, vol. 35, 1969, p. 152. It must be noted that the "maker" is synonymous with his concept of "Truth."
12. M.K. Gandhi, *Service Before Self*, p. 62.

be followed to achieve this goal. Gandhi has never compromised with truth and non-violence as has been mentioned earlier. In this respect his socialism[13] will differ from Marx because though both of them shared their dreams regarding the nature of the ideal society, Marx unlike Gandhi will not appreciate the path of non-violence. Gandhian economic theory, which is based on these two principles, appears to be absurd and romantic unless and until one understands the standpoint from which an individual should look at the world.

An Ideal Society

Gandhi returned to India in 1915. His first acquaintance with the Indian villages was in Champaran of Gujarat, where the fact of poverty was a stark reality that changed his life. Gandhi's close association with the poverty of Champaran, Kheda, and Ahmedabad of Gujarat compelled him to look into India's socio-economic problem from a different perspective. It became evident to him that India actually lived in its villages and a significant difference can only be brought about through their upliftment.

Gandhi's observation in this context is different from Marx's. Gandhi agreed with Marx and accepted the fact that the story of poverty in villages is essentially a story of exploitation but unlike Marx he realized that it is not the exploitation of the have-nots by the have-lots but the story of exploitation of the villages by the cities. To Gandhi the struggle to liberate Indian colonies from imperialist domination appeared as a part of a larger struggle to liberate villages from the oppression of those overgrown centres of powers and wealth that flourished in the cities.

---

13. Gandhi can never be considered as a socialist in the usual sense of the term.

The villages as Gandhi observed were suffering due to the absence of infrastructure, resources, and talents[14] but the main problem laid elsewhere. It is the absence of the availability of jobs that caused the inevitable exodus from villages to the cities. This mass displacement instead of solving the problem aggravated it. It is a job, a livelihood that makes life worth living for an individual. So the main problem that is to be addressed seriously as Gandhi correctly realized, is the problem of unemployment. Gandhi writes in this context, "How are the hungry millions to be fed? Not through charity." Gandhi realized that "they cannot be given it.[15] They must earn it and they can earn it by the sweat of their brow."

The deeper we get into Gandhi's economic thought, the more it becomes obvious that Gandhi has given maximum importance to the need for the individual man to lead a dignified life, which is nothing other than a life with dignified labour. It must be noted in this connection that any work, intellectual or physical, that enables the individual to earn his/her bread without involving exploitation of any kind will be considered to be dignified by Gandhi. In this connection it must be noted that Gandhi was always in favour of physical labour in comparison to the intellectual labour. Ruskin's *Unto This Last* played the most significant role in shaping this aspect of his proposals. Probably it won't be irrelevant to have a look at Ruskin's ideas to have a better understanding of the Gandhian position. Ruskin's ideas can be summarized as follows:

1. The good of the individual is contained in the good of all.
2. The lawyer's work has the same value as the barber's;

---

14. There was a constant influx from villages to the cities.
15. Gandhi is referring to food here.

inasmuch as all have the same right of earning their livelihood from their work.

3. The life of the labour, i.e. that the life of the tiller of the soil and the handicraftsman is the life worth living.

Ruskin's work made Gandhi realize that each and every individual must possess the right to work and there should not be any discrimination among different types of honest labour. To think that the physician's work or the lawyer's work is more dignified in comparison to the barber's is improper. Apart from Ruskin, Tolstoy also believed that no man is free from the obligation of bread labour. Gandhi was greatly influenced by these thinkers and was convinced that every individual must participate in the production of the elementary necessaries of life.

Some might argue that in the Gandhian framework society has primacy over the individual persons constituting it. Critics might argue that like Hegel and Marx, Gandhi is also concerned about the social whole and he is actually looking at the individuals through the lens of the society since Gandhi's individual man is essentially a member of a larger whole. But I would like to point out that both society and its members are equally important for Gandhi. Had it not been the case, Gandhi would not have given so much importance to the necessity of the individual members leading a dignified life in his village community. In his emphasis on the need of leading a dignified life by the individual man, Gandhi is looking at the society from the individual's point of view.

Both Gandhi and Vivekananda realized that unless and until the hungry millions of India are provided with their fundamental necessities of life, they will not understand the meaning of either "truth and non-violence" or of "Practical Vedānta" (popularized by Vivekananda). Vivekananda emphasized on the satisfaction of hunger of the individuals but Gandhi went a step further and insisted on the requirement of earning one's own bread by the sweat of one's brow which automatically takes care of the other necessaries of life.

Within the ideal social framework, the individual man[16] realizes that he is an inseparable part of the social whole, his good and social good are inseparably linked up together. Gandhi's individual man here is very similar to Marx's ideal man who gives his best to the society spontaneously without any external compulsion and takes from the society as much as he requires. Similarly Gandhi's ideal man is a member of a self-sufficient village community that is surrounded by similar other village communities, which are tied up together by the rules of good neighbourliness, mutual concern and non-exploitation. In Gandhi's community just as in Marx's communism there is no need of any external authority in the form of state or any other organization to ensure such a peaceful altruistic attitude of the individual members.

Relation Between Ethics and Economics

It is quite evident that Gandhian thought has an ethical orientation. We have already mentioned that Gandhi was not a conscious academic theoretician and thereby we cannot expect him to give us a neat model strictly confining himself only to the economic features. We have already mentioned that for Gandhi the line of demarcation between the social, political and economic issues is not very clear. In his letters, speeches and writings he has often discussed the relationship between ethics and economics stating that the two are identical and there is no distinction between the two. As Gandhi writes:

(a) I must confess that I do not draw a sharp line or any

16. The ideal social set-up and the moral development of man are simultaneous processes. One cannot be disentangled from the other, though conceptually we can separate them.

distinction between economics and ethics.[17]

(b) True economics never militates against the highest ethical standard, just as all true ethics to be worth its name must at the same time be also good economics.[18]

In today's world, as we can all realize, ethics to a large extent is determined by the economic constraints. The market forces, the global scenario of consumerism, play a very significant role in determining our values and world-view. Gandhi like many other modern economists believed that the relation between the two must be reverse meaning thereby that the economic principles and economic theories must be guided by ethical principles. This attitude is very similar to Marx's, because Marxian theory also presupposes the dependence of the economic principles on normative policies, for both Gandhi and Marx developed "need-based" ethics. It must be noted in this context that Gandhi made a distinction between "material advancement" and "real progress." As he writes:

> By economic progress we mean material advancement without limit, and by real progress we mean moral progress which again is the progress of the permanent element in us. The subject therefore may be stated thus: Does not moral progress increase in the same proportion as material progress? I know that this is a wider proposition than the one before us. But I venture to think that we always mean the larger one even when we lay down the smaller.[19]

Both moral progress and material progress are limitless but the former[20] is a wider proposition. Gandhi reiterates that the

---

17. *Selected Works*, p. 321.

18. Ibid.

19. Vivek Ranjan Bhattacharya, *Speeches and Writings of Mahatma Gandhi*, pp. 184-85.

20. Gandhi is referring to the moral progress in this context.

"real progress" consists in the spiritual or moral development of the individual.[21] The question that automatically arises is, "what is the relationship between material progress and moral development?" Again, "is there any reason for emphasizing the necessity of the satisfaction of the material needs?" To these queries Gandhi would answer that the question of the moral progress can be raised after the basic needs are satisfied, not before that. But the satisfaction of the fundamental needs can never guarantee moral progress though the former is undoubtedly a stepping-stone towards the latter.

Gandhian economic thought hammers upon two principles. They are

1. The satisfaction of the basic requirements of the individual. The most fundamental one is the right to work that enables the individual to lead a dignified life.
2. The satisfaction of the above-mentioned requirement will gradually help the individual to discover a higher, spiritual self that transcends his egoistic self. He gradually realizes that his good and the welfare of the entire village community are inseparable.

This is the point where ethics and economics converge in Gandhian framework. Economics proper, according to Gandhi, can never remain indifferent to the satisfaction of the basic requirements of the individual. In this context Gandhi writes:

> The economic constitution of India and for that matter of the world, should be such that no one under it should suffer from the want of food and clothing. In other words everybody should be able to get sufficient work to enable him to make both ends meet.[22]

---

21. We are using "moral" and "spiritual" synonymously.
22. *Young India*, 15.11.1928, p. 321.

This is the most significant aspect of Gandhi's economic model. Gandhi was sensitive as well as prudent enough to realize the most basic and fundamental requirement of an individual. He had a strong conviction that the individual can respect others only when he can respect himself, and for the right attitude towards oneself it is absolutely necessary to earn one's own bread. Gandhi will never approve of an undue material gain because that might satisfy one's hunger but can never generate the required "self-respect" of the individual. Gandhi has repeatedly expressed that a dependent existence is not a life worth living. In Gandhi's words:

> Supposing a few millionaires from America came and offered to send us all our food stuffs and implored us not to work but to permit them to give vent to their philanthropy, I should refuse point blank to accept their kind offer especially because it strikes at the root of the fundamental law of our being.[23]

Thus Gandhi's welfare economics is concerned with the "quality of life" of the individual in its relational existence.

In contrast to the present scenario Gandhi paints a picture of a dream-world where both the individual and the society are there for each other's benefit. The small self-sufficient village community will take care of the individuals and the members living in this village would be giving their best to the egalitarian community, receiving only as much as they require. It has been already pointed out that Gandhi's ideal village community is very similar to Marx's communism where both are optimistic enough to declare that the individuals are ethical and adequately responsible to perform spontaneously without any external intervention.

It must be noted in this context that Gandhi's emphasis on

---

23. *Harijan*, 7.12.1935, p. 341.

the need of "the quality of life" is not very uncommon. Economist John Keynes in his book, *The General Theory of Employment, Interest and Money* (1960), has drawn our attention to the need for increased availability of employment. Keynes approaches the problem of employment from the macro-economic point of view. He argues that the greater the national income, the greater would be the availability of employment. Keynes however has never used the term "quality of life" but one can easily understand that the concept is presupposed in Keynes's work. But to what extent his model can be applied in the context of underdeveloped countries is a big question. Economists like Amartya Sen are making a distinction between "engineering economics" and "welfare economics," where the latter gives highest value to the welfare of the individual members of the society. In these societies the yardstick of progress is not the material advancement of the individual members of the society but the improvement of their "quality of life." In this respect, like Sen many economists and social philosophers would agree with Gandhi that the "economic policies of a particular community" must be guided by certain "ethical norms."

A number of questions disturb us when we engage ourselves with a dialogue with Gandhi.

1. How one should determine the "quality of life"? What is the yardstick to determine the quality of life of the individuals living in a society? Many economists like Sen and others have tried to determine it. As far as Gandhian theory is concerned it would not be very difficult to work out the end or the ultimate goal visualized by Gandhi, but we will see that Gandhi unlike Marx has not clearly addressed the question of the method that must be adopted to bring about this change.

2. Again, how to determine where the phenomenon of "need ends and greed begins" ? Is it possible to have a clear-cut compartmentalization between the two ? Is it not very difficult to determine what is "need" and what is "greed" without looking at the context ? The "greed" in one situation might appear to be "need" in another case.

   In this paper I have tried to give an answer to these questions from the Gandhian point of view in the third section.

3. Is it ever possible to have a world so beautiful where each and every individual is always giving his best to the society and taking from the society as much as he requires? The Elephant and the ant will be enjoying equal status in the Gandhian society because the consumption will be totally need-based. The ant and the elephant will take from the society as much as they require and will be giving their best to the society in which they belong. However the views of both Marx and Gandhi appear to be unrealistic and over-romantic. History has never witnessed any period of any society in any corner of the world, which was not characterized by conflicts and other selfish desires that overpowered human beings.

In the third section I have tried to address some of these questions from the Gandhian point of view. As has been already mentioned, Gandhi has not given any solution to some of the most vital issues, for example, regarding the relation between the individual and the society, whether the ideal society preceeds or the ideal individual? Again how to bring about the desired society? In the Marxian theory we have a clear picture and an unambiguous recommendation about the path to be followed for the actualization of the end. But in the

Gandhian theory there is no clear suggestion regarding this issue. But in spite of these difficulties it is becoming increasingly obvious that one cannot ignore the value of Gandhi's insights and his novelty of ideas that can provide us with an alternative model to resolve the age-old problems of exploitation and class-conflicts existing in almost every society. It must be noted in this context that Gandhi's emphasis on the need of an individual to have an employment shows his practical bent of mind and his pragmatic attitude towards life that existed side by side with the optimism about the human nature.

II

In this section as I have already mentioned, I will try to paint a picture of the period, that is the socio-political economic background of the nineteenth and twentieth centuries in brief. This would help us to have an outline of the context that gave birth to the Gandhian view. A theory is a product of its context, and a sincere endeavour to probe into the view in abstraction (without considering the context) is to know the incomplete story; it is like the picture of a boat without the water on which it was floating.

A distinction is usually made between the two phases of capitalism, the earlier phase or the merchantile phase and the final phase where large scale production dawns. In the former stage the production is organized by and large on a household basis though the producers work according to the orders of a merchant class, gradually leading to the final stage of large-scale production. In India these two phases overlapped in the eighteenth century, setting the stage of Gandhian economic thought.

The village-based textile industry of India flourished till the beginning of the eighteenth century. A series of epoch making inventions in the British textile industry changed the entire scenario. India, who was the chief exporter of textile till the Napoleonic war, was compelled to import textile from Lancashire after the inventions in the British textile world. In Amlan Datta's words,

> The traditional cotton industry of India had already been disorganized by the extortionate methods of the servants of the East India Company, and before it could reorganize itself it was crippled by the competition of cheaper goods from abroad. In the second half of the nineteenth century India set up a few cotton mills of her own and by the 1920s her mills were producing more cloth than her handlooms; thus a very important village industry was seriously affected upsetting the balance of India's rural economy.[24]

Though India witnessed a major progress in industrialization from 1881 to 1931, there was a systematic decline in its cottage industry. The construction of railway was a turning point in the industrial front as it accelerated the growth of other industries, for example, the output of coal production increased from one million tons in 1880 to 20 million tons in 1925.[25] Apart from textile and coal this period saw the birth of iron and steel industry, but in spite of these developments there was a sharp decline in the employment rate. Census figures show that the total number of workers employed in the manufacturing units, mining, and construction declined from 21.1 million in 1881 to 12.9 million in 1931. It must be noted in this context that this devastating event was not due to the worldwide depression since the great economic depression affected only the industrially developed countries and India was obviously not one of them.

Even if we accept a wide margin of error in the census

24. Amlan Datta, p. 141.
25. In a span of 45 years the output of coal production was 20 times greater.

reports, one can still agree with the observation of the economists that the picture regarding the scope of employment was very depressing. Eminent economist Colin Clark rightly observed that:

> There was really a marked increase in the proportion engaged in agriculture between 1881 and 1911 and the proportion has been virtually stationary since that date.[26]

Economists point out that in the above-mentioned period,[27] while the modern sector of industry expanded, the traditional sector declined. The net result of the introduction of modern technology was not very positive as far as the total employment rate is concerned. The same picture was corroborated by Jawaharlal Nehru in his remarks on the economic history of the nineteenth century. Nehru has rightly pointed out that in the first half of the nineteenth century the old order of the cottage industries were not encouraged in the interest of the British authorities. The *ẓamindārī* system robbed the tillers and the farmers of the ownership right on their lands thereby preventing them from taking serious interests regarding any permanent reform related to their lands. Automatically the existence of the *ẓamindārī* system was accompanied by a steady decline in the employment of the rural force followed by a steady exodus of the rural population into the cities in search of work. The gulf between poverty and prosperity started increasing to an alarming level. Poor people both in rural and urban centres were victims of intolerable poverty, inhuman social and economic exploitation by both British as well as indigenous capitalists. The self-reliant village economy was completely ruined by the economic policy of the British government.

---

26 Amlan Datta, p. 141; also in Colin Clark, *The Conditions of Economic Progress*, London, 1957.

27. 1880–1910 approximately.

Gandhi must have had all these in mind when he proposed his economic policy. His entire philosophy, as has been already mentioned, rests on the twin principles of truth and non-violence as one cannot be actually separated from the other.[28] Gandhian economic thought is derived from these two basic premises and so the entire economic package is based on the principle of non-exploitation of any form. The socio-politico-economic set-up of the nineteenth and early twentieth centuries must have played a vital role in shaping his economic policies.

III

It has already been mentioned that Gandhian economic thought was a natural outcome of his exposure and other experiences of the British imperialism. Apart from the problem of unemployment, his main concern was the recovery of the village economy. Though Gandhi was concerned with the restructuring of the village economy, he rightly realized that it is the individual who should be the centre of authority and value. Throughout his life Gandhi was consistent and unambiguous regarding the priorities in his scheme of thought. In his words, "The individual is the supreme consideration,"[29] again "ultimately it is the individual which is the unit."[30] The belief that each individual is morally good and this moral goodness is an essential aspect of man's nature is a fundamental presupposition that played a vital role in shaping Gandhi's economic proposals of consumption, distribution and exchange of economic goods. In the economic scheme proposed by Gandhi it is extremely important that each individual must

---

28. Many commentators think that they should be treated as two aspects of one principle.

29. *Young India,* 13.11.1924, p. 378.

30. *Harijan,* 28.07.1946, p. 236.

lead a dignified life in the self-sufficient village community visualized by him.

It is interesting to note that Gandhi has explained the phenomenon of exploitation from a novel perspective. His view of colonial exploitation stands in sharp contrast to the usual theories put forward by the nationalists or the Marxists. The popular theory tells us that the British nation as a whole profited from the never-ending exploitation of the Indian colonies. Not only the British businessmen but also the British working class were enriched by the "drain of wealth" from the Indian colonies to their mother country.

Gandhi looked at the problem from a different standpoint altogether. Gandhi strongly felt that the direction of exploitation is from the cities to the villages, irrespective of whether the cities are ruled by the Indians or the British. It is a known fact that the cities that grew as the centres of wealth and power under the British imperialism conferred little benefit on India's 700,000 villages. In other countries the story was not always similar because there were alternative models of development that were put into practice. In England for example the towns and countries developed through a kind of symbiotic relationship. In this context the famous economist Adam Smith in his book *Wealth of Nations* (1776) has elaborately discussed how the commerce of cities and towns contributed to the improvement of the country as a whole. But when the British and the Dutch traders established commercial relation with the whole of East, the story was altogether different. A Dutch economist J.H. Bocke in his book *Economics and Economic Policy of Dual Societies* (1953) has described this phenomenon under the title of *Dual Society*. The dual economy described in this book consists of a modern sector and a traditional sector, where the latter is totally unaffected by the development in the modern front.

In India the situation was worse. The cities attracted resources, capital and talent, from the villages thereby gradually ruining the traditional handicrafts and disturbing the natural balance between the agricultural front and the village industry. Rural society gradually got robbed of its potentialities and wealth resulting in a gradual decline in its socio-economic stability. To Gandhi the endeavour to liberate colonies from the imperialist domination appeared as a part of the larger struggle to liberate the villages from the oppression of the overgrown centres of power and wealth in the cities.

Let us have a deeper look at Gandhi's insight on this issue. Gandhi was right in realizing that industrialization means large-scale production for distant markets that will automatically involve competition. This is generally accompanied by the de-industrialization of the rural corners and for this reason Gandhi did not support the idea of large-scale production. In reply to a question put to him by Maurice Frydman in this particular context Gandhi replied:

> Industrialization on a mass scale will necessarily lead to passive or active exploitation of the villages, as the problem of competition and marketing comes in. Therefore we have to concentrate on the villages being self-sufficient, manufacturing mainly for use.[31]

Provided this character of the village industry is maintained, there would be no objection to villages using even modern machines and tools that they can make and afford to use.[32]

It must be noted in this context that for Gandhi the significant choice did not lie between capitalism and socialism

---

31. Gandhi consistently emphasized on the policy of production that is need-oriented and not profit-based.

32. Datta, p. 144.

but between a centralized economic system and a decentralized economic structure, as Gandhi firmly believed that a centralized economic structure whether in a capitalistic society or in socialism would necessarily involve power abuse by those dwelling in cities. At times he identified industrialization with a system centred in cities and opposed it totally. In the Indian political scenario of the second half of the 1940s, when there was a constant debate on the issue of industrialization between Gandhi and Nehru we hear him[33] saying to an American journalist that:

> Nehru wants industrialization because he thinks if it (India) is socialized it will be free from the evils of capitalism. My own view is that the evils are inherent in industrialism and no amount of socialism can eradicate them.[34]

No one would deny that Gandhi's attitude in this respect is a misfit in the present context of globalization and of economic liberalization. In the present century there is an over emphasis on industrial investments along with an inflow of foreign exchange in the developing countries. The present economic trend believes that this strategy will perpetuate balance of payment problem, healthy competition and improvement in the management of the quality as well as in the quantity of production. In addition to these, in the individual front these economic programmes, which are in sharp contrast to what Gandhi desired, will provide larger employment opportunities and better and fuller utilization of natural resources. The question that keeps disturbing us is, why should we opt for an economic model that is indifferent to the changing phenomena of the twenty-first century, a model whose context insensitivity and inapplicability is so obvious? Before we address all these questions let us first try to understand

33. Gandhi is being referred to here.

34. Datta, p. 145.

Gandhi's arguments in support of his economic model, which includes not only his views on industrialization but also his views on consumption, distribution, trusteeship, *svadeśī* and many others.

Gandhi is generally misunderstood as one who is totally opposed to industrialization. But the actual picture is not as rigid and as unrealistic as it appears to be. Gandhi firmly believed that "machinery is for man and not man for machinery" should be the cardinal principle of all mechanical production. He clearly states that, "I am not aiming at the eradication of all machinery, but its limitation; the supreme consideration is man."[35] In the present world, modern large-scale technology is replacing old techniques in almost every sphere of production but in the Gandhian project large-scale industry will be allowed only when it is absolutely necessary; for example, in case of railway and electricity. In his framework the use of machinery is constrained by certain principles. The principles are:

1. The introduction of machines should not create more unemployment,
2. It should not destroy village crafts, and
3. It should not be used as a weapon for exploitation and to perpetuate economic inequality.

It is obvious that the three constraints are interlinked and it cannot be said that one is more important than the other. It will be a misunderstanding to think that Gandhi was against all kinds of machinery. He writes in this context:

> What I object to is the craze for machinery, but not machinery as such . . . men go on "saving labour" till thousands are without work and thrown at open streets to die of starvation.

---

35. N.K. Bose, *Selections From Gandhi*, 1957, p. 66.

Again in another context he says:

> I want to save time and labour not for the fraction of mankind but for all. Today machinery merely helps a few to ride on the back of millions. The impetus behind it all is not the philanthropy to save labour, but greed.[36]

One may feel tempted to criticize Gandhi that he was mistaken in generalizing about the use and application of machinery. It is indeed true that the disintegration of the cottage industry in India resulted in a mass-scale unemployment which industrialization could not tackle. But industrialization is not the sole factor that is responsible for mass unemployment; there are other important context-related features that can contribute to it. In the West we have seen that the gloomy prophecies of some nineteenth-century critics have not come true and the progress of industrialization has not necessarily been accompanied by any steady trend towards increased unemployment; for example, in the Soviet Union since 1930 labour shortage had been more acute and evident than mass unemployment.

But still there is a significant insight in Gandhian thought that cannot be easily overlooked. Western technology is usually inclined towards labour-saving devices. In India and in many other underdeveloped countries the basic ratios between the available stock of capital and the existing supply of labour are far more unfavourable than they are in industrially developed countries. The economists are of the opinion that the underdeveloped countries today must evolve methods of production suited to their resource endowments. Indiscriminate adoption of advanced Western technology in these countries will certainly produce more unemployment that is either safe or beneficial for them; this is all the more

36. N.K. Bose, op. cit., p. 378.

true because the rate of growth of population in these countries is faster than in the richer nations. Though modern technology is stressing on the need for maximizing production, Gandhi consistently emphasized on the need for providing maximum number of people with productive work. He would allow industrialization in his scheme provided it does not act as an obstacle to his ultimate goals. In this context he writes:

> Electricity, ship building, iron works, machine making and like existing (can exist) side by side with village handicrafts . . . hitherto industrialization has been planned to destroy the village and the village crafts. In the state of future it will subserve the villages and the village crafts.[37]

Since Gandhi has given space to the large-scale industry the question that automatically arises is, "who will be in the controlling position of these industries?" It can't be state because for Gandhi, "The state represents violence in a concentrated and organized form."[38] In the Gandhian scheme there will be innumerable self-sufficient village republics but no state. He says in this context:

> In this structure composed of innumerable villages there will be ever-widening never-ascending circles. Life will not be a pyramid with apex sustained from bottom, but it will be oceaning circles whose centre will be the individual.[39]

But if there are only self-sufficient village communities and no state there will be problems with regard to the decisions that ought to be taken in connection with the distribution of the thermal power or launching of the railway lines. When Gandhi was confronted with queries of these kinds it appears

37. M.K. Gandhi, *The Voice of Truth*, p. 381.
38. Buddhadeva Bhattacharya, *Evolution of the Political Philosophy of Gandhi*, p. 58.
39. Vasant Palsikar, *Gandhi's Economic Ideas*, p. 225.

from his responses that he would allow an organization similar to state to operate in such extraordinary situations provided, it is in harmony with his general scheme and there is no abuse of power. Gandhi writes in this context:

> I am socialist enough to say that such factories should be nationalized or State controlled. They ought only be working under the most attractive and ideal conditions, not for profit but for the benefit of humanity.[40]

In these village units the individual will enjoy *svarāja*. *Svarāja* is an ideal state where there is no difference between the prince and the peasant, between the landowner and the tiller of the soil, where all are equal irrespective of caste and creed. Gandhi truly realized that real *svarāja* must include economic freedom which will pave the way for political freedom, for he was right in realizing that political freedom cannot be complete without its economic counterpart. *Pūrṇa svarāja* means complete freedom from any kind of exploitation, social, political and economic. This *pūrṇa svarāja* will enable the individual to bloom, to realize his best self where his good and good of the community are inseparable. *Svarāja* can be attained by the individual if, and only if, the community where the individual belongs is self-sufficient, egalitarian and is not overpowered by any external factors politically, economically or otherwise.

Certain questions are inevitable in this context. Unlike Marx, Gandhi has not addressed the question of the means to be adopted to achieve the desired goal. The egalitarian self-sufficient village community precedes the attainment of *pūrṇa svarāja* or is it the other way round? Gandhi has not given an answer to this problematic issue, probably because there is no clear answer to this question. We only know that the goal and the means are intrinsically related and so the path that one

---

40. *Harijan*, 27.02.1937.

must follow to achieve this goal must be a path of non-violence.

Decentralization and Self-sufficiency

Gandhi strongly believed that centralization of power is the root cause of all forms of exploitation resulting in the curtailment of the individual freedom, in extreme cases leading to unemployment and poverty. Decentralization on the contrary restores human freedom and promotes altruistic human values like fellow feeling and co-operation. Gandhi in this context opines:

> The end to be sought is human happiness combined with full mental and moral growth. I use the adjective moral as synonymous with spiritual. This end can be achieved under decentralization. Centralization as a system is inconsistent with non-violent structure of society.[41]

Self-sufficiency is one of the most essential features of the non-violent village community envisaged by Gandhi. The villages must be self-sufficient not only politically but economically as well. The latter indicates that all villages must actually be self-supporting in the production of the basic necessities, sufficient enough to ensure a decent standard of living. With regard to Indian villages the main stress should be on agriculture along with small industries developed around it on a planned basis to suit its specific line of production. All the local requirements like food, vegetable, fruits and other necessary products will have to be produced. Production for use and not for profit has to be the guiding principle of such decentralized agro-industrial economy. This automatically implies that planning must be done in terms of available resources, real needs and maximum utilization of

41. *Harijan*, 18.01.1942; Also in *CWMG*, vol. 75, 1979, p. 216.

available labour. Apart from these, accommodation must be made for other vital requirements like housing, fuel and transport to ensure smooth communication.

However village self-sufficiency does not mean denial of sharing and co-operation with the surrounding neighbours. Gandhi writes in this context that:

> My idea of village svarāja is that it is a complete republic independent of its neighbours for its vital wants, and yet dependent for many others in which dependence is a necessity.[42]

Gandhi in emphasizing the necessity of self-sufficiency of the village panchayats has acknowledged the necessity of trade and other forms of exchanges that will help in maintaining a healthy relationship with the neighbours. However Gandhi would never allow any form of economic exploitation in the name of trade. One might remind the Gandhians that "vital necessity" is a relative concept and it might be different in different societies, and also might differ from individual to individual. If the Marxian dictum of "each according to his need" is followed in the Gandhian programme then also the above-mentioned predicament reappears, as the concept of need remains undefined. However we can try to understand the Gandhian concept of "need" by going through the details of the requirements of the village community envisaged by Gandhi. A self-sufficient village community structured by Gandhi will be of the following type:

1. Every village will grow its food, crops and required cotton for its cloth.
2. After the distribution of land for the production of its necessities, if there is more land, it can grow other crops excluding harmful crops like ganja, tobacco, etc.

---

42. *Harijan*, 26.07.1942.

3. Every village must ensure its own water supply through construction of wells and tanks when the required water supply is not available from the natural sources.
4. Every cottage in the village must have proper ventilation with enough light and satisfactory sanitation facilities.
5. Proper medical facilities must be made available in every village community.
6. Education must be made compulsory at least at the primary level.
7. Gandhi would insist that every village should have enough land for the grazing of the cattle and for the playing of the children.
8. Apart from the availability of the school and the medical care centres, there should be a public hall for worshipping and a village theatre for recreation.

Prices of the commodities would have to be determined by mutual co-operation and through proper understanding among the buyers and the sellers. The production and the consumption of the commodities would be guided by the principle of maximization of social welfare and not by the motivation of profit making. It was Gandhi's firm conviction that a village community organized on the basis of decentralization and self-sufficiency will ensure a happy, healthy and meaningful life for each and every individual, automatically promoting a harmonious and all-round development both for the individual as well as for the community. Gandhi writes in this context:

> When our villages are fully developed there will be no dearth in them of men with high degree of skill and artistic talents. There will be village poets, village artists, village architects, linguists and research workers. In short, there will be

> nothing in life worth having which will not be had in the villages. Today the villages are dung heaps. Tomorrow they will be like tiny gardens of Eden where (would) dwell highly intelligent folk whom no one can deceive or exploit.[43]

It is clear that Gandhi's villages would be empowered socially, economically and politically so that there is an absolute end of the exploitation of the village communities by the urban centres. The urban centres will be completely eradicated in the long run but initially the change can be brought about by making a difference in their relation.[44] The villages will enjoy the maximum possible benefit of advancement in all aspects. Though we have a satisfactory idea of the village community proposed by Gandhi, we still do not know anything about the composition of a village or regarding the ideal population of these village communities proposed by Gandhi. Gandhi has commented in this context that the size of the village communities will be determined by the geographical, social and the economic considerations of a particular region. Defining it on the basis of population Gandhi commented in this context that:

> My imaginary village consists of 1000 souls. Such a unit can give an account of itself, if it is well organized on the basis of self sufficiency.[45]

This of course will differ depending on the context and so many other related factors.

---

43. *Harijan*, 10.11.1946; also in M.K. Gandhi, *India of My Dreams*, pp. 97-98.
44. We are referring to the relationship between a village and a city.
45. *Harijan*, 04.08.1946; Also in M.K. Gandhi, *Rebuilding our Villages*, pp. 97-98.

Individual is the Ultimate Decision Maker

One might think that in the Gandhian scheme the self-sufficient village communities have primacy over and above the individual members but on the contrary in a non-violent economic structure ultimately it is the individual[46] who is the ultimate authority. The individual in such an egalitarian community enjoys maximum freedom, in his economic and socio-politico decisions. Freedom or *svarāja* in the Gandhian society does not mean liberty without responsibility. The individual must exercise his freedom keeping in mind that he is an integral part of the village community. Thus his decisions are constrained by broad guidelines. Explaining the meaning of *svarāja,* Gandhi declares that:

> The root meaning of *svarāja* is self-rule. *Svarāja* may, therefore be rendered as disciplined rule from within . . . independence may mean licence to do as you like. . . . *Svarāja* is positive and independence is negative. . . . The word *svarāja* is a sacred word, a vedic word, meaning self-rule and self-restraint and not freedom from all restraints which "independence" often means.[47]

Although the initiative and originality of the individual member is appreciated and acknowledged the adherence to the collective system is the most dominant feature in Gandhian socio-politico-economic scheme that can hardly be ignored. The twin principles of *svadeśī* and trusteeship determine individual's policy of consumption and production. Though the individual in the Gandhian framework is not neglected in the sense that Gandhi has always emphasized on the need of the individual leading a dignified life — in other words Gandhi

46. It is a related individual in the sense that individual is always related to other individuals of the society.

47. *Young India,* 19.03.1931; Also in *Gandhi in Today's India,* ed. B.C. Das, G.P. Misra, p. 48.

has always realized the importance of getting a job for an individual — it can never be overlooked that the freedom that the individual enjoys within this scheme is a space within a fixed boundary with limited options, where the "rights" and "wrongs" are fixed and well-defined.

The Principle of Svadeśī

The term *svadeśī* has a technical meaning in the Gandhian context and it must be understood from the right perspective. As has been stated by Gandhi:

> *svadeśī* is that spirit in us which restricts us to the use and service of our immediate surroundings to the exclusion of the more remote.[48]

Gandhi argues that since man's capacity to serve his environment is limited, man should always choose his immediate surroundings and select those that are immediately present before him. Thus man's first and foremost duty would be towards his family and village to where he actually belongs. Gandhi in his endeavour to clarify this concept reiterates that, in religion:

> I must restrict myself to my ancestral religion . . . if I find it defective, I should serve it by purging it of its defects. In the domain of politics I should make use of the indigenous institutions and serve them by curing them of their proved defects. In that of economics I should use only things that are produced by my immediate neighbours and those industries by making them efficient and complete where they might be found wanting.[49]

The spirit of *svadeśī* in guiding man's economic decisions induces an individual to prefer the local products. The individual as a consumer has a tendency to buy from the local producers as he tries to support the local farmers and

48. M.K. Gandhi, *The Gospel of Swadeshi*, p. 1.

49. *Speeches and Writings of Mahatma Gandhi*, p. 236.

artisans.[50] It was Gandhi's firm conviction that the breach of the sacred law of *svadeśī* caused unemployment and poverty that resulted in the general degradation of the economic life of India. In an address at a missionary conference held in Madras, Gandhi said:

> Much of the deep poverty of (the) masses is due to the ruinous departure from *svadeśī* in the economic and the industrial life. Had not an article of commerce been brought from outside India, she should be today a land flowing with milk and honey.[51]

One might argue that the above mentioned attitude is inconsistent with Gandhi's principle of non-violence, with which Gandhi has never compromised throughout his life. *Svadeśī* apparently expresses an attitude of jingoism. But it would be a misunderstanding to think that the principle of *svadeśī* encourages unhealthy competition and a bias towards indigenous products. Actually the principle of *svadeśī* was a conscious step taken by Gandhi to revive the dying rural economy of the British India. *Svadeśī* certainly opposes the intervention of foreign capital, technical know-how and entrepreneurship. This principle actually encourages the best possible use of the local raw material and manpower to promote occupational equilibrium. Producers on their part must have a co-operative attitude towards the poor customers. The co-operation between the consumers and the producers will lead to a downward shift of the cost curve making the essential commodities available to each and every customer.

The Philosophy of Khādī

In the economic sphere the principle of swadeshi was actually expressed through the principle of *khādī*. The philosophy of

50. Weavers, carpenters, cobblers, potters.
51. *CWMG*, vol. 13, 1964, p. 222.

khādī occupied a significant place in Gandhi's plan for the economic regeneration of the poverty ridden village India. He often referred to *carkhā* (the spinning wheel) as India's *Kāmadhenu*. It actually symbolized the image of *svadeśī* for the *khādī* movement aimed at restoring the spinning wheel to the millions of cottages in India, which was destroyed by the unjust tyrannical methods of British Imperialism.

Gandhi's attitude towards *khādī* changed from time to time. The idea of *khādī* occurred to Gandhi in 1919, when he had no clear picture about the wheel. At that period Gandhi realized that the chief cause of pauperization of India was the destruction of the cottage industries by the British government. In the early 1920s Gandhi looked at the prospect of *khādī* from a different perspective altogether. The problem of the production and distribution of wealth prompted Gandhi to think of popularizing the spinning wheel with a view to preventing the concentration of wealth in limited hands. By 1935 his vision took a new dimension. He strongly felt that *khādī* has the potentiality to play the most effective role in uplifting the Indian villages towards economic self-sufficiency of some kind. Gandhi writes in this context:

> *Khādī* must be taken with all its implications. It means a wholesale *svadeśī* mentality, a determination to find all the necessaries of life in India and that too through the labour and intellect of the villagers — in other words a reversal of the existing process. That is to say that, instead of half a dozen cities of India and Great Britain living on the exploitation and the ruin of the 700,000 villages of India, the latter will be largely self-contained, and will voluntarily serve the cities of India and even the outside world insofar as it benefits both the parties.[52]

52. M.K. Gandhi, *Constructive Programme*, p. 111; Buddhadeva Bhattacharya, p. 279.

The question that arises in this context is, what is the special feature about *carkhā* that makes it so special? Buddhadeva Bhattacharya in his book, *Evolution of the Political Philosophy of Gandhi*, has pointed out the reasons that might have played an important role for preferring the *carkhā*. The reasons pointed out by Buddhadeva Bhattacharya are the following:

1. The spinning wheel actually supplied occupation to the millions of unemployed underutilized youths of India.
2. It was cheap, easily available and almost known to everyone.
3. Gandhi must have realized that the philosophy of *khādī* can be effectively used for generating a we-feeling throughout India irrespective of the religious beliefs and other class and caste distinctions.
4. *Khādī* movement had the potentiality to prevent the drain of wealth that is used for purchasing the foreign cloth.[53]

Khādī actually stood for a particular philosophy that aimed at reversing the existing order. The philosophy of *khādī* symbolized a "new system" that stood as an alternative culture to the over-centralized factory civilization. As Gandhi writes in this context, "the science of *khādī* requires decentralization of production and consumption."[54] Whether *khādī* was a valid proposal for the economic development of India in the days when Gandhi launched this programme or whether it bears any relevance today in the economic growth of modern India

---

53. Buddhadeva Bhattacharyya, *Evolution of the Political Philosophy of Gandhi*, pp. 278-79.
54. *Harijan*, 2.11.1935, p. 300; also in Buddhadeva Bhattacharya, p. 279.

is a separate issue altogether.[55] At least one must appreciate that his experiments with truth were actually applied at the time when India was going through a difficult phase. Gandhi was not simply a dreamer but he could show the world that he actually meant what he said by applying his economic programmes of self-sufficiency into practice with effective results.

Need vs Want

Gandhi's entire economic proposal rests on the assumption that man is essentially spiritual and he can conquer the "selfish man" within himself and can rise above the multiplicity of wants. It was Gandhi's strong belief that a sincere quest for truth makes man "need oriented" whereas the pursuit of self-interest makes man "want oriented." The sole purpose of consumption according to Gandhi is not the pursuit of pleasure arising out of the gratification of the unlimited wants but the fulfilment of the "actual needs" that are essential for the maintenance of body and the development of the mind so that ultimately man can discover his true "related self" and can work for the service of mankind. Gandhian economics consistently denounces the conventional and the modern system of production, which is based on the principle of unlimited inculcation of wants.

Gandhi's emphasis on the need-based production and consumption shows us that his principle of trusteeship follows from his theory of the restriction of wants. According to this paradigm, God is the creator of everything and the entire creation automatically belongs to God. Since all the natural and the material goods are God's possession it should be equally shared by all and no individual has the right to consume more than his proportionate share. Thus one who

---

55. The relevance of *khādī* has not been dealt with in this paper.

consumes more than one's due is guilty of committing "theft." Gandhi writes in this context:

> The profound truth upon which the observance is based is that God never creates more than what is strictly needed for the moment. Therefore, whoever appropriates more than the minimum that is necessary, is guilty of theft.[56]

The breach of the principle of non-stealing is responsible for the poverty and the inequalities of income existing in all the societies of the world according to Gandhi. In 1916 Gandhi wrote:

> I suggest that we are thieves in a way. If I take anything that I do not need for my own immediate use and keep it, I thieve it from somebody else. I venture to say that it is the fundamental law of Nature, without exception, that Nature produces enough for our wants . . . if everybody took enough for himself and nothing more, there would be no pauperism in this world. There would be no man dying of starvation in this world. But so long as we have got this inequality we are thieving.[57]

One might argue that it is difficult to draw a line between "need" and "greed" as both of them are complex, concepts that merges into the other. Both "need" and "greed" are context dependent. Gandhi would suggest that a perpetual vigilance is required to discriminate "needs" from "wants" accompanied by a continuous effort to curtail superfluous wants. We find him suggesting that:

> We are not always aware of our real needs, and most of us improperly multiply our wants and thus unconsciously

56. M.K. Gandhi, *Voluntary Poverty*, comp. Ravindra Kelekar, Ahmedabad: Navjivan Publishing House, 1961, p. 15.

57. Ibid., pp. 14-15. Also in Sashi Prabha Sharma, *Gandhian Holistic Eoconomics*, p. 100.

> make thieves of ourselves. If we devote some thought to the subject, we shall find that we can get rid of quite a number of wants.[58]

Gandhi's Theory of Trusteeship

Gandhi's theory of trusteeship automatically follows from his principle of consumption. The need-based principle of consumption must be applicable in case of the possession of material property. According to the same principle if an individual possesses more property than what he/she actually requires, he/she should act as a trustee and shall use the wealth for the welfare of the society. In 1939 in reply to a question put to Gandhi by a member of the Gandhi Seva Sangha, Gandhi explained his view of trusteeship in the following terms:

> Supposing I have come by a fair amount of wealth — either by way of legacy or by means of trade and industry — I must know that all the wealth does not belong to me; what belongs to me is the right to an honourable livelihood, no better than that enjoyed by millions of others. The rest of my wealth belongs to the community and must be used for the welfare of the community.[59]

Gandhi proposed this theory keeping in mind the possession held by the *ẓamindārs* and other ruling chiefs. He wanted the privileged classes to outgrow their greed and realize that they had a social obligation to utilize their wealth for public benefit. Actually the idea of trusteeship was implicitly present in his holistic scheme. Pleading for the right relation between the capital and labour he remarked as early as in 1925:

> *Svarāja* as conceived by me does not mean the end of kinship. Nor does it mean the end of capital. Accumulated capital

58. Sashi Prabha Sharma, p. 99.
59. *Harijan*, 3.6.1939, p. 145; Also, Buddhadeb Bhattacharya, p. 235.

> means ruling power. I am for the establishment of the right relation between capital and labour etc. I do not wish for the supremacy of the one over the other.[60]

The principle of trusteeship actually redefines the concept of private property. Gandhi will never demand that each and every individual should have equal earning irrespective of the quality and the quantity of the work done. He has no desire to cramp the talents of the creative individuals, he only insists that they should be using their talent for the welfare of the society. He has clearly stated that:

> . . . the bulk of his[61] greater earning must be used for the good of the state, just as the income of all earning sons of the father goes to the common family fund. They would have their earnings only as trustees.[62]

The glaring economic inequalities of the society leading to the concentration of the capital in a few hands evoked Gandhi's condemnation. The state of inequality in society was completely unacceptable for him. In 1904 he was inspired by Ruskin's view, as we all know — that the lawyer's work has the same value as the barber's inasmuch as all have the same right of earning their livelihood from their work. Though Gandhi had sincerely endeavoured to plan for an egalitarian society where equality prevails in all aspects, the term "equality" has a technical sense in Gandhi's theory, different from the ordinary usage. His pragmatic attitude made him realize that the idea of equal distribution of wealth would not be acceptable to the majority at that stage. To quote him in this context:

---

60. Buddhadeb Bhattacharya, 1969, p. 232.
61. The one who is earning more than he actually requires or has a surplus of anything that can be used for the benefit of the society.
62. *Young India*, 2.6.1931, p. 368.

> My ideal is equal distribution, but so far as I can see it is not to be realized. I therefore work for equitable distribution. . . . Economic Equality must never mean the possession of an equal amount of worldly goods by everyone. It means that everybody should have enough for his needs . . . the elephant needs a thousand times more food than an ant, but that is not an indication of inequality. So the real meaning of economic equality is "to each according to his need."[63]

The Draft on Trusteeship finalized by Gandhi consisted of the following essential elements:

1. Trusteeship provided a means of transforming the present capitalist order of society into an egalitarian one. It provided the capitalist class a chance of reforming itself. It is based on the faith that human nature is never beyond redemption.
2. It did not recognize any right of private ownership of property except as much as it may be permitted by the society for its own welfare.
3. The principle of trusteeship did not exclude legislative regulation of ownership and use of wealth.
4. Under the state regulated trusteeship an individual would not be free to hold his wealth for selfish satisfaction or in disregard of the interest of the society.

Gandhi not only proposed a decent minimum living wage, he also thought that it is desirable to fix the upper limit of the income of an individual. The difference between such minimum and maximum income should be reasonable, equitable and should be open to modification from time to time so much so that the tendency should be towards obliteration of the difference.[64] The philosophical roots of the

---

63. *Young India*, 17.03.1927, p. 86; *Harijan*, 31.03.1946, p. 63.7
64. *Harijan*, 9.3.1947; Also in Ram Binod Singh, pp. 151-52.

principles of non-stealing can be traced back to *Īśa-vāsya mantra,* the first verse of *Īśopaniṣad*. Actually if we probe into the concept of trusteeship we will realize that it is very closely linked with the concept of *aparigraha*. Being influenced by the ideals of Upaniṣad Gandhi was convinced that the things of this world should be enjoyed by renunciation. Gandhi has clearly mentioned in his autobiography that concepts of *aparigraha* (non-possession) and *samabhāva* (equability) gripped him. Gandhi in addition to this was also influenced by Snell's maxim of equity. To quote in this context:

> My study of English law came to my help. Snell's discussion of the maxim of equity came to my memory. I understood more clearly in the light of the *Gītā's* teaching the implication of the word "trustee." My regard for jurisprudence increased, I discovered it in religion.[65]

However Gandhi was not the first man who came up with such a unique suggestion for solving the age-old problem of inequality present in the society. The early socialist thinkers of Europe were optimistic enough to think that the problem of economic inequality can be solved by making the members aware of the unequal distribution of wealth in the society. Owen, Charles Fourier and other eighteenth-century socialist thinkers thought that the economic difference in the society can be minimized by education and social awareness.

The theory of trusteeship proposed by Gandhi was vehemently criticized from different corners. T.K.N. Unnithan in his book, *Gandhi and Free India,* has observed that Gandhi never questions the historical existence of the institution of the rich though he dreams about the possibility of its complete eradication. It is most unlikely that Gandhi supported the historical growth of the institution of wealth. Probably Gandhi

---

65. M.K. Gandhi, *An Autobiography*, p. 195.

in order to be consistent with his principle of non-violence tolerated and avoided any form of confrontation with the wealthy section. He firmly believed that conflict cannot provide a stable foundation for a healthy society. Probably for the same reason he could not agree with Ambedkar regarding the reservation proposal put forward by the latter. Gunnar Myrdal has commented that the moral revolution of the psyche of the wealthy group is most unlikely. He felt that Gandhi's principle of trusteeship actually encourages the rich to be charitable so that the poor continues to be weak.[66]

Jawaharlal Nehru in his Autobiography has also criticized Gandhi's principle of trusteeship. He wrote:

> Again I think of the paradox that is Gandhiji. With all his keen intellect and passion for bettering the downtrodden and oppressed, why does he support a system which is obviously decaying, which creates this misery and waste? . . . And meanwhile he blesses all the relics of the old order which stand as an obstacle in the way of advance . . . the big *ẓamindārīs* and *tāluqdārs*, the present capitalist system. Is it reasonable to believe in the theory of trusteeship — to give unchecked power and wealth to an individual and to expect him to use it entirely for the public good? Are the best of us so perfect to be trusted in this way? . . . And is it good for the others to have these benevolent superman over them?[67]

We should remember that Gandhi is providing us with a holistic scheme where "Trusteeship" is a feature of the entire proposal. Nehru or Gunnar Myrdal are critiquing Gandhi by "picking up" one particular feature in isolation from the total scheme,

---

66. Gunnar Myrdal, *Asian Drama: An Enquiry into Poverty of Nations*, Penguin Books, 1968, vol. 2, pp. 755-56.
67. Jawaharlal Nehru, *An Autobiography*, Mumbai: Allied Publishers Ltd., 1962, p. 528.

overlooking the other aspects which are inseparably linked up with the proposal. Myrdal is considering the theory of "Trusteeship" from his leftist perspective; on the other hand, Nehru is considering "Trusteeship" from socialist standpoint, thus none of them are doing justice to the holistic complex network of the Gandhian scheme. Moreover Gandhi's theory of "Trusteeship" can be interpreted as a stepping-stone towards the ideal society envisaged by Gandhi. Since Gandhi would not approve of any conflict or tension among the individuals or the economic classes existing in the society, "Trusteeship" can be looked as a time-appropriate proposal in a social context where there is a sharp difference between the "have-lots" and the "have-nots." In such a context the class with surplus property can participate in this programme and thus can utilize their wealth for social benefit and public welfare. Gradually the society can evolve better schemes of distribution so that the difference between the higher and the lower income group can be minimized in such a way that the institution of "Trusteeship" becomes redundant.

We have already mentioned that the Gandhian economic theory is a step towards his holistic proposal of *svarāja*. The aim of *svarāja* was not the replacement of "one form of coercive rule by another." *Svarāja* was actually an endeavour to alter the entire socio-economic set-up in which the individual is located. Gandhi as we all know correctly realized that the political freedom without its economic counterpart is a vacuous concept. As he writes:

> Let there be no mistake about my conception of *svarāja*. It is complete independence of alien control and complete economic independence. So at one end you have political independence and at the other end economic. It has two other ends. One of them is moral and social, the corresponding end is *dharma*. Let us call this the square of

> *svarāja*, which will be out of shape if any of its angles is untrue.[68]

In the square of *svarāja* the relation between the political and the economic is clear, but the relation among social, moral and *dharma* remains vague. The other writings of Gandhi on this issue seems to suggest that *dharma* is the highest state that can be achieved after the first three, i.e. political, economic, and social parameters are taken care of.

Before I wind up the entire discussion on the Gandhian economic model let me highlight the contrast between the modern trend and the Gandhian scheme to have a clearer understanding of the issue.

Modern Trend

Centralization of the entire production system resulting in,

1. Diffusion of large-scale industry.
2. Mass production.
3. For perpetuating 1 & 2 there is constant emphasis on the multiplication of wants.
4. State is being used for the above-mentioned purpose leading to inevitable inequality and marginalization of villages.

Gandhian Proposal

1. Emphasis on small-scale production, cottage industry, handicrafts except in a few sectors where mass production is unavoidable. Decentralization through widespread village ownership and trusteeship.
2. Limited state ownership.

---

68. Budhadeva Bhattacharyya, p. 77.

3. Emphasis on the minimization of wants.

We can relook at the entire scheme to see that Gandhian project is in absolute contrast to the modern economic trend.

Modern Trend	Gandhian Proposals
1. Diffusion of large-scale industry.	1. Emphasis on small-scale technology, cottage industries, handicrafts co-existing with some large-scale industry.
2. Mass production.	2. Emphasis on small-scale production except in a few sectors where mass production is unavoidable.
3. Centralization of the economic process.	3. Decentralization through widespread spread village ownership and trusteeship. Limited State ownership.
4. Constant encouragement of the multiplication of wants.	4. Emphasis on the minimization of wants
5. Rapid urbanization, marginalization of the villages.	5. Self-governing village republics Based on the concept of *svadeśī, svarāja*.
6. Inevitable inequality.	6. Equality in Gandhian sense prevails.

In the present scenario the Gandhian model seems too unrealistic, completely alien in the modern trend of consumerism. Gandhi as I have mentioned condemned this concept of progress and civilization. He challenged the claim that modern civilization is a leveller in which the productive capacities of human labour rise exponentially resulting in increased wealth, prosperity, ample leisure, and comfort finally contributing to individual's health and happiness. Gandhi argued that far from attaining these objectives modern civilization perpetuates an ever-increasing greed and a sense of competition resulting in inequality, poverty, insecurity and constant sufferings of various sorts. This is precisely because modern civilization treats man as a "limitless consumer" and thus opens the floodgates of production leading to constant oppression and violence. We all have gradually realized to what extent Gandhian anticipations are true. The self-defeating position of the present system would compel us to give a serious thought to the alternative scheme proposed by Gandhi with its emphasis on need minimization, decentralization and self-sufficiency. Many economists argue that the counter-finality of the consequences of our actions would ultimately compel us to opt for the Gandhian model; at some point of time we would be forced to appropriate it with certain modifications.

References

Bhattacharya, Buddhadeva, *Evolution of Political Philosophy of Gandhi*, Kolkata: Calcutta Book House, 1989.

———, "Gandhi's Political Thought", in Krishna Roy (ed.), *Political Philosophy: East and West*, New Delhi: Jadavpur University and Allied Publishers, 2003.

Bhattacharya, Vivek Ranjan, "Economic Thoughts of Mahatma Gandhi", in S.C. Biswas (ed.), *Gandhi's Theory and Practice: Social Impact and Contemporary Relevance*, Shimla: Indian Institute of Advanced Study and K.P Bagchi and Company, 1969.

Biswas, S.C. (ed.), *Gandhi's Theory and Practice: Social Impact and Contemporary Relevance*, Shimala: Indian Institute of Advanced Study and K.P Bagchi and Company, 1969.

Bose, N.K., *Selections From Gandhi*, Ahmedabad: Navjivan Publishing House, 1948.

Datta, Amlan, "Aspects of Gandhian Economic Thought", in Sibnarayan Roy (ed.), *Gandhi, Gandhism and Our Time*, Kolkata: Renaissance Publication, 2003.

Gandhi, M.K., *From Yerada Mandir*, Ahmedabad: Navjivan Publishing House, 1932.

———, *Hind Swaraj or Indian Home Rule*, Ahmedabad: Navjivan Publishing House, 1938.

———, *The Story of My Experiments with Truth*, Ahmedabad: Navjivan Publishing House, 1940.

———, *Constructive Programme: Its Meaning and Place*, Ahmedabad: Navjivan Publishing House, 1941.

———, *Khādī*, Ahmedabad: Navjivan Publishing House, 1955.

———, *India of My Dreams*, Ahmedabad: Navjivan Publishing House, 1957.

———, *Economic and Industrial Life and Relations*, Ahmedabad: Navjivan Publishing House, 1959.

———, *The Gospel of Swadeshi*, Mumbai: Bharatiya Vidya Bhavan, 1967.

———, *Service Before Self*, Mumbai: Bharatiya Vidya Bhavan, 1967.

———, *Rebuilding our Villages*, Ahmedabad: Navjivan Publishing House, 1969.

Gyanchand, "The Substance of Gandhian Economic Approach", in S.C. Biswas (ed.), *Gandhi's Theory and Practice: Social Impact and Contemporary Relevance*, Shimla: Indian Institute of Advanced Study and K.P Bagchi and Company, 1969.

Kelkar, Ravindra (comp), *M.K. Gandhi, Voluntary Poverty*, Ahmedabad: Navjivan Publishing House, 1961.

Krishna, Raj, "Some Reflections on Gandhian Economics", in S.C. Biswas (ed.), *Gandhi's Theory and Practice: Social Impact and Contemporary Relevance*, Shimla: Indian Institute of Advanced Study and K.P Bagchi and Company, 1969.

Myrdal, Gunnar, *Asian Drama: An Enquiry into Poverty of Nations*, Penguin, 1968.

Narayan, Shriman (ed.), *The Selected Works of Mahatma Gandhi*, Ahmedabad: Navjivan Publishing House, 1968.

Paliskar, Vasant, "Gandhi's Economic Ideas and their Present Relevance", in S.C. Biswas (ed.), *Gandhi's Theory and Practice: Social Impact and Contemporary Relevance*, Shimla: Indian Institute of Advanced Study and K.P Bagchi and Company, 1969.

Parekh, Bhikhu, *Gandhi: A Very Short Introduction*, Oxford: Oxford University Press, 1997.

Sharma, Sashi Prabha, *Gandhian Holistic Economics*, New Delhi: Concept Publishing Co., 1992.

Singh, Ram, Binod, *Gandhian Approach to Development*, New Delhi: Concept Publishing Co., 2006.

6

Varṇa and Jāti

Indrani Sanyal

ONE of the perennial problems that afflict Indian society is the problem of caste. The Indian psyche, especially the Hindu psyche, has been held responsible for being the breeding ground of caste mentality. Undoubtedly, the caste structure continues to persist as one of the main features of Indian society. The notion of caste, its nature, its origin and structure defy any straight-cut characterization. Attempts are often made to relate the notion of caste with that of religion, morality, politics and law. There are some like Louis Dumont, the author of *Homo Hierarchicus,*[1] who argue that caste is essentially a Hindu phenomenon and maintain, "The caste system is . . . different from our own social system in its central ideology . . ."[2] But there are others who consider it to be an utter misconception to regard caste to be peculiar to the Hindu culture and connected with the Hindu faith. In many countries in ancient times as in Persia, Rome and Japan caste system based on birth and occupation did prevail. Any proper attempt to explore ali the issues and associated values and disvalues of the caste system needs to take into consideration its empirical-sociological-anthropological aspects as well as its

---

1. *The Homo Hierarchicus, The Caste System and Its Implications,* 1998.
2. Ibid., p. 1.

conceptual-philosophical aspects. The study of caste systems has been carried on either from the angles of the sociologists and anthropologists through empirical descriptions or from the angle of the philosophers through conceptual analysis with focus upon conceptual issues. In spite of the pronouncement in the Indian Constitution that any discrimination on the basis of caste, creed and religion is illegal, the real scenario of the society here is often markedly different.

While commenting on the caste system of India, philosophers, historians, sociologists, politicians, social anthropologists as well as the man on the street have expressed mixed responses. Thinkers, theoreticians and pragmatists alike, both within the country and outside, were occupied in exploring the connotation of *jāti* and its implications. One is surely to be taken aback by the diversity of conflicting responses elicited from different quarters on this single phenomenon of caste system. Sidney Low, a century ago in his *Vision of India*, says:

> There is no doubt that it is the main cause of the fundamental stability and contentment by which Indian society has been braced up for centuries against the shocks and politics and the cataclysms of Nature. It provides every man with his place, his career, his occupation, his circle of friends. It makes him at the outset a member of a corporate body, it protects him through life from the canker of social jealousy and unfulfilled aspirations; it ensures him companionship and a sense of community with others in like case with himself. The caste organization is to the Hindu his club, his trade union, his benefit society, his philanthropic society.[3]

Abbe Dubois remarks in his *Hindu Manners, Customs and Ceremonies*:

---

3. pp. 262-63, 2nd edn. of 1907, Reference obtained from *History of Dharmaśāstra*, Pandurang Vaman Kane, vol. 2, part 1, chapter 2, 1974.

> I consider the institutions of castes among the Hindu notions as the happiest effort of their legislation, and I am well convinced that if the people of India never sink into a state of barbarism and if, when almost all Europe was plunged in that dreary gulf, India kept up her head, preserved and extended the sciences, the arts and civilizations, it is wholly to the distinction of castes that she is indebted for that high celebrity.[4]

Meredith Townsend in *Europe and Asia* maintains:

> I firmly believe caste to be a marvellous discovery, a form of socialism, which through ages protected the Hindu society from anarchy and from the worst evils of industrial and competitive life — it is an automatic poor law to begin with and the strongest form known of trade union.[5]

Again there are writers who have expressed totally different views about castes. Maine in his *Ancient Law* says about the caste system that it is "the most disastrous and blighting of all human institutions."[6] Sherring in his *Hindu Tribes and Castes* says, "It is the most baneful, hard-hearted and cruel social system that could possibly be invested for damning the human race."[7] Thus we find contradictory characterizations come forth in descriptions about the caste system.

We are aware about the problem of caste. Questions relating to the origination and source of castes are being relentlessly asked. The further question that is being asked is, "what has actually provided support for its survival for so many centuries without any break?" In order to find any

4. *Hindu Manners, Customs and Ceremonies*, Rupa Paperback edition, 2007, p. 4.
5. 1901, p. 72. Reference obtained from P.V. Kane's *History of Dharmaśāstra*, 1974.
6. 1930, p. 17.
7. Vol. 3, 1881, p. 274.

suitable reply to such queries an empirical study about the features that are associated with the caste system may be helpful. However, even empirical descriptions about the nature of the caste system have failed to reach any unanimous standpoint. This is largely due to the fact that even empirical descriptions about the caste system are coloured by the perspective from which the system has been viewed by the describer. Sociologists like Joan P. Mencher[8] accuses the majority of authors from the earliest writings on the subject till the present day, barring a few exceptions, of viewing the caste system from a top-down perspective. He proposes to redress the situation by viewing caste system from the bottom-up or "upside down" perspective as opening up the alternative possibility for the discussion about the caste system. Following the trends of social-cultural-anthropology wherein a distinction is maintained between "emic" *versus* "etic" conceptualizations, the caste system may be alternatively investigated and conceptualized. The so-called "emic" perspective is the representative of the insider's or native's interpretation or model in the context of culture, whereas an "etic" analysis is the representative of the viewpoint of the outsider's, the anthropologist's interpretation or model. Dumont has pleaded to undertake the macro level as the only legitimate level for Indian sociology as the model of research on the caste system. In fact, questions relating to methodology to be pursued, or the model of research to be adopted in carrying on any significant research and reinterpretation about the caste system have no single unanimous reply. In this essay all these issues, though very important and worthy of consideration, are to be side-tracked. Very broadly speaking, without entering into all the nuances relating to the nature of understanding, it may be maintained that the understanding of the complexity of

8. "The Caste System Upside Down", in *Social Stratification*, Oxford University Press, 2007.

the caste system rests on the understanding of the main features of the caste system and also the very nature of the ideology, if any, that is supportive of the caste system. The study about the origin of *varṇa* order in classical Indian literature and subsequent extensive practice of the caste system in India have given rise to varied speculations. Two primary objectives would define the goal of this essay: in the first place an attempt will be made to bring out some of the salient features of the caste system as prevalent in the present Indian society. In this connection we would consider views of sociologists, social anthropologists and historians as and when required. Sociologists, anthropologists and people of allied perspectives have provided a clear account of the caste-phenomena in the empirico-social context. The second important thing is to have a re-look at the *varṇa* ideology which is often supposed to have translated its perception of values to empirical reality. In other words, the question as to the relation between the caste as it is in fact, and as it is subsumed by the traditional concept of *varṇa,* remains the focal point for discussion. In common talk caste is considered as a natural corollary of *varṇa* order. How far the prevalent belief would support the attempt to de-link *varṇa-dharma* from caste? *Varṇa-dharma* is a Vedic concept and in its germane form it was contained in the Vedas and the Upaniṣads. The second section of the present article will try to present an exegetical account about *varṇa, varṇa-dharma* as available in the Śruti and the later Smṛti literatures especially as found in the *Mahābhārata* and the *Gītā*. This is followed by the concluding section, which accounts for *varṇa-jāti* ideology in the light of Sri Aurobindo's view about the psychology of social development.

I

One of the most valued aspects of the modern age is the recognition of individual liberty, for an individual is viewed no longer as only a member of a social unit; each individual's being, his right to be what he chooses to be, his demand for freedom, for space, and his own initiative are undeniable. Modern society has learnt to respect an individual's freedom. The related valued aspect of modern society is its focus upon human equality and its effort to eradicate all sorts of economic, social and political inequality. The advocacy of the belief in natural rights during the seventeenth century in the Western world and its assumption of equality of natural order among all human beings led to the rejection of the postulate that human beings are unequal by nature — that there was a natural human hierarchy. The modern society with its announcement of the Universal Declaration of the Human Rights[9] is committed to the principle of equality. No doubt the struggle for the recognition of human rights and the struggle against oppression, injustice and inequalities are as old as human civilization. Dumont while complimenting Western society as egalitarian in outlook, perhaps had in mind the origin of the conception of human rights which may be traced back to the Declaration of Independence[10] adopted by the American colonies and the formation of the United States of America and to the Declaration of the Rights of Man and Citizen[11] by the National Assembly of France in 1789. The Declaration of Independence says:

> . . . that all men are created equal, that they are endowed by their Creator with certain unalienable rights, that among

---

9. On 10 December 1948, the General Assembly of the United Nations adopted and proclaimed the Universal Declaration of Human Rights.
10. On 4 July 1776, with the adoption of the Declaration of Independence, the United States of America was formed.
11. The Declaration of the Rights of Man and Citizen adopted on 26 August 1789 by the National Assembly of France.

> these are Life, Liberty, and the pursuit of Happiness.[12]

The Declaration of the Rights of Man and Citizen says:

> Men are born and remain free and equal in rights. Social distinctions may be based only on common utility.[13]

The disvalue that is associated with the caste system is born out of the perception that the ideology of the caste system is directly contradicted by the ideology of egalitarianism.[14] The British philosopher John Locke defended the claim that men are by nature free and equal. According to Locke natural rights were those enjoyed by the pre-historic man in their original "state of nature."[15] Rousseau in the *Social Contract*[16] defines equality as a political norm:

> The fundamental compact substitutes for such physical inequality as Nature must have set up between men, is an equality which is moral and legitimate.[17]

But among the egalitarians, however, there are differences of opinion regarding the exact connotation of equality. Speaking

---

12. *Human Rights: A Source Book*, National Council of Educational Research and Training, 1996, p. 3.
13. Ibid., p. 6.
14. Egalitarianism, derived from the French word *égal*, meaning *equal*, holds that all people should be treated as equals and have the same political, social, civil and economic rights.
15. *Two Treatises of Government* (1680-1690), book 2, chapter 2, "Of the State of Nature", http:/www.lonang.com/exlibris/index.html.
16. Jean-Jacques Rousseau, *The Social Contract, Or Principles of Political Right*, 1762, tr. by G.D.H Cole, Rendered into HTML and text by Jon Roland, Constitution Society, Austin, TX 78757-1102.
17. *Origins of Inequality*, Selected passages from Jean-Jacques Rousseau, tr. by Anuradha Mukherjee, Aseema Prakashanee, Kolkata, p. 29.

very broadly, an egalitarian is one who views equality as intimately related to justice though he may differ from other egalitarians in interpreting the very concept of equality in terms of either intrinsic goodness or instrumental goodness or constitutive goodness. Equality as a social value, henceforth, receives great impetus from all quarters.

The most obvious feature of Indian society is its division into castes. Hence the question has arisen, "how do we corroborate these ideals of equality and justice in the context of the Indian society?" If these are not the only ideals or values to be pursued by any society, does the Indian society by its adherence to other values, supplement these with any other model of values? Or, are these sheer disvalues embedded in the Indian society? To seek answers to these questions it is necessary to look into the pioneering studies of the missionaries, colonial administrators-turned-historians, sociologists and others who not only recorded their field observations about the social institution of caste in India but also tried to explain the origin of this system by identifying what they considered to be its essential contributory element or elements. Abbe Dubois, the noted anthropologist, who lived for long years among the population of southern India, while commenting on the nature of the Hindu society, said:

> They set out from the cardinal principle common to all ancient legislators, that no person should be useless to the common wealth.[18]

Now broadly speaking, two approaches are discernible in attempts to narrate the empirical reality of the caste system in contemporary India, though other alternatives may as well open up; according to one such approach the caste system is representative of a typical social stratification, whereas others

18. *Hindu Manners, Customs and Ceremonies.*

like Louis Dumont define caste system in terms of hierarchy. Dumont penetrates the façade of observables to get at the core of ideas and values which the people recognize and express themselves while situated in a caste ridden society. Those who look upon caste as social stratification, Dumont accuses them of falling victim to the Western socio-centric model. Dumont defines hierarchy as follows:

> A hierarchical relation is a relation between larger and smaller, or more precisely, between that which encompasses and that which is encompassed.[19]

The cure to socio-centrism lies in trying to look at caste as the indigenes do. The institution of *varṇa* presents, according to Dumont, the purest example of "hierarchy" though it is intriguing that there is no distinct word for hierarchy in any Indian language. While Indian society is hierarchical, modern Western society is egalitarian and the dichotomy of hierarchy-equality is part of the larger dichotomy of the traditional and the modern. Holism is a necessary attribute of hierarchical societies just as individualism is of modern societies. Hierarchy and holism may be taken to be marks of traditional society as equality and individualism are marks of modern societies. Dipankar Gupta and many others do not subscribe to Dumont's way of conceptualizing caste in terms of hierarchy for he is sceptical about the existence of true hierarchy as assumed by Dumont and draws attention to the fact wherein actual reality believers in caste system are not at all following the dictates of true hierarchy. The notion of social stratification,[20] which also needs further clarification, signifies a multi-layered phenomenon which is comparable, though not quite accurately,

---

19. *Homo Hierarchicus*, p. 24.
20. Dipankar Gupta, "Hierarchy and Difference: An Introduction", in *Social Stratification*, Oxford University Press, 2007, p. 5.

with earth's crust. In the case of social stratification as conceived by sociologists, unlike the geological stratification, the concept is not necessarily tied with the notion of hierarchy. In other words, the concept of social stratification may be said to be wider for it may or may not involve social stratification in terms of hierarchy only. These are important issues no doubt and sociologists and anthropologists are still debating about the exactness of the concept to characterize caste system.

What is a caste? As the question admits no simple answer, we may concentrate on some broad-based features of caste. According to H.H. Risley:[21]

> A caste may be defined as a collection of families or groups of families bearing a common name which usually denotes or is associated with specific occupation, claiming a common descent from a mythical ancestor human or divine, professing to follow the same professional callings and are regarded by those who are competent to give an opinion as forming a single homogeneous community.[22]

Thus from the above account, it follows that members of any particular caste (1) bear a common name, (2) claim a common descent, (3) follow the same profession, and (4) form a homogeneous community. To emphasis the characteristic feature of hereditary specialization, it is maintained that in

---

21. Herbert Hope Risley was a British ethnographer and a colonial administrator who did extensive work on castes in India. He entered the Indian Civil Service and had a distinguished career. Herbert Risley was commissioner for the census of 1901. Risley believed that the hierarchy of Indian society matched with the teachings of the literary texts. He hoped to categorise thousands of *jāti*s in terms of the four *varṇa* order.
22. Herbert Hope Risley, *The People of India,* ed. W. Crooke, 2nd edn., London, 1915.

the caste model the son of a blacksmith will be a blacksmith, just as the son of a warrior will be a warrior. The son can only continue the profession of the father and the son cannot choose any other occupation than that of his father. Professions become the monopolies of families, to perform them is not merely a right but a duty imposed by birth upon the children:

> Caste is essentially hereditary; it is the transmission of the same situation and potentialities from father to son. Where there is no heredity, there is no caste.[23]

It is thought to be quite natural and not abominable for a Hindu to take recourse to starvation by following a family profession than to prosper by adopting a profession which is not his family profession.

Critics, however, urge that the division of labour brought about by the caste system is not a division based on choice. Individual sentiment, individual preference has no place in it. "Some have dug a biological trench in defence of the caste system."[24] In the context of the present-day society we do not generally find all the members of a particular caste in a society following a common "family" profession. It is not uncommon to find that the son of a blacksmith is an accomplished MBA earning a handsome salary in a white-collar job, whereas the son of a warrior becomes a teacher in a school.

It is said that the object of caste was to preserve "purity of race and purity of blood."[25] It has been stated that within the caste ranking has been done on the basis of the principle of purity and pollution. Generally, it is supposed that whoever accepts the ideology of caste system must be guided by the principle of purity and pollution. The higher castes are pure

23. Guizot, *La Civilisation en Europe*, Paris, 1828, p. 138.
24. B.R. Ambedkar, *Annihilation of Caste*, p. 264.
25. Ibid.

in relation to the lower and the two have to be kept apart in order to safeguard the purity of the higher. The higher would become impure if they come into contact with the lower. From the perspective of a brāhmaṇa ideology, the brāhmaṇas are the most pure and the levels of purity decrease as we come to the other end where we have no purity at all. Thus we find mainly three tendencies characterize the spirit of caste: these are separation, relating to marriage and contact; hierarchy, relating to ranking of groups as relatively superior or inferior to one another; and hereditary specialization relating to profession of their own which members of each group can hardly abandon. Thus, one aspect, as we have already noted, is hierarchy, by which is meant that pure is superior to the lower; Dumont very carefully brings out the sense of hierarchy understood as value in the context of caste.[26] The common sense view of hierarchy is generally conveyed in terms of "ladder of command" and in this sense "higher rungs encompass lower rungs." Another sense of hierarchy may be called "military hierarchy" where the commander-in-chief is in a commanding position over the people who are in lower ranks. Any sense of hierarchy may be taken to convey the notion of "systematically graduated authority." The other important aspect of caste is separation, whereby the pure must be necessarily kept apart from the impure. When we say that the spirit of caste reigns in a society, we mean that the different groups of which that society is composed, bear a feeling of repulsion against each other, that each confines within itself, isolates itself, makes every effort to prevent its members from contracting alliances.[27] Looked at from this perspective, it would seem that the caste system was designed to seclude members of a class in a society from the members of another

26. "Pure and Impure", in *Homo Hierarchicus,* pp. 46-49.

27. C. Bougle, *The Essence and Reality of the Caste System*, p. 28.

class. It seems to us that we must be able to recognize the existence of different levels in that society, the existence, in other words, of a hierarchy. It has been argued that the word caste makes us think not only of the hereditarily appointed work but also of unequally divided rights. "Personal status for life is determined by the rank of the group to which one belongs."[28] The greatest importance attached by Senart[29] to the principle of exogamy or prohibition of marriage within one's *gotra* as a fundamental basis of the Indian caste system and he traces it to the Indo-European period. It has been pointed out by some that this custom was not in existence among the Ṛgvedic people, it was practised during a later period. The idea of pollution by touch with lower classes, and the prohibition of inter-caste dining, were absent in the earlier Vedic period. This feature of caste has been variously looked upon by scholars. To quote a few lines from the writings of B.R. Ambedkar:

> That prohibition, or rather the absence of inter-marriage — to be concise, — is the only one that can be called the essence of caste, when rightly understood . . . thus the conclusion is inevitable that endogamy is the only characteristic that is peculiar to caste. . . .[30]

Ambedkar says, "Caste system is a negative thing. It merely prohibits persons belonging to different castes from intermarrying."[31] Ethnologists of the recent times are of the opinion that men of pure race exist nowhere and that there has been a mixture of all races in all parts of the world. D.R.

---

28. C. Bougle, op. cit., p. 29.

29. Emile Charles Marie Senart (1847-1928), the French ethnographer, advocated the religious theory about the origin of castes in *Les Castes d'Inde*, Paris, 1896.

30. *Castes in India*, p. 241.

31. Ibid., p. 245.

Bhandarkar on "Foreign Elements in the Hindu Population" has stated, "There is hardly a class or caste in India which has not a foreign strain in it. . . ."[32] The caste system cannot be said to have grown as a means of preventing the admixture of races or as a means of maintaining purity of blood.

II

The caste system is characterized as the "sacralization of a social order"[33] to stress that the ancient social institution was the necessary sociological manifestation of the moral-philosophical presupposition of Hinduism. Weber,[34] Bougle[35] and many other later interpreters like Hocart[36] and others each in their own way maintained that the caste system in India manifested itself as an interplay between social and

---

32. Reference is provided in Kane's *History of Dharmaśāstra,* vol. II, part I, Pune, 1974
33. Harold Gould, *Politics and Caste: The Hindu Caste System,* 1990, p. 1,
34. Maximilian Karl Emil Weber (1864-1920), German political economist and sociologist. His most famous essay, "The Protestant Ethic and the Spirit of Capitalism" laid foundations for research on the impact of cultures and religions on the development of economic systems. Weber created anti-positivistic, hermeneutic tradition. Some of his important publications related to this field are: *The Religion of India: The Sociology of Hinduism and Buddhism* (tr., 1958), *The Religion of China: Confucianism and Taoism* (tr., 1951), and *Ancient Judaism* (original 1917-20, tr., 1952).
35. Celestin Bougle (1870-1940) was a French philosopher. Bougle was regarded as one of Louis Dumont's foremost inspirations in viewing Indian caste system as forming an ideological system.
36. Arthur Maurice Hocart (1883-1939), a British anthropologist.

cultural forces. Weber and Bougle saw that caste was a social structure which depended for its reality on the Brāhmanic codes. It was the systematic nature of this phenomenon which set it apart from rigid forms of social stratification found elsewhere.

Unlike the Egyptians, Mesopotamians or Greeks, the Vedic people, who called themselves Aryas have not left behind any architectural, sculptural or numismatic evidence of the nature of their society and civilization. Archaeological excavations in Moheṅjo Dāṛo, Haṛappā and a few other sites in northern and western India have not yielded any structures or artefacts that can be clearly identified as Vedic Aryan or can give a clear idea of the Vedic social organization. The only historical evidence of the existence of the Aryan society, culture, and civilization is of a primarily literary character, consisting of the four Vedas. For determining the class structure of ancient Vedic society and its dynamics, therefore, there is no better alternative before us than to focus our attention primarily on the internal literary evidence of the Vedas. There are many others who are in favour of assigning the beginning of the caste system in the shape of *varṇa* division to the Indo-Iranian period of history. Thus, in ancient Persia, there were the *atharva*s (priests), *rathaestha*s (warriors), *vastriya Fshuyant*s (cultivators), and *hui ti*s (artisans). Corresponding to this ancient Persian model of four classes consisting of priests, warriors, cultivators and artisans, Risley suggested, the Brāhmanical order of four *varṇa*s has originated. The only difference lay with regard to the fourth class, which was the artisan class in Persia, and the servile or śūdra class in India. This is not a unanimous view about the origin of castes in India.

This Vedic tradition is especially held responsible for caste and all the issues relating to caste that we experience in contemporary India. Puruṣa-Sūkta,[37] one of the hymns of *Ṛgveda* has been specifically cited by many interpreters as responsible for sowing the seeds of a thoroughly obnoxious caste system in India. Some writers have gone to the extent of nicknaming Puruṣa-Sūkta as the "ideology of class exploitation."[38]

> The full text of the Puruṣa-Sūkta (*ṚV*, 10.90) is without doubt intended to establish the divine origin of the four-tiered class structure of the prevailing Vedic society, to legitimize and sanctify it in the eyes of the people and thus create a pseudo-religious disguise for the oppression and exploitation of the masses by the ruling class.[39]

We need to see what actually was there in that famous Puruṣa-Sūkta which has often been cited as the source of all evils? The Puruṣa-Sūkta presents a story of creation referring to the supreme being *Puruṣa,* who is a self-conscious being and the ultimate cause of all creation. It depicts a fanciful mythology of a divine *Puruṣa,* with thousand heads, thousand eyes, and thousand feet who pervaded the entire primordial universe. The *Puruṣa,* by his *saṅkalpa* or resolution produced *Virāṭ* and after that *Puruṣa,* was born. *Virāṭ* means the cosmos or totality of all existence. The *Puruṣa* who came after *Virāṭ* is Brahmā or Hiraṇyagarbha. The first born *Puruṣa,* Brahmā or *Virāṭ* produced gods, men, etc. and the inanimate cosmos and entered into them as their souls. The present hymn conceives of the act of creation as representing the self-sacrifice of *Puruṣa.* The first born *Puruṣa* undergoes sacrifice in order to create the world or cosmos. From the oblation smoke first *ṛk-yaju-sāma* appeared. From the body of the *Puruṣa,* horse, cattle,

37. *brāhmaṇosya mukhamāsit* । *bāhu rājanyah kṛtaḥ* । *ūru tadasya yad vaiśyaḥ* । *padābhyam śūdra niyata* ॥

38. *Class and Religion in Ancient India,* p. 20.

39. Ibid.

goat, sheep, etc. were born. In the same *sūkta* it was stated that from the mouth of *Puruṣa* brāhmaṇa was born, from the two arms of *Puruṣa* kṣatriya was born, from his two thighs vaiśya was born and from his two feet śūdra was born. The story of creation does not end here. The mind of *Puruṣa* turned into the moon, eyes into the sun, ears into directions and *loka*s. This is the first statement about four *varṇa*s available in the Vedas. However, it is to be noted here that nothing specific about superiority or inferiority of any *varṇa* whatsoever has been stated in this *sūkta*. This solitary *Ṛk* in the Puruṣa-Sūkta relating to the four castes (brāhmaṇa, rājanya, vaiśya and śūdra) born from parts of a gigantic divine personality is often believed to be a later inclusion in a more modern language, as there would have been other references in the vast volume of *Ṛgveda* if the caste system was in operation. Among the older texts, mention must be made of *Bṛhadāraṇyaka Upaniṣad*,[40] wherein we come across a story of creation of brāhmaṇa gods, kṣatriya gods, vaiśya gods and śūdra gods. In the later Smṛti literatures,[41] in the *Mahābhārata* and also in the *Gītā*[42] we find reference to *varṇa*. In the *Bhagavad-Gītā* we find a metaphysical speculation and a normative exposition about *varṇa*.

The *Gītā*[43] speaks about three *guṇa*s, viz. *sattva, rajas* and *tamas* as qualities of *Prakṛti*; these three *guṇa*s, according to the Sāṁkhya philosophers represent latent potentialities of which *sattva* is the principle of assimilation, harmony and

40. 1.4.11-15.

41. *sattvam jñānam tamojñānām rāgadveṣau rājaḥ smōtam* ।
etadvyāptimadetesām sarvabhūtasoitam vapuḥ ॥
— *Manu-Smṛti*, 12.26.

42. *brāhmaṇakṣatriyaviśāṁ śudrānāṁca paraṁtapa* ।
karmāṇi pravibhaktāni svabhāvaprabhavairguṇaiḥ ॥
— *Bhagavad-Gītā* 18.41.

43. 4.13.

equilibrium; *rajas* is the principle of creative endeavour, motion and impulsion; and *tamas* is the principle of inertia, passivity and responsible for creating disharmony and thwarting dynamicity. *Gītā* maintains further that these three qualities of nature are evidently present and active in all existencies including human beings and none can be said to be devoid of one another or free from any one of the three *guṇa*s; none is cast in the mould of one *guṇa* to the exclusion of the other. These three *guṇa*s are juxtaposed or combined in a very complex manner in all existences, in all aspects of their existence — physical, mental and moral. These three *guṇa*s are present in all existencies including human beings but the order is not the same in which one *guṇa* predominates and the other *guṇa*s play a subservient role to it. There is a general rule of mind and action for all men, but each individual acts not only according to the common laws, but according to his own nature constituted by the inherent potentiality, tendency or whatever bestowed upon by the order of the constituting *guṇa*s; each man fulfils different functions or follows a different bent according to the rule of his own circumstances, capacities, character, and power. What place is to be assigned to this variation, this individual rule of nature in the moral discipline? It lays down that one's own nature, rule, and function should be observed and followed, — even if it is defective, it is better than the well-performed rule of another's nature.

> To follow the law of another's nature is dangerous to the soul, contradictory as we may say, to the natural way of his evolution, a thing mechanically imposed and therefore imported, artificial, and sterilizing to one's growth towards the true stature of the spirit.[44]

---

44. *śreyān svadharmo viguṇaḥ paradharmāt svanuṣṭhitāt* ।
svabhāvaniyatam karma kurvannāpnoti kilviṣam ॥
— Sri Aurobindo, *Essays on the Gītā*, 18.47

This *svadharma* is of four general kinds formulated outwardly in the action of four orders of the old Indian social culture, *caturvarṇa*. In other words, there are four distinct orders of the active nature, or four fundamental types of the soul in nature, *svabhāva*, and the work and the proper function of each human being corresponds to his type of nature. The actions of brāhmaṇas, kṣatriyas, vaiśyas and śūdras are divided according to the qualities (*guṇas*) born of their own inner nature, spiritual temperament, and essential character (*svabhāva*). Moral actions performed under the predominance of *sattva guṇa* are called *sāttvika karmas*; similarly we see there are provisions for *rājasika karma* and *tāmasika karma*. Thus if we look into the *Gītā* text, we do not find any reference to birth or hereditary feature in accounting for *varṇa*. In the *Mahābhārata* also we find that it has been asserted that *varṇa* is not hereditary. It has been said that *varṇa* depends solely on natural temperament or inborn vocational aptitude. It has been very clearly said that neither birth, nor *saṁskāra*, nor *vidyā* nor family is the cause of being a brāhmaṇa, but only profession. In the Vana Parva of the *Mahābhārata* it has been further stated that a śūdra, if he has acquired good character traits may be treated as a brāhmaṇa and a brāhmaṇa by his defiling deeds may be turned into a śūdra.

In the Smṛti literatures including *Manu-Smṛti*,[45] frequently elaborate references to all these *varṇas* are available. In the writings of Manu we find lots of praises are bestowed on the brāhmaṇas. It is stated in 1.96:

> Among the created beings, living beings are superior, among the living beings rational beings are superior, and among

45. It is maintained that the current *Maṇu-Saṁhitā* is based on the ancient Mānava Dharma-Sūtra with the later additions and alterations.

the rational beings, brāhmaṇas are superior.[46]

It is found in the *Manu-Smṛti* further, "brāhmaṇa is the lord of all created beings,"[47] and "brāhmaṇa who is conversant in the Vedas, is the ruler of the world."[48] In the *śloka* 10.3 Manu says clearly that among all the *varṇas*, brāhmaṇas are superior to all others for their nature, for upholding laws and for performing some specific sacraments (*saṁskāras*).[49] Thus we find that in the writings of Manu clearly brāhmaṇas are granted superior status. It has been stated that it is the duty of the king to look after the well-being of brāhmaṇas. No true brāhmaṇa ought to suffer from hunger. It is the duty of a king to make provisions for the maintenance of the dependents of brāhmaṇas. If the king does not take cognizance of brāhmaṇa's hunger, then that would torment the kingdom.[50] However, the brāhmaṇa also needs to be a true brāhmaṇa. If the brāhmaṇa deviates from his duty, then he is considered to be a *brāhmaṇa-brūva,* i.e. one who is called a brāhmaṇa but not a true brāhmaṇa. *Atri-Saṁhitā* mentions certain characteristics which are specifically of a brāhmaṇa. These are purity (*śauca*), doing good to others (*maṅgalam*), absence of exertion (*anāyāsa*), absence of jealousy (*anasūya),* absence of acquisitiveness (*āspṛhā*), self-restraint (*dama*), charity (*dāna*), and mercy (*dayā*). In the text some explanation is also provided about these features. Firstly, an account is provided about what is meant by *anasūya,* i.e. absence of jealousy. A person who does not

46. *bhūtānām prāṇinaḥ śreṣṭhaḥ prāṇinām buddhijīvinoḥ* ।
buddhimatsu narāḥ śreṣṭhāḥ nareṣu brāhmaṇāḥ smṛtāḥ ॥

47. *sarvsyaivāsya sargasya dharmato brāhmaṇaḥ prabhuḥ* — 1.93

48. *īśa sarvasya jagato brāhmaṇo vedapāragaḥ* — 9.245

49. *vaiśesyāt prakṛtiśraisthyāt niyamasya ca dhāraṇāt* ।
saṁskārasya viśeṣācca varṇānām brāhmaṇaḥ prabhuḥ ॥ — 10.3

50. *yasya rajñastu viṣaye śratriyaḥ sī dati kṣudhā* ।
tasyāpi tatkṣudhā rāṣṭramacirenaiva sīdati ॥ — 7.134

try to belittle another person's achievement, rather speaks highly about that person's achievement or does not joke about anybody's defects is considered to be one devoid of jealousy. In the Indian *dharma* tradition especially in accounting for *varṇa* we will frequently come across the notion of *śauca* or purity. *Atri-Saṁhitā* says:

> *Abhakṣyapārihāraśca,* i.e. rejecting those food which are not to be eaten; avoiding interaction with those who are criticized, *saṁsargāścāpyaninditaiḥ;* and *acāreṣuvya-vasthānam,* i.e. committed to established rule of conduct.[51]

The expression *ācāra* may mean conduct, behaviour as well as established rule of conduct. In my rendering of *ācāra,* my preference is for "established rule of conduct." While explaining the concept of *maṅgala,* they bring two further opposite notions one of *praśasta ācaraṇa* and the other *apraśasta ācaraṇa,* without much clue as to their exact connotation and maintain that *maṅgala* is synonymous with *praśasta ācaraṇa. Praśasta* literally means what is recommended or considered to be fit or good. Hence this explanation of *maṅgala* in terms of *praśasta ācaraṇa* does not add anything more to our intuitive understanding of *maṅgala* or good. A brāhmaṇa should not torment his body with over-exertion whether good or bad, for a brāhmaṇa *anāyasa* is his distinctive mark. The brāhmaṇa must be satisfied with whatever he has. He should never covet for another person's wife and this sort of lewd mentality is called *spṛhā. Dama* is a quality which marks a brāhmaṇa for he is such that even if anybody either externally or spiritually brings harm upon him, he does not take any revenge for that for he is a self-restrained personality. Charity or *dāna* that has been spoken of here refers to an altruistic trait of a brāhmaṇa and in order to be benevolent one need not give a huge amount of

51. *Atri-Saṁhitā, śloka* 35.

wealth. What has been stated in the *Atri-Saṁhitā* is that the brāhmaṇa should donate (even) from a limited income regularly with zeal and internal feeling. The brāhmaṇa is supposed to have compassion (*dayā*), and to look upon his friend or foe as himself (*ātmavatvartitavyam*).

The brāhmaṇa is required to perform certain actions which are called *iṣṭa*. Maintenance of sacred fires and adoration of *viśvadeva* (holy ceremony or sacrifice) are such work. The excavations of tanks, wells, and other watery expanses, the construction of temples, the distribution of food, laying out of pleasure gardens are called *pūrtta,* i.e. acts of pious liberality. The brāhmaṇa should do both the *iṣṭa* and *pūrtta karma*s that are prescribed. A śūdra must perform *pūrtta karma*s but śūdra has not been allowed to perform Vedic rites.

In the *Mahābhārata* it has been stated that kṣatriya is one who protects from being afflicted with wounds, in other words, kṣatriya is the redresser of wrongs (*saḥ eva kṣatriya proktaḥ kṣatāt trāṇam karati yaḥ*). It has been further stated that it is the duty of kṣatriya not merely to be ready for the defence of the country but to actively seek the evil out and crush it. It is the duty of a kṣatriya to engage himself in just violence. If an enemy attacks, he should be killed. It is honourable for a kṣatriya to die in a battlefield. It has been very specifically mentioned that *svadharma* or duty of a kṣatriya is not to run away from the battlefield.

Vaiśya were allocated a separate class of duties. Agriculture, rearing of cattle, looking after business — these were considered to be duties of a vaiśya. It is stated in the *Manu-Smṛti* that it is the duty of a vaiśya to make the provision for food for every living creature.

The work of a śūdra is to serve all communities. In the *Bṛhadāraṇyaka Upaniṣad,* as already mentioned, the story of creation begins with the creation of four types of gods belonging to brāhmaṇa *varṇa*, kṣatriya *varṇa*, vaiśya *varṇa* and śūdra *varṇa*. One interesting thing has been said about the śūdra *varṇa* god who is Pūṣā, i.e., Pṛthivī and whose task is *pūṣaṇam (sa naiva vyabhavat sa śaudram varṇamsṛjat pūṣnāmīyam vai puṣeyam hidam sarvam puṣyati yadidam kiṁca)*. The Sanskrit word *pūṣaṇam* is derived from the root √*puṣ*, which means to cause to prosper, thrive, nourish, fulfil, etc. Hence there is enough scope for interpreting the work of śūdra in a nobler way.

It has already been mentioned that there are many literary evidences to suggest that divisions into different *varṇa*s are not very rigid in the sense that these are determined by birth. In the Vana Parva of the *Mahābhārata*, we also find illuminating statements relevant to this context, wherein a *ṛṣi* had made the following statement: A brāhmaṇa who indulges in vicious acts and is very haughty, in spite of his intelligence is to be considered as śūdra; and a śūdra who is always truthful and dutiful and has self-restraint is to be considered as a brāhmaṇa. In the Ajagarādhyāya of the Vana Parva, Rājarṣi Nahuṣa is found to remark that if truth, charity, forgiveness, and mercifulness, which are said to be qualities of a brāhmaṇa are discovered in a śūdra, then that śūdra should be regarded as a brāhmaṇa. In reply to this remark of Nahuṣa, Yudhiṣṭhira admitted that in many instances qualities of a brāhmaṇa are discernible in a śūdra and qualities of a śūdra are discernible in a brāhmaṇa. Hence the contention that just by birth one is not a brāhmaṇa or śūdra, rather it is by their *vyavahāra,* i.e. through the mode of action one person may acquire the qualities of a brāhmaṇa or that of a śūdra. In the *Mahābhārata* there are instructive suggestions at places in favour of accepting a non-rigid stand regarding classification of *varṇa*. Passages have been cited from the *Mahābhārata* specifically suggesting that a person born of śūdra parents pursues good practices, is not to be regarded as a śūdra.[52] Thus, arguably, in one of the senses, *varṇa* signifies character or inner trait of an individual.

In the *Mahābhārata* there are passages that suggest non-existence of any difference relating to *varṇa*. No doubt there is some metaphysical twist to this belief which suggests that this world is born of brāhmaṇa, so initially there was only one *varṇa*, that is brāhmaṇa, gradually the criterion for deciding who is brāhmaṇa, or kṣatriya or vaiśya or śūdra depended on the type of character of the individual.[53]

However, the question remains, how do we then justify *varṇabheda*, or difference among *varṇa*s, which is also an accepted matter? In this regard we have some suggestive hints from the epics and other *dharma* literatures. It has been stated that among the original brāhmaṇas some were regarded as kṣatriya for they became interested towards material property, and were rough by nature, more prone to anger and were adventure-loving and gave up their own *dharma* and the colour of their body was red.[54] Among the brāhmaṇas some earned their livelihood by animal husbandry, agriculture and were yellow in colour and were vaiśya.[55] Lastly, those brāhmaṇas who were fond of violence and falsehood, used to perform those tasks in order to assist other people, were devoid of

---

52. *śūdra caitadbhavellakṣma dvije cecca na vidyate* ।
na vai śūdra bhavecchudra brāhmaṇo brāhmaṇo na ca ॥
—Vana Parva, 151.25

53. *satyam dānam kṣamā śīlamanṛśamīsyam tapoghṛṇā* ।
dṛśyante yatra nāgendra ! sa brāhmaṇa iti smṛdaḥ ॥
— Vana Parva, 151.21

54. *kāmabhogapriyāstiṣṇāḥ krodhanāḥ priyasāhasāḥ* ।
tyaktasvadharmma raktāgāste dvijāḥ kṣatratām gatāḥ ॥
— Śānti Parva, 181.11

55. *gobhyo vōttim samāsthāya pītāh kṛṣyupajīvinaḥ* ।
svadharmannanutiṣṭhanti te dvijāḥ vaiśyatām gatāḥ ॥
— Śānti Parva, 181.12

tidiness and were black in complexion were called śūdra.[56] True brāhmaṇas were sincere to Vedic rites and rituals and they observed the Vedic tradition and kept themselves busy in penance, or *tapasyā*.[57] Thus, from the above it would not be too rash to conclude that birth was not the only deciding factor in case of determining difference between one *varṇa* and another. The intellectual capacity of the individual, his temperament, his ethical nature, his spiritual stature all are important factors in determining *varṇabheda*.

The interesting point to note is that from within the tradition the justification for maintaining difference among various *varṇa*s was questioned. In the Mokṣa Parva of the *Mahābhārata*, in the section entitled *Bhṛgubhāradvājasaṁvāda* we find Bhāradvāja questioning the legitimacy of *varṇabheda*. His argument is as follows:

> Since each of us have desire, anger, fear, greed, sorrow, thought, hunger and labour, how can we be different from one another?[58]

Further it is argued, since equally all of us have experience of excreting perspiration, urine, stool, cough, bile and blood from our body, how should we be different from one another?[59] One concept that frequently occurs in connection with castes

56. *hiṁsānṛtapriyā lubddhāḥ sarvakarmopajīvinaḥ* ।
kṛiṣṇāḥ saucaparibhraṣṭāste dvijāḥ śūdratām gatāḥ ॥
— Śānti Parva, 181.13

57. *brāhmaṇā brahmatantrastaḥstapesteṣām na naśyati* ।
brahmadhārayatām nityam bratāni niyamāmstathā ॥
— Śānti Parva, 181.16

58. *kāmakrodhabhayamlobhaḥ śokościntākudhāśramaḥ* ।
sarveṣām noḥ prabhavati kasmadvarṇa vibhajyate ॥
— Śānti Parva, 181.7

59. *svedamutrapurīsāni sleṣmāpittam saśanitam* ।
tanuḥ kṣarati sarveṣām kasmadvarṇa vibhajyate ॥
— Śānti Parva, 181.8

and sub-castes is *varṇa-saṁkara,* i.e. admixture of *varṇa*s, which may remind one of the criterion of purity and pollution as admitted by sociologists as a criterion for maintaining difference among the castes. In *Manu* X.12 and 24 the word *varṇa-saṁkara* is used in the sense of mixed castes, mixture or intermingling of *varṇa*s. On account of the great emphasis laid on the prevention of *varṇa-saṁkara,* the Smr̥tis ordain that it is one of the principal duties of the king to punish people if they transgress the rules prescribed for *varṇa*s and to punish men and women if guilty of *varṇa-saṁkara.* The *Bhagavad-Gītā,* the normative text *par excellence* of the Hindus, outlines collapse of the social and moral order when there are leakages in the closed structure of marriages. Ideally both parents must be of the same caste. The anxiety about polluting the ritual order and the quality of blood through women is demonstrated in the horror of *varṇa-saṁkara.* Most polluting are those castes which are the products of reprehensible unions between women of a higher caste and men of a lower caste. In fact, in later Dharmaśāstras concern about purity of *varṇa* became very important. [60]

III

To trace back the origin of *varṇa* ideology is indeed a long journey into the remotest past. The occurrence of the concept of *varṇa* in the Puruṣa-Sūkta appears quite innocuous, just as a complementary idea to support a creation theory. However, in the *Mahābhārata* period there is no denial of the fact that the *varṇa* ideology was one of the important factors in the social context. In fact, during the period of Smr̥ti literatures including *Mānavadharma-śāstra, Manu-Smr̥ti* and other Dharmasūtras rigidity in the domain of *varṇa* is quite apparent. Philosophers desperately search for, if any, missing link that connects *varṇa* ideology to the discomforting caste practices. Among the

60. *The Human Cycle,* p. 4.

nineteenth-twentieth-century galaxy of Indian thinkers who expressed their reaction towards caste system and sought an explanation for this anomalous system, names of Bankimchandra, Sri Aurobindo, Vivekananda, Gandhi, and Ambedkar are worthy of mention. Within the scope of this article it would not be possible to do justice to all these views, hence I would stick to the observation, interpretation and approach of one of the most thorough thinkers, Sri Aurobindo. In Sri Aurobindo's various writings we find attempts to explain distinctively the *varṇa* as ideal or norm and also as a social practice and their interconnectedness. Sri Aurobindo cautions us:

> The ancient *cāturvarṇya* must not be judged by its later disintegrated degeneration and gross meaningless parody, the caste system.[61]

Acknowledging "the difference between the ideal theory of the system and its rougher unideal practice," he endeavours to highlight the missing links between the two. Views on *varṇa* of a versatile thinker like Sri Aurobindo lie scattered in his major works like *Essays on the Gītā, The Human Cycle, The Foundations of Indian Culture* and in his various other writings. Sri Aurobindo is focussing upon *varṇa* from different angles: In the *Essays on the Gītā* the very concept of *varṇa,* its ideology and the triple aspects of the *varṇa* order, viz. the economic or social, the cultural, and the spiritual have been elaborated. Secondly, *The Human Cycle* in its attempt to narrate the actual historical phenomenon of social development elaborates the sociology of the caste. In the *Foundations of Indian Culture,* Sri Aurobindo refers to the societal frame of four graded classes as providing the basis for relating the natural life of man to the freedom to exceed himself through fulfilment of spiritual life. In the present section a holistic account of Sri Aurobindo's view on *varṇa* and *jāti* will be attempted.

---

61. *The Foundations of Indian Culture,* p. 118.

Sri Aurobindo tries to make sense of the *varṇa* concept by situating it in the larger context of civilization, development and society. While delineating the process of any social development, he accords importance to the role of psychology that lies behind that development. To uphold the psychology of the social development and to assign it a pre-eminent role in tracing the course of historical development of a society is to embrace a paradigm which is contradictory to the *Cours de Philosophie Positive* as envisaged by Auguste Comte. Sri Aurobindo believed that development forms a sort of psychological cycle through which each nation or each civilization is bound to proceed. In this regard, Sri Aurobindo was very close to the point of view of Lamprecht who says in his *Deusche Geschichte:*

> History in itself is nothing but applied psychology, and so it is clear that theoretical must be the key to its thorough understanding. . . . But it is one thing to know of this relationship and quite another to corroborate it. For the latter is necessary that historical appreciation should include the deepest elementary processes or precisely those that psychology first of all elucidates, and necessary too, that the development of individual psychology should at least . . . progress far enough towards intellectual comprehension of these elementary processes.[62]

Aurobindo in his *The Ideal of Human Unity* shows his disapproval for the ordinarily understood notion of history. He remarks about that sense of history:

> History teaches us nothing; it is a confused torrent of events and personalities or kaleidoscope of changing institutions. . . . We do not seize the real sense of life in the

62. This quotation is derived from Ernst Cassier, "Positivism and its Ideal of Historical Knowledge" in *The Problem of Knowledge*, tr. by William H. Woglom and Charles W. Hendel, Yale University Press, New Haven, 1950, pp. 284-85.

> channels of Time. . . . What we seize are current or recurrent phenomena, facile generalizations, partial ideas.[63]

Sri Aurobindo tries to get rid himself of the obsession of the modern science with the strong bias towards its physical discoveries and consequently from its preoccupation with "external data, laws, institutions, rites, customs, economic factors and developments" in interpreting history and sociology. Sri Aurobindo tries to interpret history of civilization in general, Indian history in particular, and *varṇa* ideology specially by focussing upon deeper psychological elements.

Following the German historian Lamprecht, Sri Aurobindo in his *The Human Cycle* classified the course of historical progress into distinct psychological stages as symbolic, typal, conventional, individualist and subjective. In the symbolic stage, the first hypothetical stage that marks the beginning of the cycle of human civilization, a sort of symbolic mentality prevailed and because of this mentality men believed everything in terms of symbols — their thoughts, customs, institutions all were permeated with symbols. During this period symbols are taken to represent things which man feels to be present behind himself, his life and his activities. These symbols represent the Divine, the gods, the vast and deep unnamable, a hidden living and mysterious nature of things. These symbols are expressions of mystic influences that are behind his life and shape and govern it or at least intervene at times. Men of this period of civilization were imaginative and religious no doubt, but were not much intellectual or sceptical.

This stage is followed by the typal stage wherein a social order was developed. In the subsequent period it took the shape of convention and in the end these conventions remained as a tradition. The conventional stage of human development

63. *The Ideal of Human Unity*, p. 261.

presented a system of rigid grades and hierarchies in the society. During this stage education and training depended on certain unchangeable traditional norms. The tendency of the conventional age was to subject thoughts and beliefs to some infallible authority. This conventional stage is also characterized as the pre-individualistic age. Pre-individualist age banned true knowledge and science. During this period the role of religion was to impose upon human minds certain dogmatic ideas. Religion is often identified with a mass of ills. In many instances an irrational viewpoint was responsible for confusing religion with a particular creed, sect, cult, religion, society or church. Religion failed to provide any principle for the guidance and control of human society because of its association with sectarian attitudes. During this period men had forgotten how to deal freely with facts and forces, they lived in a world of stereotyped thoughts and customary action. Conventional standards lost contact with the truth from which initially those conventions were derived. Sri Aurobindo believed that the full cycle of historical development would be completed by a civilization by passing through the age of reason and finally the stage of spiritual age. Sri Aurobindo spells out conditions for the coming of the Subjective Spiritual age.

The analysis of the psychology of social development as provided by Sri Aurobindo is important in understanding his view about *varṇa.* The institution of *varṇa,* according to him is a symbolic and typal institution which with the passage of time got conventionalized into caste. How do we interpret the concept of *varṇa*? According to the symbolic interpretation of *varṇa,* based on the Puruṣa-Sūkta, one finds that the brāhmaṇa signified the divine as knowledge in man, the kṣatriya the divine as power, the vaiśya, the divine engaged in production, enjoyment, and neutrality and the śūdra, the divine engaged in service, obedience and work. According to Aurobindo initially these divisions answer to cosmic principles:

> The Wisdom that conceives the order and principle of thing, the Power that sanctions, upholds and enforces it, the Harmony that creates the arrangement of its parts, the Work that carries out what the rest direct.[64]

Out of this idea there developed a firm but not yet rigid social order based primarily upon temperament and psychic type with a corresponding ethical discipline and secondarily upon the social and economic function. Thus, Sri Aurobindo thought that human society was for the Vedic peoples an attempt to express in life the cosmic *Puruṣa* who has expressed himself otherwise in the material and the supraphysical universe. The system of *varṇa* supported the plasticity and catholicity of Hindu society by making room for a graded working out of the latent potencies and capabilities of human nature. "The ancient Indian idea was that man falls by his nature into four types."[65] Thus it was admitted there were the men of learning, thought, and knowledge, there were the men of power and action, there were the men of economics, production, cultivation. Lastly, there were people who were intellectually undeveloped and without the capability of intelligent production and so were fit for only unskilled labour and menial service, the śūdra. Sri Aurobindo further envisages the economic order of society to be based on these four types. The brāhmaṇa class gave to the society scholars, religious leaders, and priests; the kṣatriya class gave to the society its kings, governors, and administrators; the vaiśya class supplied producers, agriculturists, craftsmen, traders, merchants, and the śūdra class provided servers of society in general. Thus in the Hindu society the order is fixed by reference to the inner nature or capacities of the individual. In fact, this period of history of *varṇa* may be called after Sri Aurobindo as the typal stage. The belief that originally the

---

64. *The Human Cycle*, 1997, p. 6.

65. *The Foundations of Indian Culture*, p. 118.

division of society was based on inner nature (*svadharma*) and capacity (*adhikāra*) of the individuals was very much loaded with metaphysical speculations.

But in the process of its historical evolution the rigidity of the caste system became an obstacle to further social experimentation. In his *The Human Cycle,* while delineating the cycle of society, Sri Aurobindo conceives of this typal stage in which the symbolic idea of four orders expresses itself. The first, the symbolic stage, is supposed to be spiritual and religious; the other elements psychological, ethical, economic, physical are there but subordinated to the spiritual and religious ideas. The second stage, which we may call typal, is predominantly psychological and ethical. This typal stage is supposed to be such that it creates the great social ideals which remain impressed upon the mind even when the stage itself is passed. During this stage of development the brāhmaṇa-type stands for purity, a disinterested possession and exclusive pursuit of learning and knowledge. The kṣtriya-type lives in courage, chivalry, strength, a certain proud self-restraint and self-mastery, nobility of character and the obligations of that nobility; the vaiśya-type maintains itself by rectitude of dealing, mercantile fidelity, sound production, order, liberality, philanthropy; and the śūdra-type stands for obedience, subordination, faithful service, a disinterested attachment.

But these more and more cease to have a living root in the clear psychological idea or to spring naturally out of the inner life of man. In the conventional stage of human society outward expressions of the spirit become more important than the ideal, the body or even the clothes more important than the ideal. Thus in the evolution of the caste, the external factors like birth, economic function, religious ritual and sacrament, family custom, each began to exaggerate itself enormously and project its importance in the scheme. At first birth does not have any importance in the social order since individual human's faculty and capacity were considered to be important; but afterwards, the type got fixed:

> The tendency of the conventional age of society is to fix, to arrange firmly, to formalize, to erect a system of rigid grades and hierarchies, to stereotype religion, to bind education and training to a traditional and unchangeable form, to subject thought to infallible authorities, to cast a stamp of finality on what seems to it the finished life of man.[66]

During the conventional age of a society everything need not be necessarily reprehensible. But the historical evolution of India or Europe has shown that a period comes when the gap between convention and the truth widens. If the Aurobindonian explanation is accepted then it is not difficult to guess what led to the decadence of *varṇa* during the conventional age. During the conventional age, the qualities born of each individual's own inner nature, spiritual temperament, and essential character were no longer respected and accepted as the standard for drawing a division in the caste system. The son of a brāhmaṇa was a brāhmaṇa, the son of a trader became a trader, and the descendants of shoe-makers remain shoe-makers till the end of their lives. Thus it was birth that was the basis for determining *varṇa* divisions. Though this was observed by Sri Aurobindo, it did not have any pessimistic influence on him.

Sri Aurobindo believes in the highest traditional Indian value of liberation, and he believes that the development of the spirit will ultimately liberate him out of the lower nature of the triple *guṇa*s into the supreme divine nature beyond the three *guṇa*s. (*Gītā*, II.45). Sri Aurobindo's explanation in this regard is very much influenced by the *Gītā* and in his *Essays on the Gītā* he sounds very encouraging when he mentions that

66. *The Human Cycle*, pp. 7-8.

every human being can achieve this human evolution. How that evolution is to be achieved by each human being? Sri Aurobindo interprets and explains the answer of the *Gītā* as follows:

> But while the general rule of mind and action is the same for all men, we see too that there is a constant law of variation and each individual acts not only according to the common laws of the human spirit, mind, will, life but according to his own nature; each man fulfils different functions or follows a different bent according to the rule of his own circumstances, capacities, turn, character, powers.[67]

Now, this individual rule of nature is nothing but his *svadharma* or *varṇa dharma* and it has been assigned a very important role in the context of spiritual development.

At the very beginning of the *Bhagavad-Gītā*, the reference to Arjuna's "own rule of nature" or *svadharma* occurs — *svadharmam api ca vekṣya* (II.31). The *Gītā* text emphasizes that *svadharma* or "one's own nature, rule, function" should be observed and followed — even if defective, it is better than the well-performed rule of another's nature. Sri Aurobindo translates *svadharma* as one's rule of nature generally; it may as well be translated as inner capacity or potency of an individual. The idea *svadharme nidhanam śreyaḥ*, i.e. "death in one's law of nature is better for a man than victory in an alien movement," is a pressing one in the context of Indian ethics. It has often been alleged that these verses of the *Gītā* are incitements to casteism and provide encouragement for caste systems. Sri Aurobindo is emphatically negative in his reply; he says:

> In point of fact the verses in the *Gītā* have no bearing on the existing caste system, because that is a very different thing from the ancient ideal of the four clear-cut orders of the Aryan community, and in no way corresponds to the

67. *Essays on the Gītā*, p. 491.

> description of the *Gītā*.[68]. . . The *Gītā*'s words refer to the ancient system of *caturvarṇa,* as it existed or was supposed to exist in its ideal purity, — there is some controversy whether it was ever anything more than an ideal or general norm more or less loosely followed in practice — and it should be considered in that connection alone.[69]. . . In fact, it (*Gītā*) lays great stress on the internal law which the *varṇa* system attempted to put into regulated outward practice.[70]

The optimism of Sri Aurobindo lies in pointing out that "men in spite of the natural conservatism of the social mind are compelled at last to perceive that the Truth is dead in them and that they are living by a lie."[71] At times caste ideology has sometimes preached gross intolerance and contempt for those below. Even Aurobindo refers to the prevalence of "economic serfdom" created by the existence of "the proletariat, called in India the śūdra":

> In the full economic period of caste the priest and the puṇḍit masquerade under the name of the brāhmaṇa, the aristocrat and feudal baron under the name of kṣatriya, the trader and money-getter under the name of the vaiśya, the half-fed labourer and economic serf under the name of śūdra."[72]

What lesson do we get from Sri Aurobindo in trying to understand the nature of the relation between the *varṇa* and the caste, between the Ideal and the stark empirical reality of the caste-ridden Indian society? First and foremost, just by looking at the external surface of the society, its existing institutions, practices, and customs no answer is possible. Secondly, in spite of admitting that "the psychology of man

68. *Essays on the Gītā*, p. 493.
69. Ibid., p. 494.
70. Ibid., p. 497.
71. *The Human Cycle*, p. 7.
72. Ibid., p. 8.

and his societies is too complex, too synthetical of many-sided and inter-mixed tendencies to satisfy any such rigorous and formal analysis,"[73] he suggests to explore the psychology of social development to unearth the veiled secret of history. The task of unearthing psychology of social evolution is a difficult task no doubt and it does not lend itself to any easy answer. Thus, we see that in order to find an answer to the question as to how *varṇa* ideology was translated into caste ideology one must try to grasp the psychology of social development. In his opinion *varṇa* is a symbolic and typal institution, and caste, which is the result of economic and political causes, is a conventional institution. Aurobindo's social philosophy indicates going beyond the *varṇa* principle. He pleads for an integral manifestation of the concealed divine within the individuals and collections. Sri Aurobindo clearly states:

> Each man contains within himself the whole divine potentiality and therefore the śūdra cannot be confined within his śūdrahood, nor brāhmaṇa in his brāhmaṇahood, but each contains within himself the whole divine potentiality and the need of perfection of his other elements of a divine manhood.[74]

Thus, it is clear that on the foundation of an integrated spiritual monism Aurobindo would plead for going beyond the social conservatism of the distorted *varṇa* order expressed through hierarchies of the caste system.

Thus we see the conceptual difference between *varṇa* and *jāti* is really difficult to bridge. There are four *varṇa*s with definite orders. *Varṇa* as an ideal should have remained always distinguished from the non-ideal practice of caste. The necessity inherent in the historical cycle, as Sri Aurobindo

---

73. *The Human Cycle*, p. 2.

74. *Essays on the Gītā*, p. 493.

would make us believe, has to be admitted as giving rise to the ridiculous accident of confounding two opposite tendencies into one. "The fourfold order was created by Me," says Kṛṣṇa, "according to the divisions of quality and active function."[75] On the other hand, *jāti*s are too numerous and complex and are difficult to subsume under any principle of division or classification. Sri Aurobindo very carefully brings out the triple aspect of the *varṇa* order, viz. (1) economic or social, (2) the cultural, and (3) the spiritual. On the economic side, it recognized four functions of the social man in the community. The cultural ideal associated with the religious custom, ethical rules, family ideal and discipline has a historical or evolutionary significance. The spiritual significance in general of the *Gītā* as such and *varṇa* order specifically, is the real kernel of the teaching of the *Gītā*. The principle, viz. "each according to his own inner capacity should act" has a universalistic appeal:

> As has been said elsewhere, not alone the brāhmaṇa with his ideal of spirituality, ethical purity and knowledge and the kṣatriya with his ideal of nobility, chivalry and high character, but the wealth-seeking vaiśya, the toil-imprisoned śūdra, woman with her narrow, circumscribed and subject life, the very outcaste born from a womb of sin, *pāpayonayaḥ*, can by this road rise at once towards the highest inner greatness and spiritual freedom, towards perfection, towards the liberation and fulfilment of the divine element in the human being.[76]

To conclude, in this essay, mainly attempts are made to grasp the true nature of caste and *varṇa* both from the externalistic empirical perspective and the internalistic perspective. However, it is needless to add that within the span of a single essay it is absurd to try to comprehend all the

75. *Essays on the Gītā*, p. 495.

76. *Essays on the Gītā*, p. 498.

nitty-gritty of caste and *varṇa*. In this essay, Sri Aurobindo's interpretation of caste and *varṇa* has been given much emphasis because as an internalist with a reformist zeal he has given an interpretation of *varṇa*, which seems to be quite logical in its approach. *Varṇa* and caste have some links but no necessary links as such between the two are to be found. Puruṣa-Sūkta may be viewed as a heuristic device to represent differences in personality, especially moral personality. *Varna* represents broad types of moral agency and it is not uncommon among the Buddhists or the Jains to admit unequality at the moral levels. The rational, logical reading of *varṇa* provides enough scope for each individual to improve oneself and to be promoted to the higher moral order by performing his duties according to his capability. Caste is the product of politics of power and it got itself associated with *varṇa*. If Sri Aurobindo's interpretation is to be accepted, nothing other than the psychology of the society is to be held responsible for this oversight.

References

Ambedkar, B.R., "Annihilation of Caste", in Valerian Rodrige, ed., *The Essential Writings of B.R. Ambedkar*, New Delhi: Oxford University Press, 2002.

(Sri) Aurobindo, *Essays on the Gītā*, Pondicherry: Sri Aurobindo Ashram, 8th reprint, 1970.

———, *The Foundations of Indian Culture*, Pondicherry: Sri Aurobindo Ashram, 4th edn., 1998.

———, *The Human Cycle: The Ideal of Human Unity, War and Self-Determination*, Pondicherry: Sri Aurobindo Ashram, 7th impression, 1997.

Bandyopadhyaya, Jayanatanuja, *Class and Religion in Ancient India*, Delhi: Anthem Press, 2007.

Bougle, C., "The Essence and Reality of the Caste System", in Dipankar Gupta, ed., *Social Stratification*, New Delhi: Oxford University Press, 14th impression, 2007.

Comte, Auguste, *General View of Positivism* (1830-42), tr. J.H Bridges, Robert Speller and Sons, 1957.

Dev, Arjun; Indira Arjun Dev and Supta Das, *Human Rights: A Source Book*, New Delhi: National Council of Education Research and Training, 1996.

Dubois, Abbe J.A., *Hindu Manners, Customs and Ceremonies*, tr., Henry Beauchamp, New Delhi: Rupa & Co., 10th impression, 2007.

Dumont, Louis, Homo Hierarchicus, *The Caste System and its Implications*, tr., Mark Sainsbury, Louis Dumont and Basia Gulati, Kolkata: Oxford University Press, 1998.

Dutt, Manmath Nath, *Atrisaṁhitā in the Dharam Śāstra (Hindu Religious Codes)*, vol. 2, New Delhi: Cosmo Publications, 1979.

Dutta, Hirendranath, *Manur Varnasramadharma*, Kolkata: Jadavpur University.

(Swami) Gambhirananda, ed., "Bṛhadāraṇyaka Upaniṣad" in *Upaniṣad Granthāvalī*, Prathama Bhāga, Kolkata: Udbodhana Kāryālaya, 7th impression, 1962.

Gould, Harold A., *The Hindu Caste System*, vols. 1-3, New Delhi: Chanakya Publications, 1988-90.

Guizot, Francois, *Histoire generale de la civilisation en Europe* (General History of Civilization in Europe), vols. 1-3, Paris: Librairie Academique, 1882.

Gupta, Dipankar, "Hierarchy and Difference: An Introduction", in *Social Stratification*, New Delhi: Oxford University Press, 14th Impression, 2007.

———, *Interrogating Caste*, Penguin Books India (P) Ltd., 2000, 14th impression, 2007.

(Swami) Harshananda, *The Puruṣasūkta: An Exigesis*, Bangalore: Ramakrishna Math, 3rd edn., 1999.

Kane, Pandurang Vaman, *History of Dharmaśāstra*, vol. II, part I, Pune: Bhandarkar Oriental Research Institute, 1974.

Karl Gotthard Lamprecht, *Deutsche Geschichte*, 12 vols., 2 incomplete vols., Berlin, 1891-1909.

———, *Die Kulturhistorische Methode*, Berlin, 1900.

———, *What is History*? Five Lectures on the *Modern Science of History*, tr. E.A. Andrews, New York: Macmillan Co, 1905.

Locke, John, *Two Treatises of Government, Of the State of Nature,* http : / www.lonang.com / exlibris / index.htm/Senart, Emile, Les castes dans I" Inde : les faits et le system, Ernest Leroax, 1896.

Low, Sidney, *Vision of India,* 2nd edn. 1907, as cited in Pandurang Vaman Kane, *History of Dharmaśāstra,* Pune: Bhandarkar Oriental Research Institute, 1974.

(Sri) Madhusudan Saraswati (Tika), *Śrīmadbhagavad-Gītā,* Varanasi: Chowkhamba Sanskrit Series, 1962.

Maine, *Ancient Law,* new edn., 1930. Reference obtained from P.V. Kane, *History of Dharmaśāstra* , vol. 2, part 1, 1974.

Mencher, J.P., "The Caste System Upside Down or the Not So Mysterious East?" in *Current Anthropology,* vol. 15, 1975.

———, "The Caste System Upside Down", in Dipankar Gupta, ed., *Social Stratification,* New Delhi: Oxford University Press, 14th impression, 2007.

Risley, Herbert Hope, *The Tribes and Castes of Bengal,* 2 vols., Calcutta: Bengal Secretariant Press, 1891.

———, *The People of India,* ed. W. Crooke, 2nd edn., London, 1915.

Rousseau, Jean-Jacques, *Origins of Inequality,* Selected Passages, tr., Anuradha Mukherjee, Kolkata: Aseema Praksani, 2001.

———, *The Social Contract, Or Principles of Political Right,* 1762, tr., G.D.H. Cole, Rendered into HTML and Text by Jon Roland Constitution Society, Austin, TX78757-1102.

Sanyal, Indrani, "Socio-Political Thoughts of Sri Aurobindo", in Siuli Saha Dalal and Sukanya Mitra, eds., *Proceedings of the National Seminar on "Sri Aurobindo's Contribution to Education and Society: His Message for the New Age",* Kolkata: Department of Philosophy, Baruipur College, 2007.

Senart, Emile, *Les Castes dans I'Inde* : *les faits et le system,* Ernest Leroax, 1896. This book has been digitized by Google.

Sherring, M.A., *Hindu Tribes and Castes,* 3 vols., 1872-81. Reference obtained from P.V. Kane, *History of Dharmasastra,* vol. 2, part 1, 1974.

Vedavyāsa, Śrīkṛṣṇadvaipāyana, *Mahābhāratam,* Bengali tr., Haridassiddhāntavāgīśa, Kolkata: Visvabani Prakasani, 1444 (Baṅgābda).

7

Rising above Self-interest Prescribed Value

Ratna Dutta Sharma

CLASSICAL Indian philosophical texts provide a list of two sorts of actions accordingly as they are enjoined by the Śāstras or prohibited by the *Śāstras*. One such list of actions has been offered by Vātsyāyana in his commentary on *Nyāya-Sūtra* (1.1.1). The actions which are never encouraged are distinguished from those actions towards which an agent is incited or motivated, and are marked as prohibited actions. The act of overruling *self-interest* can be taken to be a prescriptive act, that is, as worthy of being pursued, provided it can be shown on analysis, to form the foundation of any sanctioned acts whatsoever. In the same way, if the actions that are prohibited are shown to have self-interest as their driving force, then indirectly self-interest turns out to be unworthy of pursuance. The question arises as to what does it actually mean when one is instructed to rise above the self-interest. The aim of the paper is to specify the sense of *disinterestedness* as a moral value.

Misdeeds that can be done by the operation of body, as stated by Vātsyāyana, include among others (a) violence (*hiṁsā*), (b) stealing (*steya*) and (c) indulging in prohibited sexual intercourse (*pratisiddha maithuna*). The vices relating to speech as stated by him are (d) telling lies (*mithyā vacana*), (e) speaking harshly (*kaṭu vacana*), (f) incoherent babbling (*asambandha vacana*), etc. (g) Hostility (*paradroha*), (h) covetousness for others' belonging (*paradravyābhipsā*), and (i) rejecting authority of the Vedas, scriptures (*nāstikya*) are the vices relating to mind. The corresponding virtues relating to the body comprise (a) saving the distressed (*paritrāṇa*), (b) charity (*dāna*) and (c) social service (*paricarṇa*). Virtues relating to speech, as mentioned by Vātsyāyana, are (a) truthfulness (*satya vacana*), (b) agreeable speech (*priya vacana*), (c) beneficient speech (*hita vacana*) and reading of scriptures. Virtues relating to the mind include (a) kindness (*dayā*), (b) non-attachment (*aspṛhā*), (c) reverence (*śraddhā*).[1]

One way of trying to understand the nature of actions that are considered to be baneful is by tracing the source of such actions. It is a matter of common experience that in certain specific situations people do not hesitate to cause injury to others. But what makes them behave in that way? When we are not able to acquire an object of desire for instance, whereas someone else has managed to possess the same, we feel a tinge of jealousy towards that person. Jealousy often culminates in hatred that has the potential to cause immense violence to the person concerned. Ordinary people have an intense sense of possession for the object, which adds to their pleasure. Excessive possessiveness towards something often brings about a fear of insecurity. The fear of loss regarding objects of pleasure results in severe violent reactions like causing injury and harassment to the person from whom the threat of loss comes.[2] Sometimes one does not hesitate to adopt unfair

1. Vātsyāyana — *Bhāṣya on Nyāya-Sūtra* (1.1.2), *Nyāyadarśana*, vol. I, ch. I, ed. Pandit Anantalal Thakur, 1967, p. 150.

2. *"Saṅgā" sukhahetutvajñālakṣaṇāt "Saṁjāyate Kāmaḥ" mamaivete bhavantviti tṛṣnāviśeṣaḥ. Tasmāt "kāmāt" kutaścit pratihanyamānāt pratighātakaviṣayaḥ "Krodhaḥ"* →

means to obtain an object, which he failed to possess in a fair way. A person may be desirous of possessing an object, which would enhance his pleasure even though the object is in the possession of somebody else.[3] Sometimes the gratification of sensuous desire becomes so important to an individual that he transgresses the limit of the accepted norm and indulges in prohibited and forbidden acts. Often we come across such persons who make unfair criticisms or derogatory remarks about other persons to defame them and cause suffering to them. This, of course, can be a source of satanic pleasure for the perpetrators. Often a person tells lies to serve his own interest. Sometimes people take recourse to incoherent babbling to confuse other people to get maximum benefit from a situation.[4]

A person indulges in performing prohibited actions, by body, mind or speech to derive sensuous pleasure. This shows that an individual performing such acts gives priority to self-interest. The issue of one's own pleasure or satisfaction is the primary concern for him; hence the objects that gratify his desires are of utmost importance to him. People hanker after objects that contribute to their pleasure. They care for the pleasure of the self as self is the dearest thing to him.[5] On the

---

→ *abhijvalanātma abhijāyate.* Sri Madhusudana Sarasvati, *Gurārthadīpikā, Śrīmadbhagavad-Gītā,* Dvitīya adhyāya — *śloka* 63.

3. *Saṁgāt sukhahetutvajñānalakṣaṇāt saṁjāyate kāmaḥ mamaivete bhavantiti tṛṣṇāviśeṣaḥ.* Madhusudan Sarasvati — *Gurarthadīpikā on Gītā* 2.62-63.

4. *"Krodādbhavati Sammohaḥ" kāryākārya vivekābhāvarūpaḥ sammahāt smṛti bibrahamah" smōteḥ sāśtracaryyopadiṣṭārthānusandhānasya bibrahmaḥ vicalanam bibrahṁśa* — Ibid.

5. *Ātmanastu kāmāya sarvampriyam bhavati*
— *Bṛhadāraṇyaka Upaniṣad* 2.4.3.

other hand, people often contribute to charities, extend the hand of co-operation to the victims of natural calamity and perform many other such acts without any expectation for a definite return. These actions are counted as altruistic in contrast to those which are done for the sake of self-interest. We contribute to some fund for the benefit of others at the call of our conscience. If we are not ready to sacrifice our own interest we cannot think of doing anything for some one else's benefit. Similarly in order to help or rescue someone from danger or distress we sometimes have to place ourselves in unfavourable situations. Unless our spirit of disinterestedness gives the requisite boost to embrace the danger for the sake of another in distress we would not at all be in a position to act as the rescuer.

The list of sanctioned acts to be performed through the operation of speech as discussed by Vātsyāyana includes, among others, speaking the truth and endearing words. To abide by the dictates of truth one is required to be strong enough to embrace the untoward consequences, if any, resulting therefrom. It is a matter of common experience that soothing, encouraging, assuring, endearing words have magical effects in lessening the suffering of other people. One who has been able to rise above the domain of personal interest would try to alleviate the suffering of others. A person who is in the habit of glorifying himself is unable to appreciate the admirable qualities of others. Such a person may be proud of himself but he is really impoverished in his mentality.[6] Such

6. *"Akta ye vikatākār" kintu rāhu tāhār sakal prasamsāi grās kariyā thake, se rāhuti ar keha nahe, se tāhar angahin "āmi", tāhar aparitripta khudita ahaṁkāra. Se daitya, tāhar prasamsāsudhā khaibar adhikār nai, ai janya sakal sudhākar chadke malin nā karia thakite pare nā."* Rabindranath Tagore, "Kintuoyala", *Rabindra Racanavali*, vol. 14, Visva-Bharati, *Vividha Prasaṅga*, p. 681.

a person in spite of having admirable qualities in himself feels insecure if he is not appreciated by others. But one who does not try to glorify oneself is not at all affected in case others fail to appreciate the admirable qualities in him.[7] Whoever is respected must have the capacity to evoke a specificfic response by virtue of some of his attributes. Unless one restrains himself from self-glorification his attention cannot remain focused within the parameters of those attributes which renders him admirable. On the basis of the above observation, I would like to bring out that the virtue of disinterestedness assumes a great significance when we try to act in compliance with any of the prescriptions or prohibitions of the Śāstras. It is to be noted that whenever one tries to engage himself in the performance of actions in accordance with the prescription of the scriptures he needs to be respectful to the scriptures.

II

When can one be supposed to act out of self-interest? One can be assumed to be guided by self-interest if he acts for the benefit of his own self. One may come forward with the suggestion that to act rising above self-interest is to act without any interest for any advantage for oneself. But had it been the case, one would not be able even to sustain himself. This cannot certainly be the prescription of the scripture, for this devalues human life. It is suggested that the actions performed for mere subsistence are not at par with actions done out of self-interest. But the problem is that the concept of subsistence does not convey the same sense to all. Moreover, the question

---

7. *"Daser chokher upare ye dinaratrir vas karite chahe, parer chokher uparei yahar bari ghar, tahar ar nijer ghar bari nai. Sei janyai se rongchong diya parer chokh kinite chay, sekhan haitebhraṣta hailei se vyakti akebare nirāśraya hoia pore"*. Rabindranath Tagore, *Rabindra-Racanabali*, "Ghar O Basa Bari", vol. 14, Visva-Bharati, *Vividha Prasaṅga*, p. 702.

may be raised as to the very motive for subsistence. The plausible answer is this: since one considers oneself worthy of subsistence one should take every possible step to possess things which contribute to one's subsistence and pleasure. One may come forward and say that there is nothing wrong with it. Why should I not care for my own pleasure? If I have a feeling of goodness about myself, I will have a feeling of goodness towards the world. In fact, one may be tempted to justify acts of self-interest on different grounds.

It is a matter of common experience that sometimes pursuance of self-interest by an individual in turn contributes to the promotion of other's interest as well. A case may be cited where an economically backward family with very limited resources faces even more hardship when one of its members seeks to enhance his personal goal of attaining a dignified existence through higher education. The particular individual is here no doubt motivated for higher education out of self-interest. But actually when he succeeds in his goal and shares his subsequent higher income with other members of his family, the family as a whole enjoys the benefit of his act. Similarly, an individual on whom the duty of protecting others from enemies has been entrusted needs to protect himself first, in order to be able to discharge his duties adequately.

Some of the acts sanctioned by the Śāstras are done for the interest of the doer himself. For instance, one has been instructed to perform actions for the purification of the body and the mind as a necessary prerequisite for being liberated. Performance of this first act is necessary for being eligible to do sacrifice and other rituals, whereas performance of the second one is the prerequisite for being competent for acquisition of knowledge. Are not these acts guided by pure self-interest? One may argue that it is easier to keep oneself clean both physically and mentally than to make others keep themselves clean. Again, one who follows this instruction of the Śāstras can definitely set an example for others. In this way his act has an impact on others.

It is true that some of the actions prescribed by the Śāstras have direct reference to the benefit of the doer himself, just like the acts of keeping oneself clean both physically and mentally. One possible answer may be that this cannot be treated as guided by self interest when someone is guided by the motive for the satisfaction of his short-term desire, particularly say, by the desire for material gain he may be said to act out of self-interest.[8] But if one acts for his spiritual upliftment he can, in no way, be said to be guided by self-interest. The question that would naturally arise as to why acting for one's spiritual benefit is not to be counted as selfish as acting for one's material gain.[9] It is argued that if an act has been enjoined by the Śāstras; and also if it promotes self-interest then the person engaged in the performance of such an act should not be regarded as acting out of his own self-interest.

This issue will be taken up in the next section. One important thing is to be noted that there are several occasions when the prescription of the scripture is not followed blindly. We are to follow it consciously according to the requirement of the situation. For instance, the scripture has advised us to adhere to truth. But we can cite an instance from the *Mahābhārata* where the performance of a prescribed act has also been condemned for causing injury to other innocent persons. Once a brāhmaṇa named Kauśika saw that a group

8. *Nalini Brahma, Gitar marma o upadesh, Śrīmadbhagavad-Gītā* with Bengali tr. of *Gurārthadīpikā* of Madhusudan Sarasvati, 1345, Kolkata, p. 1257.

9. *yajñārthāt karmaṇah anyatra loka ayam karma vandhana* ।
yadartham karma kaunteya mukta saṅgaḥ samācara ॥
— *Śrīmadbhagavad-Gītā*, 3.9.

of robbers were running after an individual. The helpless individual while hiding himself behind the bushes requested Kauśika not to disclose it to the robbers. But when the robbers asked Kauśika about the individual Kauśika told them the truth. Subsequently the robbers found the individual and killed him. In this case in spite of telling the truth Kauśika had incurred *pāpa* (sin) for his adherence to truth caused the death of an innocent man.[10]

This instruction of the scripture to adhere to truth can be interpreted to mean that one should stick to truth so long as it does not harm another. So, if circumstances demand, we have to follow the scripture consciously on the basis of our own judgement. The scripture has not only instructed us to desist from doing what is injurious to others but to do good for others as well. How do we evaluate the worth of an act if it is done both for the benefit of one's own self and for the benefit of others as well? Let us take an example — suppose, at the very sight of a ravaging fire in the house of my neighbour I inform the fire brigade. Though I do it primarily to help my neighbour a tinge of self-interest is surely there. If the fire spreads it will definitely harm me. Can my action of informing the fire brigade be taken to be selfless in nature? It is not altruism or sacrificing one's own interest for the sake of other. Nor is it sacrificing others' interest for one's self-interest. Actually it is an instance of adhering to the principle, viz. "One for all, all for one"; since my own interest is included in the interest of all.

Those who believe that the world is created by God, and it is our duty to preserve the creation of God, consider that one should aim at the well-being of everything created by God. But this cannot be done excluding myself. So there is no question of sacrificing my own interest for the interest of

10. *Mahābhārata*, (69.51-53).

others. One should care for the interest of each and everything created by God including one's own self. Thus the intention of the God is served.

We obey the instruction of the scriptures and avoid telling lies, killing others, stealing other's property, for if we do whatever we want to do to others, regardless of the consequence, then life would become miserable. For others would also behave in the same way with us.

We should not treat others in a way in which we are not ready to be treated.[11] How can a man who seeks help, sweet words, assistance from another be himself cruel, intimidating, and damaging to the others? For this reason we should treat others in a way which is desirable for ourselves and should not act towards others in a way which is undesirable or unpleasant for us. If we are guided by this principle then harm and risk can be avoided, benefits can be accrued as well. To see the whole world in the analogy of one's own self implies seeing the pleasurable and painful experience of all in the analogy of one's own self. In the verse 6.32 of the *Bhagavad-Gītā* a *yogī* is described as one who sees everybody in the analogy of his own self.[12] As we desire to be free from all hazards and troubles, so must we desire the same thing for other individuals as well. As we are fond of our self-esteem, welfare and well-being so must we be respectful towards the self-esteem, welfare and well-being of each and everyone. This sort of awareness encourages one to have a merciful attitude towards other people and other living creatures.

---

11. *yathā smaryate prāṇāh yathātmanobhistā bhutānāmapi te tathā* ।
ātmaupameyena bhūteṣu dayam kurbanti sādhavaḥ iti ॥
Madhusudana *Gurarthadipika* on *śloka* 6.32 of *Bhagavad-Gītā*.

12. *ātmayupamyena sarvatra samam pasyati yo arjuna* ।
sukham vā yadi vā dukham sa yogī parama mataḥ ॥
— *Śrīmadbhagavad-Gītā*, 6.32

Guided by this mentality we may try our best to prevent ourselves at least from becoming a source of any harm to others. If any such practice can be followed it will definitely help in curbing instances of vengeance and would make room for more congenial and harmonious co-existence. If one develops an intimate relationship with the other members of a society he will be able to feel others' pleasure and success as his own. This feeling will prevent him from being jealous of others' happiness and success. Consequently, one would cease to develop anger towards the successful persons. By developing a favourable attitude towards all he becomes happy at others' happiness and considers others' success as his own.[13]

Man is primarily a social being. He knows very well unless the social condition is stable it would not be feasible for all including himself to pursue his goal. Being a member of a society we should not indulge in such an act which would provoke others to retaliate against any of our actions leading to an unstable social condition. Each one of us desires the benefit of living in a society based on reciprocity. In such a situation the interest of the society includes the interest of each one of the individual members. So, some of the acts prescribed by the Śāstra have definite social implications at least in the sense that they are grounded on a consideration of fellow beings living in the society.

Since everybody is desirous of living in a stable social

---

13. *evam sukhnisu maitrim bhāvayato na kevalam rāgo nivartate, kintuasuyersādayopi nivartante. paraguṇeṣu. dosāviṣkaranamasūyā, paraguṇānāmasahanamṛṣā* ।

yadā maitrivasāt parasukham svīyameva sampannam ।
tadā parguṇeṣu kathamasūyādikam samvaveta ॥

— Madhusudana *Gurārtha-dīpikā* on *śloka* of *Bhagavad-Gītā*, p. 587

condition, the action prompted by the vision of such a goal cannot be considered to be selfish in nature. Even where the goal is not common the action motivated by the desire to attain that goal cannot be said to be selfish if it does not cause harm to others. There is nothing like it if the action is beneficial towards others as well. *Īśopaniṣad* has also sanctioned those acts which contribute to the enjoyment of the doer. But the enjoyment must be well regulated so as not to hamper others' interest.[14] We find the reflection of the same thought in the writings of the contemporary thinkers as well. There is nothing wrong in seeking my own pleasure. But it should not stand in the way of others' pleasure. *Ami parke sukhe rakhia yadi apnio sukhe thakite pari, tabe taha na kariya icchapurvaka kasta sahiba keno*?[15]

On the basis of the above discussion we can make the following classification of action:

1. The action that has been performed (for) the desire of some material gain.
   (a) It does not cause any harm to other persons.
   (b) It causes harm to other persons.
   (c) Persons other than the doer may also be benefited by the act.
2. The action that is undertaken for the attainment of spiritual goal.
   (a) The action does not cause harm to others.
   (b) It causes harm to others.
   (c) The action does help others to reach their spiritual goal.

---

14. *īśāvasyameda sarvam yat kiñca jagatyām jagat tena tyaktena bhuñjīthā mā gṛdhaḥ kasya śrīddhanam* — *Īśopaniṣad* I.
15. *Bankimchandra Vividha Prabandha, Bankim Racanābalī*, vol. 2, Sahitya Samsad, Kolkata, 1376, p. 271.

It seems to me that the actions 1(c) and 2(c) can be regarded as being above self-interest or disinterested in the strict sense of the term whereas 1(a) and 2(a) can be so in a somehow loose or weaker sense. But 1(b) and 2(b) cannot be regarded as above self-interest or disinterested act. To rise above self-interest is nothing but to regulate the lower propensity by the higher one. The natural inclinations of man go in favour of his own interest. So far man is confined to himself he is taken to be guided by animal propensity, by lower interest. But his inclination is higher when he is concerned with others as well. The scriptures instructing us to rise above self-interest is suggesting to negate the lower propensity by the higher one. This is a necessary prerequisite for a stable social condition.

III

The question arises as to whether one who strives for his liberation can be said to act by rising above self-interest. Let us try to get a possible answer to this question.

Generally true cognition about the nature of self which is conducive to the attainment of liberation is attained through the process of *śravaṇa, manana* and *nididhyāsana.*[16] Persons who have received instructions (*śāstriya upadeśa*) are under obligation to their cultural forefathers. The idea of such duty involves the notion of repayment.[17] One who considers teaching to be his duty does not simply repeat or narrate the truth as received from his preceptors. Prior to teaching or instructing what he has been learnt, he subjects the truth to critical examinations. It is his duty to defeat in open debate another person who is

16. *ātmā vā are śrotovyaḥ, mantavyaḥ, nididhyāsitavyaḥ* ।
— *Bṛhadāraṇyaka Upaniṣad* (2.4.5)

17. *jāyamano vai brāhmaṇastribhirnaiṛnavā jāyate, brahmacaryeṇa ṛṣibhyaḥ yajñena devebhyoḥ prajayā pitṛbhya* — quoted by Vātsyānana in his commentary on Nyāya-Sūtra (4.1.58).

unduly attached to a particular viewpoint out of false beliefs. A defeat in the debate makes the person sceptical of the position he adopted so long and makes him eager to know the truth.[18] The attainment of truth is not enough, the received truth is to be preserved, and the preserved truth is to be applied in practice. Just as one has been advised to follow this procedure, one must at the same time make others follow the same.[19] So one who aspires after liberation can in no way be taken to be motivated by self-interest alone. He is under obligation to help other people to attain the truth which is necessary for liberation. One who acts for the attainment of the highest goal is advised to help others to pursue the highest goal through the attainment of truth. But it is true that when he himself is engaged in the attainment of truth he is totally absorbed in the process. Still he is to be careful enough not to harm others by his endeavour. In this connection we may refer to Patañjali's classification of actions performed by ordinary people (*ayogī*) into three types — (1) *śukla,* (2) *kṛṣṇa,* and (3) *śuklakṛṣṇa.*[20] According to him *svādhyāya* or recitation of the Vedas, and *tapasyā* or meditation are included among others in the first variety of actions. Speech is active in the case of the recitation of the Vedas. *Manas* is active in the case of meditation. These actions are conducive to happiness only and

---

18. *asandigdhapi tattvapratipādanāya kāuruṇikena sandigdhaḥ kṛtvā pratipādyata iti* — Vācaspati Miśra, Tātparyaṭīkā, *Nyāya Darśana of Gautama,* vol. 1, Ch. 1, ed. Pandit Anantalal Thakur, Benaras, 1967, p. 26.

19. *anutpannasya hi tattva nirṇaysyasya utpādanam, utpannasya pālanam, pālitasya ca viniyogaḥ* I *sa ca svayamabhyāsaḥ, kāruṇikatayā paravyutpādanam* II Udayana, Pariśuddhi, *Nyāya Darśana of Gautama,* vol. 1, ed. Anantalal Thakur, Benaras, 1967, p. 620.

20. Śrīmad Hariharānanda Āraṇya *Pātañjala Yogadarśana,* paścimbhāga, Kolkata: Rajya Pustak Parisad, 1988, p. 801.

never cause harm to others. Once the truth is attained it is to be transmitted to keep the tradition alive. How can these acts be treated as motivated by self-interest? If one's upliftment is a necessary condition for making upliftment of others possible, then it is one's foremost duty to make oneself eligible for providing help to others in achieving the goal. Attainment of the required knowledge of truth leads one to the desired goal. Only thereafter one can pitch in for the improvement of others.

From the above discussion it is evident that the Śāstra prescribes that we ought to rise above self-interest. Here ought implies can. Had it been impossible for us to rise above self-interest it would not have been prescribed by the Śāstra. Actually this springs from the nature of human being. Unlike the animals man is not merely bound within the limits of his bare necessities. He has got the capacity of appreciating the aesthetic aspect in addition. Due to this resource of emotional energy human being surpasses individual interest.[21]

References

Brahma, Nalini, ed., *Śrīmadbhagavad-Gītā*, Kolkata: Nava Bharat Publishers, 1345 BS.

Chattopadhyay, Bankimchandra, *Bankim Racanāvalī*, vol. 2, Kolkata: Sahitya Sansad, 1376 (Baṅgābda).

Durgacarana Sāṁkhya Vedāntatīrtha, *Bṛhadāraṇyaka Upaniṣad*, part 2, Kolkata: Dev Sahitya Kutir, 1371 BS.

Miśra, Vācaspati, Tātparyaṭīkā, *Nyāyadarśanam*, New Delhi: Munshiram Manoharlal Publishers, 1985.

Sāṁkhya Yogācārya Śrīmat Svami Hariharānanda Āraṇya, *Pātañjala Yoga Darśana*, Kolkata: Rajya Pustak Parsad, 1966.

---

21. *saundarya prayojaner vārā* ı *eiyanya tāhākei amrā aiśvarya baliā māni* ı *eiyanya tāhā āmādigake nichhak svārthasādhaner dāridrya haite premer madhye mukti dey* ı Rabindranath Tagore, Sahitya, *Rabindra Racanāvalī*, vol. 4, Visva-Bharati, 1909, p. 635.

Sarasvati, Madhusudan, *Gudarthadīpikā, Śrīmadbhagavad-Gītā*, 1345 BS.

Swami Gambhirananda, ed., *Īśopaniṣad, Upaniṣad Granthāvalī*, vol. 3, Kolkata: Udbodhan, 1383 (Baṅgābda).

Tagore, Rabindranath, *Rabindra Racanāvalī*, vol. 4, Kolkata: Visvabhārati, 1909.

———, *Rabindra Racanābalī*, vol. 14, Kolkata: Visvabharati, 1909.

Taranath Nyāya, Tarkatīrtha, Amarendranath, Tarkatīrtha, eds., *Nyāyadarśanam*, New Delhi: Munshiram Manoharlal Publishers, 1985.

Thakur, Anantalal, *Nyāyadarśana of Gautama*, vol. 1, Ch. 1, Varanasi: Mithila Institute Series, 1967.

Thakur, Rabindranath, *Rabindra Racanābalī*, vol. 14, Santinikitan: Visva-Bharati University, 1985.

Udayana, Tatparyapariśuddhi, *Nyāyadarśana of Gautama*, vol. 1, Chapter 1, ed. Anantalal Thakur, Benaras: Mithila Institute Series, 1967.

Vātsyāyana, Bhāṣya on Nyāya-Sūtra, *Nyāyadarśana of Gautama*, vol. 1, ed. Anantalal Thakur, Benaras: Mithila Institute Series, 1967.

Vedavyāsa Mahābhārata, tr. Kaliprasanna Singha, Kolkata: Tuli Kalam, 1984.

8

Exploring Ao Values and Ethics

Sashinungla

WITHIN the dominant philosophical discourse both Indian and Western, tribal values and ethics have often been assessed to be mainly negative in nature compared to the corresponding mainstream or written one.[1] This type of unfavourable assessment, no doubt, has led to the devaluation of tribal thought and demoralized the tribals. This has also stirred them to bring into focus their viewpoint. However, in recent times this misconception is on the wane and scholars are discovering promising features of tribal culture. A tradition represents more than just a way of life. It also includes "a way of thinking, a way of doing things, a way of conceiving, and a way of conceiving what a good life is."[2] The *Ao*'s vision of the world is characterized by the term *sobaliba,* as implying thereby their idea of what is good and bad, right and wrong, ought to be done and ought not to be done and so on.[3] *Sobaliba* is defined as the origin, source, foundation, base, purpose, process and

1. For the view that tribal thought has no elements of a moral code and that it is a mere system of ceremony, see for instance J.P. Mills, *The Ao Nagas*, London: Oxford University Press, 1926, p. 115.
2. Sujata Miri, *Rationality and Tribal Thought*, Delhi: Mittal Publications, 2004, p. 3.
3. For this purpose I have explored and considered their poetry, legends, proverbs, songs, idioms and forms of speech- →

end of all reality. Since, *sobaliba* is the *tamendaktak* (foundation) and *ozung* (principle) of *ajak* (all beings), which holds all things and sustains human society and the world, it is followed and preserved. The concept of *sobaliba* is generally equated with their concept of *yimsu* (religion), to spell out the relationship between God, man and the world. It is because of this relationship with God, according to the *Ao* thinking, *sobaliba* is *yimli* or *ochi*, everything that is Truth, right order, the overall plan and design of the Creator Himself. Therefore, man belongs entirely to God, and manifests this total belonging to God by executing *yimli* of God, and in particular by earning righteousness. *Yimli* or *ochiba* is God Himself as manifested in this created universe. It means, God Himself governs and rules the world in an invisible but effective manner. So, *sobatiyaba mesuka* means to recognize the manner in which God acts and then to model our human conduct on God's way of dealing with the world. They say, accepting man is to accept God, the invisible, and what has been done to man has been done to God.[4] Because of this, *sobaliba* is not merely a way of life in accordance with laws and customs as is usually meant by the word righteousness. It characterizes the traditional etiquette, social manner, honesty, integrity, virtues and much more than that.[5]

→ making to unpack the key terms and concepts. See Sashinungla, "Collection of Ao Folk Narratives", in Desmond L. Karmawphlang, ed., *Folk Narratives of the North-east*, vols. 1 and 2, Shillong: North Eastern Hill University, 2003; P.K. Bhattacharya, ed., *Folk Tales of Nagaland*, Kohima: Naga Institute of Culture, 1971; Renthy Keitzar, ed., *Ao Dictionary*, Impur: Ao Theological Literature Society, 1999.

4. Panger Imchen, *Ancient Ao Naga Religion and Culture*, Delhi: Har-Anand Publications, 1993, p. 77

5. Renthy Keitzar, "Tribal Theology in the Making", in K.C. Abraham, ed., *New Horizons in Ecumenism : Essays in Honour* →

Sobaliba has been characterized as both *yimden-yimli* and *yimsu-yimli*. This means the principle of knowing man and knowing the truth. This suggests both the intellectual and experiential knowledge. It also means that to understand who human beings are, we must accept them as they are, and deal with them in accordance with this knowledge. The maintaining of a positive attitude towards human beings is the starting point of their relationship with truth. *Yimden-yimsu* is a condition *sine qua non* of *yimli*. It means, not only the intellectual knowledge of *sobaliba*, but also its acceptance as the truth and a life of communion with it. In matters of conduct, *sobaliba* emerges as the higher principle, signifying the sense of right and wrong. *Sobaliba* is the fountainhead of the morality of society, and is also described as *ochiba takum*, designating thereby the perfect moral behaviour of man. The moral life or righteous life includes love, recognition, respect, equality and justice.[6] Hence good moral life or the righteous life, that is *ochiba takum*, is a life, lived according to *ochiba*, that is righteousness or morality.

According to the *Ao* way of thinking, man's moral life begins with his interaction with other fellow human beings, and it accomplishes its completeness by relating itself with the man-nature-truth continuum. Thus, it is the *ochi* (truth) basis of all things, the *libukum* (nature) nurtures them and the *meimchir* (man) preserves them. Though man is having responsibility and is the "role" player in all aspects, the possession of faculty of intellect does not give him the right to exploit and dominate over others unfairly. As *sobaliba* is characterized as *yimli*, which is justice, love and kindness, it

→ *of Bishop Samuel Amrithan*, Bangalore: BTESSC & BTTBPSA, 1993, p. 48.

6. N. Talitemjen Jamir, *Asen Sobalibaren*, Kohima: State Rural Development Agency, 1986, pp. 5-21.

demands that the right order should be maintained through mutual respect and reciprocity avoiding any confrontation, conquest or exploitation of one by another.[7]

From the *Ao* perspective, the very essence of good life depends on fostering a generous outlook which consists in viewing everything — people, their groups, land and varied life forms, as related to one another.[8] The notions of man's liberation and morality include the well-being and dignity of human beings along with the whole creation. According to their view, to segregate his own good and dignity from that of his fellow human beings, the family of nature and the divine is to lose the actual meaning and purpose of life itself. "If you do not act responsibly towards the well-being and dignity of others, it will in turn jeopardize your own life" is the motto that guides the ideal relationship of man with the universe. The liberation is understood by *Aos*, as *alang*, literally meaning "worth" or "worthy," in relation to the well-being and dignity of others. It means that each moral act, each good deed or bad is not to be taken only in the sense of "personal self-regarding duty." A life is worthy that has concern for the protection, restoration, sustenance and the proper continuance of society and the environment. *Alang*, therefore, signifies the condition, context or the space in which human well-being and the ultimate fulfilments are made possible. It is the condition that helps to establish justice and unity.[9]

Sobaliba is also characterized as the principle of correct observance of norms and practices. *Sobaliba* complements

7. A. Wati Longchar, Yankahao Vashum, eds., *The Tribal Worldview and Ecology*, Jorhat: The Tribal Study Centre, 1998, p. 58.

8. Jamir, *Asen Sobalibaren*, p. 11.

9. Sashinungla, *Environment Preservation : A Philosophical Critique*, Delhi: Decent Books, 2005, pp. 121-23.

libaliro, which is social conduct; the practice of morality or righteousness should be according to the norms laid down in *sobaliba*.[10] These practices are performed according to the needs. Though the norms and practices are many and differ from place to place and from time to time the underlying principle is the same. It is a principle which demands our knowledge of its fundamental features. *Sobaliba* emphasizes the sanctity and importance of the inter-group relationships, governance, institution of marriage, interpersonal relationships, duties and etiquettes. This has the force of a customary law and is a basis of the *Ao* values and ethics. From this viewpoint a person's credibility and respectability are closely linked to his belonging to the society and guiding himself according to the moral principle adopted by the society. This interactive cohesiveness between a society and its members provides the basis for security of life and property because all the collective efforts are aimed at providing a safe and secure condition for all. Thus the social institutions provide the place for man's existence and for asserting his identity as a moral being.[11] This prompts him to accept that his individual "identity" is always in relation to an "other." The interactive cohesiveness between the individual and the society provides us with an insight into the working of the moral principle in a situation where it was imperative to evolve a system, which would guarantee security, justice and good governance for all. In such an order, "individual identity," as we understand the term in the modern context, to a great extent, is included within the larger identity of the unit. The individual accepts this because the principle to which he has "submitted" his individuality is the

---

10. M. Horam, *Religion and Society of the North-east India*, New Delhi: Vikas Publishing House, 1980, p. 15.

11. Imchen, *Ancient Ao-Naga Religion and Culture*, p. 106.

same with the one which worked for the good of all, including his own good.[12]

Another important aspect of *sobaliba* is expressed by the saying *tatalokba temangi tekia ajangukudango,* which means that nothing happens without a cause. All events and happenings have causes behind them.[13] It is this aspect of *sobaliba* that helps man to make a right decision and guides him on the right path of life. It is also the basis of that eternal relationship between God and man. Because of this, according to the *Ao* way of thinking, God would not listen to a man if that man has no reason and the man himself never goes to God without a reason. This is one of the reasons why they laid much importance on retaining individual purity and honesty. They believe that by observing and following the principle of *sobaliba,* life is reasonably and rationally led.

It is because of this they give so much importance to the idea, *salang menna, ken o medema* which means, consultation, consensus, participation in decision making, co-operation and a caring concern for the well-being of other members of the society. In the *Ao* creation-poems, the representation of the whole community as discussing together, through mutual consultation, and consensus, words of wisdom from *sobaliba,* searching for order, tracing the eldest and giving him his due, dividing duties, etc. is indicative of a moral system based on the consent, participation and co-operation of all members in decision making and carrying out respective roles.[14]

---

12. Temsula Ao, "Human Resource Management in Ao Society", in Sujata Miri, ed., *Rationality and Tribal Thought*, Delhi: Mittal Publications, 2004, p. 187
13. Imchen, *Ancient Ao-Naga Religion and Culture*, pp. 86-90. See also Joseph Puthenpurakal, *Baptist Missions in Nagaland*, Shillong: Vendrame Missiological Institute, 1984, pp. 5-6.
14. Imtilepden Longjang, *Aor Tatakrutsu*, Imtilepden, Longjang,

→

If we examine their social structure not just in terms of how it appears, but also consider how far it spreads the horizon of its life world, we might discern a society where a unified endeavour is not dependent upon some superseding organ of an institution or society. The different ways, at different times, in which people aligned towards certain leaders for protection or for opposition may be considered as forming an alliance for a principle or a purpose. The power lies at the primary level of the society that functions everyday. Their notion of power-sharing is explicated through highly organized and well-established patterns of social, moral and political structures and functions.[15] According to their understanding, every discussion should lead to some conclusions. Once a decision is reached after a thorough debate, arguments and questioning, it is to be accepted. It is here one discerns the value of remaining neutral between "liberty" and "rule-following." Though he exhibits a strong sense of individual self-awareness and liberty, he is very much aware of his duty to keep his commitment. Another value discernible here is that power ascends upwards from the people below unlike the model where power is from the top down, from a sovereign body above to the people below. In this regard *Ao* society is to be seen as one that is antithetical to centralized control. The underlying principle requires that no one should unfairly overrule anyone else; mutual agreement and acceptance and

---

→ 1968, p. 1. See also Joseph Puthenpurakal, *Baptist Missions in Nagaland*, p. 6; M.M. Clark, *A Corner in India*, Guwahati: CLC, 1978, p. 45.

15. Verrier Elwin in his book (*The Nagas in the Nineteenth Century*, 1961) observed "each village amongst the Aos is a small Republic, and each man is as good as his neighbour, indeed it would be hard to find anywhere else more thoroughly democratic communities. Tatar (village leader), does exist, but his authority is very small" (see p. 234).

harmony in the process should prevail.[16]

In matters of justice, *sobaliba* assumes itself as the principle for determining justice. *Sobaliba* in this sense comprehends a wide compass of meanings, ranging from being true, just, right, proper, upright, honest to being personally and culturally correct. *Sobaliba* augments the rationale of authoritativeness and control, in addition to its previous exercise of moral authority. *Sobaliba* can be characterized as law in its broadest sense. However, *sobaliba* does not imply a static set of rules. This is so because the entire *Ao* judicial system was founded on values, and being a value-based system, *Ao* adheres to principles rather than a set of rules. It is true that there are rules like *kidang, kilamet,* and *jencha*[17] for matters like adultery, violence, criminal offence, etc. but it will be erroneous to see *Ao* custom in terms of rigid rules. In fact, they were by and large successful in keeping their values to the fore.

Thus, the *Ao* value concept has been commonly explicated in terms of compassion, giving and sharing, caring for others, love and promotion of others' welfare, equity, and the maintenance of harmony and balance. Certainly, a degree of unselfishness and promotion of others' welfare is necessary for co-operative endeavours, and the *Ao*s place a high value on such service. They say, "haughtily ridiculing one who has sacrificed his interest for others has permanent consequences."[18]

*Ao*s believe that giving and sharing are essential for a fruitful relationship among people. For instance, they go out of their way to give freely "community" land to the landless

---

16. Jamir, *Ao Kin Sobalibaren*, p. 116.

17. Imchen, pp. 121-22. See also Tajen Ao, *Ao-Naga Customary Law,* Aowati Imchen, Mokokchung, 1980, pp. 147-50.

18. N. Tali Jamir, *Aor Tar Nunger Otsu,* Jamir, Mokokching, 1962. See also Mills, p. 314.

for rehabilitation and residential purposes.[19] According to their thinking, by getting the land the receiver is indebted to acknowledge the virtuous acts of generosity and sharing, and to support and practise it. Here they are doing their part of giving liberally in order to generate lasting responsibility on the beneficiary and to enhance the power of the very act of generosity and sharing. As such, they give much importance to *liromedem ajemalu,* that is, the maintenance of balance and self-restraint in both thoughts and actions. It means they believe in never overdoing things *wapowaji, talitapong* because they say anyone who over-indulges has to pay a price.

The concepts of *ochi* and *ochiba takum* are central to the understanding of *Ao* values and morality. Concepts of *ochi* and *ochiba takum* are related to each other. But they do not convey the one and the same meaning. It pervades all spheres of life, social, political, economic and moral life of the man. It is *yimden-yimli, yimsu-yimli* in the sense of law, value and morality, that regulates all his thoughts and actions.[20] It is also in this sense, *ochi* or *ochiba* is the right order. Because of this, they say, everything that is right and orderly has *ochi* or *ochiba* as its principle. Therefore, man does everything by *ochi* in accordance with the direction given by *sobaliba.*[21] This is the reason why right order is the desired objective of their life and actions. This implies that they have always the possibility and hope of earning righteousness, if they so desire. Because of this fact, consequently, man can think always righteously and also act righteously.

The modern cultural perspective has offered conflicting

---

19. A. Wati Longchar, *The Traditional Tribal Worldview and Modernity*, Jorhat: Eastern Theological College, 1995, pp. 67-68. See also Ao, p. 170.

20. Jamir, p. 9. See also Ao, *Ao-Naga Customary Laws*, pp. 1-3.

21. Imchen, pp. 106-07.

and often erroneous judgement on the nature of the tribal values. As a result of such evaluations, several parallel views have evolved, proclaiming, for example, that tribal culture is a mere nature-based religion or animism without any element of consistent moral code or that tribal culture is not "logical" or "reasonable."[22] Even setting aside any cultural resurgence, in capturing lived experiences of individuals and communities there is no adequate reference to the depth of the system nor is there any attempt to find out the extent to which these values had continued to influence and guide human thinking and action at different points of time. It is imperative to appreciate such value system and distil values and apply them to our present context in understanding human actions and social problems more accurately. Traditional and academic evidences in fact depend on each other. They are not in conflict.[23] It is necessary to revise the notion of tribal values such as compassion, sharing, peace and inclusion.[24]

I would like to identify a few ways in which I find the *Ao* paradigm discreet. Their concept of value makes provision for mutual co-operation and interaction, for a caring attitude and compassion towards others, the maintenance of balance and harmony between humans and humans and between humans and nature. The recent model of value seems to be essentially individualistic, materialistic and prey to consumerism and unchecked power-based domination. The acceptance of a

---

22. For further discussion on this view, see E.B. Taylor, *Primitive Cultures*, Harper and Brothers, New York, 1958, pp. 8-10. See also A.W. Davis, Census of India, vol. 1 (Assam, 1891), pp. 230-51.
23. T. Kuhn, *The Essential Tension: Selected Studies in Scientific Tradition and Change*, Chicago: University of Chicago Press, 1977, p. 234.
24. Louis T. Mayeux, *Tribal Values: Faulkner's Vision*, New York: New York Times, August 8, 2002.

value model for a certain kind of social harmony, without division and fragmentation is quite promising. The way they holistically delineate their relationship with others seems to represent a viable perspective on this account. In such a scheme we may see ourselves as parts of a larger whole, and as being responsible for the impact of our choices on those around us, and on our environment. It also may imply getting to know the values that are at the core of all existence and appreciate the new definition of power based on each receiving a fair share rather than on hierarchical domination.

References

Ao, M. Alemchiba, *A Brief Historical Account of Nagaland*, Kohima: Naga Institute of Culture, 1970.

A. Wati Longchar, Yankahao Vashum, eds., *The Tribal Worldview and Ecology*, Jorhat: The Tribal Study Centre, 1998.

A. Wati Longchar, *The Traditional Tribal Worldview and Modernity*, Jorhat: Eastern Theological College, 1995.

Bhattacharya, P.K., ed., *Folk Tales of Nagaland*, Kohima: Naga Institute of Culture, 1971.

Charles, M., *Varieties of Human Values*, Chicago: The University of Chicago Press, 1956.

Clark, M.M., *A Corner in India*, Guwahati: CLC, 1978.

Davis, A.W., Census of India, vol. 1, Assam, 1891.

Giri, K. Ananta, *Conversations and Transformations: Towards a New Ethics of Self and Society*, Lanham: Lexington Books and Rowman & Littlefield, 2002.

Heidegger, Martin, *Being and Time*, tr. John Macquarrie, Edward Robinson, Oxford: Basil and Blackwell, 1973.

Horam, M., *Religion and Society of the North-east India*, New Delhi: Vikas Publishing House, 1980.

Imtilepden Longjang, *Aor Tatakrutsu*, Imtilepden, Longjang, 1968.

Jamir, N. Tali, *Aor Tar Nunger Otsu*, Mokokching, Published by the Author, 1962.

———, *Asen Sobalibaren*, Kohima: State Rural Development Agency, 1986.

Kappen, S., *Tradition, Modernity, Counter-culture : An Asian Perspective*, Bangalore: Vistar, 1994.

Mills, J.P., *The Ao Nagas*, London: Oxford University Press, 1926.

Miri, Sujata, ed., *Rationality and Tribal Thought*, Delhi: Mittal Publications, 2004.

Panger Imchen, *Ancient Ao Naga Religion and Culture*, Delhi: Har-Anand Publications, 1993.

Perry, R.B., *"The Definition of Value"*, *Journal of Philosophy*, vol. 11, New York: Columbia University.

Putnam, Hilary, *Realism with a Huma Face*, Cambridge: Harvard University Press, 1990.

Puthenpurakal, Joseph, *Baptist Missions in Nagaland*, Shillong: Vendrame Missiological Institute, 1984.

Rapp, Fredrich, "Distrust of Reason", in Joseph Agassi, Robert S. Cohen, eds., *Scientific Philosophy Today*, London: D. Reidel Publishing Company, 1980.

Renthy Keitzar, ed., *Ao Dictionary*, Impur: Ao Theological Literature Society, 1999.

———, "Tribal Theology in the Making", in K.C. Abraham, ed., *New Horizons in Ecumenism : Essays in Honour of Bishop Samuel Amrithan*, Bangalore: BTESSC & BTTBPSA, 1993.

Sashinungla, "Collection of Ao Folk Narratives", in Desmond L. Karmawphlang, ed., *Folk Narratives of the North-east*, vol. 1 and 2, Shillong: North Eastern Hill University, 2003.

———, *Environment Preservation : A Philosophical Critique*, Delhi: Decent Books, 2005.

Sundara Ranjan, R., *Beyond the Crisis of European Sciences*, vol. 1, Shimla: Indian Institute of Advanced Study, 1998.

Tajen Ao, *Ao-Naga Customary Law*, Mokokchung: Aowati Imchen, 1980.

Tambiah, Stanley, *Magic, Science and Religion, and the Scope of Rationality*, Cambridge: Cambridge University Press, 1990.

Taylor, E.B., *Primitive Cultures*, New York: Harper and Brothers, 1958.

Toulmin, Stephen, *Return to Reason*, Cambridge: Harvard University Press, 2003.

Verrier, Elwin, *The Nagas in the Nineteenth Century*, 1961.

9

Love and Sexuality in the Kurmi Culture

Arun Mahata **and** ***Aditi Dasgupta***

THE Kurmis are the aboriginal inhabitants who occupy the vast area covering the western part of Paschim Medinipur, the whole of Purulia district, and some parts of the adjacent states — Bihar, Orissa and Jharkhand. These Kurmi people worship Nature and are very sensitive about the preservation of the uniqueness of their own culture. They are determined to protect their own colourful cultural practices from the modern and post-modern influences. Researchers think that these Kurmis have originated from the valley of the Kurum hill and migrated to different lands in various directions for their survival. Scholars like Dalton maintain that these people are the descendants of the Aryans. But Risley and others do not accept their view.[1] The modern researchers fail to arrive at any unanimous conclusion regarding the origin of the Kurmis. Their way of living; their gods and goddesses such as *Karam, Garam, Dharam, Buram;* their festivals like *Makar, Bandhana,* etc.; their practice of worshipping trees, hills, stones, ponds; their custom of dancing, singing and torturing the body on the occasions of birth, death or marriage; and their acceptance of widow re-marriage, divorce, re-marriage[2] are supposed to

1. H.H. Risley, *Tribes and Castes of Bengal*, p. 529.
2. Ibid., p. 531.

bear the traits of pre-Vedic aboriginal culture. The familiar proverb says:

kol, kurmi, kora,
ved śāstra chhara.

The Kols, the Kurmis and the Koras do not abide by the Vedic norms.

This article primarily intends to explore the philosophical concept of love and sexuality as depicted in the folk songs of the Kurmis. These songs convey the essence of their everyday lives. It is however not an easy task to present a catalogue of all Kurmi folk songs nor are we engaged in this endeavour. We may try to capture the different moods and colours of love and sexuality, by analysing the inner meaning of some of the Kurmi songs.

Love, Sexuality and those Songs

Love essentially plays the most significant role in human lives. The well-groomed elites may often keep their brains busy with conceptual dissection of the notion of abstract love. Elite literatures seem to have a mission for serving people with the intellectual taste of love and sexuality and so most of the time they keep themselves busy with exploring new dimensions of those two concepts. But at times a refined linguistic mind fails to touch and comprehend the sensuality of true love. Abstract Platonic love is a debatable issue. Can love between two sexes ever be indifferent to any kind of bodily pleasure? The proponents of *love with sexuality* often claim that one can reach the pinnacle through bodily pleasure. It is maintained that Platonic love is accompanied by a latent sigh of frustration as it fails to attain its desired climax — the bodily pleasure.

The Kurmi love songs are to be considered as the reflection of the mentality of the Kurmi society on love and sexuality.

The passages of songs depicting the witty comments among the young Kurmi boys and girls are very common. Their love songs express the relationship between man and woman in an unpretentious manner. These are often stigmatized as "obscene" by the cultural crusaders. These songs are misinterpreted though these songs continue to be the original expressions of their hearts — the true saga of their love and are wild as the wild rivers of Chhota Nagpur plateau.

Some maintain that love brews the passion for music in humans. Kurmi folk songs too testify to this very fact. But their love is essentially different from the love depicted in the *Vaishnai* literature. The Kurmi love songs are not descriptions of any *transcendental love* like that between *sādhaka* and his object of worship. Love that is nourished within the Kurmi culture is rather sensual in nature. Love without sexuality is rather absurd from the perspective of the Kurmi culture. The pleasure of creation is the driving force behind heterosexual attractions and creation is not possible without copulation. The Kurmi culture views a sex-starved body as purposeless, and upholds that love can attain completeness only through sexual satisfaction. An enticing gesture, or a glimpse can strike the right note in love, which hundreds of well-chosen explicit words can never possibly do. So the Kurmi girl sings:

shishire ki gachh banche, bina barasane he
chithite ki prem jame bina darashane he.

A rough translation of the above song is as follows:

> Neither a tree can survive on dew drops alone without a shower of rain nor can love flourish on letters alone without a glimpse (of the beloved).

There are hundreds of such folk songs in the Kurmi culture, which have been sorted out by scholars in several categories and sub-categories, such as *Tusu, Vadu,*[3] *Janoa, Karam, Jhumur,* etc. But it seems that such watertight demarcations among songs hinder the prospect of their proper evaluation. The folk poets must have composed those songs unmindful of any such divisive mechanism and the folk singers too do not care for any kind of categorization or grouping of those songs.

The Blooming Body

Adolescence brings in certain changes in a girl's physical appearance, which naturally attract the boys. The boys begin to move around the girl and a sort of narcissistic attitude of admiring herself germinates in her mind — for a few months back she was a child, with no importance whatsoever, but now it is herself who is the centre of so much attraction. She cherishes this novel experience along with the anxieties and hesitations of a novice. She requests her lover not to provoke her at such an early stage to get involved in sexual acts, unless she is physically and mentally matured. So she says:

kachi Kadamer kali,
koro na go bhalabhali
pakle kadamer asvadan
kachi kadam chhuina ekhan.

A rough, not very literal, translation of the above quoted lines runs as follows:

> Tiny and tender buds of *kadama* (a variety of fruit), are too sensitive to withstand tortures of love. These may be better enjoyed when they are in full bloom. Please do not disturb them now.

The Kurmi culture and folk songs accord much importance to the role of the body in the life of an individual, especially in his sexual life. This is supported by their explicit statement in

3. *Tusu, Vadu* — local goddesses.

folk songs. There are folk songs candidly advertising midwifery practices prevalent among the tribes to enhance the sexuality of female body parts. Sexuality and relationship between boys and girls are important topics for discussion in the Kurmi society.

In the Full Bloom

When the teenage girl blossoms into a young woman she enjoys her conjugal life with her partner. They believe that the bodily pleasure is the master key to the pleasure of a living being. The fragrance of flowers, the buzzing of the honey bees, all are meaningful only when humans themselves are sexually attractive to one another and feel the sexual urge to mate with the opposite sex. The lovers buzz around that woman who is young and attractive. When the youthful grace dies out nobody cares to glance a second look at her. The Kurmi girl does not believe in mere verbal love with the deprivation of the body. Life is short and the love life is shorter, so she desires to participate in the feast of youth with her partner. She sings:

jusna dubile andhakar
bhabe ke ba kar,
ei dudin premeri bazaar.

> There remains nothing but darkness when the moonlight dies out, then no one belongs to you. So enjoy for the two days the carnival of love.

A Kurmi folk poet thinks that only two days are reserved for love. The total span of human life is allegorically explained as lasting for a week. Birth and death are supposed to occupy one day each. So there remain only five days, the half of which is spent by a man in sleep. Childhood and old age cover the half-day of the remaining two and a half days that are spent in the wakening state. So ultimately only two days are left for the enjoyment of the youth. The Kurmi lyricist portrays:

dhan jouban araidin
najar bhore manush chino.

> Wealth and youth last only for two and a half days. So, one should engage oneself in trying to know people.

However, one may infer from the above discussion that in the Kurmi culture love is associated with nothing but erotica. Though sexual satisfaction is projected as the ultimate achievement of love, the psychological aspect of sexuality, which is the asset of human sexuality, has also been given great importance in their love songs. Courtship is an important chapter in the development of love in the Kurmi society. This psychological aspect of love achieves its true objective only when the love between the two sexes culminates in quenching the erotic thirst.

Just like most other civil societies, the Kurmi society, too, thinks that in a woman's behaviour passion plays the most vital role. Thought and reflective analysis play no part in their decision-making, and so women easily get into passionate affairs without any second thought. A chauvinist attitude towards women prevails in the following song:

lal shaluk phuler buddhi nai,
raite lal shaluk phute
jar sange jar gopan pirit
orai maja lute.

> The red water lily lacks intelligence, so it blossoms at night. A woman in whom passion is more intense than reason surrenders herself secretly to her lover without any judgement and they enjoy the fun of making illicit love.

Generally a Kurmi girl chooses her partner from her own community. The incident of a girl's engagement with someone from a different community is not favourably treated by the men of her society. They say:

charkunya pakharti
labanga latai ghera re
dal bhangi phul tule
vindeshi bhamra.

> The square shaped pond is surrounded by clove-creepers. The alien hornet is plucking flowers by breaking the branches.

It is interesting to note that the poem mentioned here through a symbolic expression refers to the female genital organ and the act of sexual intercourse between a Kurmi girl and an outsider from the Kurmi community.

The male singers have highlighted the intense sexual urge of a Kurmi girl. However, it is also a fact that men are not free from such passions. In an aboriginal society the predominance of body is accepted in true love and not intellectual speculation about body. A Kurmi poet, as a member of that society, naturally surrenders himself and his creation to this worldly pleasure. Despite being a poet he does not crave for transcendental or heavenly pleasure and his creativity is always filled with the aroma of earthly love that finds its climax in the real physical union with the loved one.

The path of love does not always run smooth and simple. The Kurmi society, in spite of their relatively permissive attitude towards love and sexuality, often shows intolerance to its lovers. Sometimes conservative attitude, family pride and practised norms governing the match of the members of the clan stand as obstacles to the union between two lovers.[4] The lovers often protect the honour of love by elopement, but

4. In the ages of the Purāṇas, the Vedic sages made the structure of Vedic society by introducing different *gotra*s according to the inheritance of different sages like Vasiṣṭha, Bharadvāja, →

the unlucky ones are forced to marry according to the choice of their elders. So, longing for the lost lover is also a part of Kurmi life.

Marriage and Questions about Marital Bliss

The Kurmi marriage does not require the performance of sacrificial rite or recital of hymns by any priest. The *Ambiha* and *Mahulbiha* are two rituals in the Kurmi marriage, which take place in the groom's and bride's place respectively. The brothers-in-law (in this context, sisters' husbands) tie the leaf of a mango tree on the right wrist of the groom. The leaf of a *mahuā* tree is tied on the left wrist of the bride by her brothers-in-law. The mango seed symbolizes masculinity. A *mahuā* stem carrying ten to twelve blossoms signifies the concept of integrity. It symbolizes family integrity and each bride is expected to uphold and preserve integrity of the family. Generally the married life of a Kurmi girl seems to be happy. But different pictures are also available. The Kurmi girl sings:

guru-kara marile singjorā bhai nishan thake
manush marile bhai kiba nishan thake
birthai gelo din, nari janam parer adhin.

> Cows and other animals die, leaving behind a pair of horns as their remnants but human beings die leaving no remnants whatsoever. A woman spends her worthless life being subordinated to someone else.

So, what we see is that in the permissive Kurmi society too, a woman is considered as a dependent being, and her life has no value of its own. The society accepts the sexual liberty of a

→ Śāṇḍilya, Kāśyap. But the totems of the Kurmis, which are accepted as *gotras* do not bear that Vedic trait. They are actually the symbols of different clans. They originated before the birth of religion. These totems are neither gods nor goddesses; they are various kinds of trees and animals.

man but it gets impatient on the question of women's sexual liberty. A man, married or not, enjoys every right to have a second wife also. In such cases, he may be in disrepute in his society but the promiscuity of a man is not considered to be a punishable offence. He may develop a relationship with any married or divorced woman who may have been his former lover. He may even have an affair with an unmarried girl. However, the woman's case is treated differently. A woman, married, unmarried or divorced has no such liberty. So, the married Kurmi woman sings:

khalbhara hamake santachhe
khabar bela gabur gubur khachhe
ghare ase khachhe dhuchhe
porer ghare mou khachhe
parer ghare kiba maja ache?

> That deceitful man is cheating me. He takes his meals with great relish. He returns home at his own will only for refreshment. Actually he is sucking honey in another's house. What is the fun in another's house?

Some women, however, care little for the social regulations directed against the sexual liberty of women. They have no inhibition, whatsoever, to enjoy carnal desires. A woman's extramarital affair is an issue of public scandal to which the society shows the least tolerance. In such a case, a woman is subjected to physical punishment, social boycott and divorce. Attraction for a particular man is not the sole cause for which a Kurmi woman engages herself in such an affair. A woman takes recourse to the prohibited path to take revenge on the promiscuous husband. Such a woman, when she elopes with her lover, is stigmatized as a *Bahrahnai Jaoa,* i.e. outsider to her society. The agony of an outcast woman finds expression in the following lines:

elach labang paner khili
kenere tui khaoali
amni tor bhaber nisha
chha chhanar ma bhulali.

> Why do you treat me with betel leaf, spiced up with cardamom and clove! you have seduced me! What a skilful womaniser you are that a mother of six children gets obsessed with you!

All these poems are loaded with symbolic expressions. The betel leaf, cardamom and clove indicate the sexual experience of the extra marital affair. Betel leaf itself plays a very significant role in the expression of mutual love. In a village market or in a fair, if a girl receives a betel leaf from a boy, it is taken as a mark of their mutual love.

Marital bond, in the Kurmi society is not considered as something eternal or everlasting. Husband or wife, anyone, can ask for a divorce from his/her partner. The process of marriage or divorce is very simple in this society. When a Kurmi boy throws some vermillion on the forehead of a girl in a public place, they are accepted by the society as husband and wife. Such a marriage is called *Sindhur ghasa biya,* i.e. marriage by rubbing vermillion. A man can declare the end of his marriage by erasing the vermillion from the forehead of his wife. He takes off her iron bangle (*noa*) that is another symbol of a married woman. The *Māhāto* heads of the society end a marriage by tearing off a *śāla* leaf into two parts. On various grounds, a Kurmi man may seek divorce; it may be due to his incapability to meet the monetary requirement of his wife, it may be due to his wife's resistance towards his extra-marital relationship, or it may be due to his wife's promiscuous behaviour. The grievance of one such deserted wife finds expression in the following verse:

kulchi muray tanatani le laha jabo hāmi
khalvarar eto mone chhilo
āsin tane laha lute lilo
ādha dine kule dagā dilo.

My husband has rejected me by snatching away my bangles in the public. He has defamed my family by disowning me. Just half way through my life, I was too innocent to predict the intention of that treacherous fellow.

Society has also granted some right to a wife to forsake her husband on the charges of promiscuity or impotency and seek divorce.

A married Kurmi girl is often a victim of domestic violence by her in-laws. The rudeness of the intoxicated husband increases her agony. The poor exploited woman unleashes her emotions to a childhood friend:

ek diner halud bata
tin diner basi
olo-o-soi
mai bapke bole dibi
damei sukhe achhi
jakhan sanjhe phute jhinga phool
takhan danton kathi
olo-o-soi
mai bapke bole dibi
damei sukhe achhi.

The turmeric paste for cooking one day's meal has to be miserly saved for three days. O, my friend, tell my parents how happy I am! I can manage myself to have some time for brushing my teeth only at the evening when the *jhinga* blossoms start to bloom. O! My friend, tell them how happy I am.

However, a Kurmi girl often does not compromise with such

wretched conditions. She returns to her parents and they, in their turn, often provide shelter to their daughter, and do not encourage her to go back to her husband's home. Such a determined Kurmi girl sings:

sasur gharer khalvarara legte āschhe
nai jabe ga hāmār māthā dukachhe
kal sakāle jabāb dibo desher majhete.

> The intolerable in-laws are coming to take me back. I have the excuse of a headache. Tomorrow morning I am going to declare that I am not ready to stay with them anymore.

After the Divorce

After ending her marriage, the girl rejects every symbol of a married woman. She erases the vermillion from her forehead and takes off the iron bangle (*noa*) from her hand. But she is not ready to spend her life like a spinster nor as a widow. The earlier sex experience drives her crazy for deriving renewed erotic pleasure again at any cost. She does not bother, at all, about social regulations. Such a girl is, often, labelled by the society as *udma chhuri* (the lunatic girl) or *udma shanri* (the mad oxen). Her attire and posture often go against their commonly accepted social norms. Sometimes they are considered to be audaciously provocative. Often, she accepts ornaments and toiletries from any man in exchange of her body.

Her appearance and behaviour narrate her social position.[5] On many occasions treacherous men try to exploit their helplessness. There are many songs depicting the condition of those poor girls, such as:

tanti chinhai paire
chasha chinhai āire

5. Bankim Chandra Mahato, *Jharkhander Lokasahitya*, p. 265.

bhatar chara magi chinhai
khachar khichir chaile.

These songs are difficult to translate. Roughly the above lines state:

> The weaver is recognized by the border of a sāṛī, the (skill of a) peasant is recognized by the border erected between one land and another, and a woman is recognized to be without husband by her quickly changing glances.

However, remarriage or *saṅga* may emancipate such a poor woman from sexual exploitations. Generally, a divorced woman can remarry only a divorced man. A girl, widowed in her early youth, is often married off to the brother of her husband. But those who leave their husband's home forever and get no chance to be remarried often have to spend their life in humiliation in the family of brothers after their parents' death. They go crazy for some pleasure in life and are often engaged in secret sexual relationships with one or more than one person.

Right to Love, Right to Live

A Kurmi woman, be she a teenager at her early puberty, or a matured woman — married, unmarried, widow or divorcee — always seeks her liberty. She struggles for absolute and exclusive rights over her own physical and mental domains. The changing time and modern education have made her conscious about her own rights. She now realizes that her claims are not to be clubbed as issues relating to social disagreement but are to be taken into consideration as an inevitable outcome of the social justice that she deserves. Her sentimental and sensual demands are backed by ethical values that encourage the illiterate girl to face the dire consequences of such a struggle. The Kurmi girl is determined to protect her right to love, and right to live the life of an autonomous individual which she is; no longer willing to sacrifice her love or her life either for the so-called "social reputation" or for fulfilling the wish of her family. She sings:

lal shaluker phul phute
phute adha raite he
jar sange jar gopan pirit
marile ki tute bandhu
eto rait kise?

> The red water lily blooms at midnight. The secret love never ends, even death is not powerful enough to put an end to it. There is nothing to be labelled as "late" in love.

It is wrong to conclude that a Kurmi woman always looks for erotic fun. The physical relationship plays a central role in Kurmi love-life. Emotional attachment too plays a very powerful and significant role in choosing the love partner or in the continuation of that love affair open or secret. Her secret dating with her lover (*avisar*) are by no means altered negatively by social apprehension. She dreams of her own cosy nest — this, to her, is the saturation of her affair. So she sings to her lover:

ekhan tumar mon janali
moner matan sukh pali
chutobelay kothai tumi chhile
sindur ghanshe kene nai dile.

> Now after knowing your mind I am contented. Why have you not come, earlier, in my childhood? Why did you not rub vermillion on my forehead?.

Now, naturally comes the most important aspect of Kurmi girls. What kind of lover does a Kurmi girl prefer? The Kurmi girls are generally very witty, jolly and outspoken and it is quite natural that they will choose partners of the same kind. A Kurmi girl dreams for a man who charms everyone by his

Jhumur. It is his flute, the melodious tune of which is echoed from the hills to the forests. The hills, the jungles, the rivers, the villages — all are reverberated with the sound of his *Dhamsa* and *Madol*. It is he who cheers her up, shelters her, offers her the warmth of his mind and body and promises her a cosy, sweet home.[6]

Struggle for Power : In a Different Sense

The struggle of a Kurmi girl for a proper love life appears to be a struggle for her existence. But what we see is that a Kurmi society, in spite of its cultural uniqueness, fails to present any unique outlook on the question of woman's sexuality. Like most of the traditional societies it also bears that conservatism which views a woman not as an individual — with her own feelings, emotions and sexual urges — but as a mere medium used by man to satisfy his lust. It is accepted, without any question, that man's sexuality is something which is to be satisfied at any cost but women are born to serve others, and their sexualities have to be satisfied only within the barriers of various stipulations. And these stipulations, as we see, are made by the society with vested interest. In spite of its permissive attitude towards love and sexuality, the Kurmi society, too, is not ready to accept *sex for its own sake* in case of a woman. The Kurmi women's struggle for satisfying their "right to love" and "right to have sex with the loved one," are actually struggles for achieving a particular *power*.

Here, she struggles with men for her right to love a particular man. Such a power-struggle is not an andocentric power struggle that is associated with domination and control. She is not eager to achieve that power by which she can take a revenge on the menfolk by control and domination. Rather

6. Pashupati Prasad Mahato, *Jharkhandi Lokadarshan*, pp. 94-95.

she struggles to achieve that power by which she can make herself free from any kind of authoritarianism that controls and dominates the expression of her emotional and sexual urges. Now, we have distinguished two notions of power:[7] (i) Power as domination and violence and (ii) power as the condition of linking human beings together.

The desire for power in the first sense is often attributed to women by the society and even, by the family. In her songs, the Kurmi girl does not express any desire for occupying the position of a man. Rather, in her song she expresses her long cherished wish for love, and making a nest with the loved one. She struggles to attain a condition that enables her to love and be loved without being a victim of domination. Hence, we can evaluate that she wants to achieve the *power* in the second sense.

Love, for a Kurmi girl, is not any psychological exercise with a particular concept. She owns that vitality and practical courage by which one can face and enjoy the practical situations of life. So, the Kurmi girl has no time to "love" a figure of her own fantasy. Love without any correspondence or without any physical contact is something meaningless to her. She is positive and, of course, practical in her attitude towards love. Nevertheless, it seems clear that in her love songs, the Kurmi girl highlights the values of positive emotional aspects of love and commitment.

Note

Questions may be raised as to whether the Kurmi woman's attitude towards love represents the "care perspective" of the modern theories of justice and power? The actions that follow from love may not always produce suitable results for people

7. Cristina Shües, "On Freedom, Power, Justice: Feminists Perspectives", 1998, p. 197.

close to her. For instance, when a mother of a child or children elopes with her lover, her action throws the poor children into a miserable condition. Should such women be denied the right to love? Or should her attitude towards love be criticized? Love itself is not to be criticized for a particular action that is proved to be "cruel." We may say with Zeno Vendler, that loving is not an action and hence cannot be done deliberately and carefully; can we be held responsible for it as for an action.[8] However, we can be responsible for acting for love in certain immoral ways.[9] The response from the Kurmi perspective may be explored.

References

Beauvoir, Simone de, *The Second Sex*, London: Vintage, 1997.

Brown, Robert, *Analyzing Love*, Cambridge: Cambridge University Press, 1987.

Ghosh, Saswati, "Purush Bihane", *Ananda Bazar Patrika*, September 9, 2001.

Kamilya, Mihirchowdhury, *Rarer Jana-Jati O Lokasanskriti*, Uchchatara Vidya Characha Kendra, Bangla Vibag, Burdwan University, 2006.

Mahato, Bankim Chandra, *Jharkhander Loksahitya*, Kolkata: Banishilpa, 2000.

Mahato, Binoy, *Lokayata Jharkhand*, Kolkata: Nabapatra Prakasan, 1984; first published, Mahalaya, 1391 (Baṅgābda).

Mahato, Pashupati Prasad, *Jharkhandi Lokadarshan*, Kolkata: Prashik, 2004.

Mahato, Radhagobinda, *Jharkhander Kurmi: Itihas-O-Sanskritir Aloke*, Kolkata: Indian Publications, 1985.

Mahato, Sristidhar, "Manbhume Kurmi Bhasa O Bhasacharcha", in Subodh Basuroy (ed.), *Chhatrak*, Purulia: Banami-nadiha, Issue, 1, 1999.

---

8. Zeno Vendler, *Linguistics in Philosophy*, 1967, p. 106.
9. Robert Brown, *Analyzing Love*, Cambridge, 1987, p. 124.

Moitra, Shefali, *Feminist Thought*, New Delhi: Munshiram Manoharlal, 2002.

Risley, H.H., *Tribes and Castes of Bengal*, Kolkata: Firma Mukhopadhyay, 1981.

Shües, Christina, "On Freedom, Power, Justice: Feminist Perspectives" in Chhanda Gupta and Debiprasad Chattopadhyaya (eds.), *Cultural Otherness and Beyond*, Leiden Brill, 1998.

Vendler, Zeno, *Linguistics in Philosophy*, Ithaca: Cornell University Press, 1967.

10

Communicating Moral Values to Adolescents

Atashee Chatterjee Sinha

EVERYONE agrees that instilling good values in children is important. Yet not many parents are thoughtful and systematic in their effort to communicate values in the young minds. Values bear special significance in human lives. They constitute a set of principles or standards of behaviour, which are regarded as desirable, and necessary by all/most humans or by particular society in which a person lives. Values are objects of our intentional feelings, such as approving, non-approving, and so on. In the traditional view values are grounds of our obligations, beliefs, ideals, and attitudes. Such values are transmitted most effectively in human relationships, right from birth till the end of life. Among various kinds of values, moral values are especially important for adolescents because they are inseparably associated with each significant aspect of life — such as social, religious, moral and political spheres.

In modern emerging societies in India, there has been a revolutionary change in the field of values due to many factors in addition to the influence of industrialization, modernization, and multiculturalism. In the last decade, science and technology have immensely changed our life-conditions. Every aspect of human life and growth is influenced as well as altered by this transformation. Advanced communication system has created a common shared space of information and has increased the speed of communication while there has been a decrease in time for social relation and interactions. Although in most societies particular sets of values are transmitted in and outside educational institutions, yet the present generation is found to be confronted with a host of anti-values, such as acts of violence, glorification of superficial qualities, excessive consumerism, selfishness, competition, denial of moral responsibility, lack of accountability, and so on. It is also found that in many cases young adolescents take recourse to these anti-values, with the belief that it would be profitable for them. On the other hand, the significant positive values are not conveyed appropriately due to which they are hardly taken up and followed by the young minds. Hence it is important to consciously help and motivate young adolescents to think, identify and understand the importance of moral values in life. At the present time, ethical or moral issues are as important as scientific and technological advancements. On the one hand, science and technology provide us with the capacity to possess systematic knowledge of natural and human realities, which in turn improve the conditions of our material life. On the other hand, ethics helps us to identify moral values whose application improves our internal harmony, quality of life and balances our individual and social lives. Unlike scientific values, ethical values vary according to the culture or society in which they are derived. The ethical conduct of individuals often depend upon the value system of the family where one is born, the system of education, various institutions and one's native constitution.

Family is the most profound of all influences on who we are and what we do. The families, in which we are born and where we grow up as adults, shape us from birth to maturity. The urban Indian metamorphosis is directly affecting the family. Many of the adults in the urban areas are confused, caught in between two social realities — one in which they were raised: authoritarian, traditional, value-based, communal, single income upbringing; and the other that they find as popularly acceptable today: characterized by permissiveness, liberalism, imbalanced parenting style, individualistic, academic, materially driven, career oriented upbringings. As a result of this, parents are confused with respect to their own identities, choices and values and there is a dearth of role models from whom to learn or whom the young can emulate. In this confusion, the so-called moral values being adopted by default result in homes that are torn apart by individualistic aspirations and expectations. Competition, independence, exclusion, and self-righteousness have taken over co-operation, mutual trust and empathy in primary relationships. Children growing up in such environments are often at a loss regarding values that are reaffirmed by family, various social institutions, media, and peer group. Consequently they grow to be maladjusted, frustrated, and constantly seeking to conform to media-peer-parent models in the absence of a stable, positive, dependable relational guidance. Often this sense of void or lack of positive support leads adolescents to increased loneliness and anxiety, leading to perception of self as a failure, depression and other extreme outcomes.

Two Opposing Philosophical Views on Moral Values

Our moral values and choices are largely dependent upon our ability to think critically and to understand how far our own values are desirable for others. Our moral values are occasionally influenced by changing ideologies, cultural and religious perspectives, socio-political and economic conditions in which an individual lives. Philosophers generally talk about a "hierarchy" of moral values. We often look for the "highest good" or the greatest moral value that will unify the other values — that which is intrinsically valuable — good in itself, as opposed to being a value merely as a means or instrument — good for something else. When we talk about moral values, in the Western philosophical tradition, we are often faced with two opposite views. One adheres to a kind of absolutism, which says something like "others" must share the values that we endorse while the contrary view upholds a form of extreme relativism which might suggest that "anything goes." An immediate problem with all systems of absolute morality is that they set themselves to be final arbiters of truth, and rightness/wrongness, thereby creating two compartmentalized worlds of good and evil, right and wrong, true believers and heretics. Kant's Categorical Imperative is a secular rational attempt to establish absolute morality, based on universalizability and goodwill. An orthodox objectivist stand is prevalent in our traditional moral theories which regulated all our practices on the basis of some universal objective principle. This suggests a rational, unemotional or detached way of observation, thinking and behaviour. Such a stance presupposes that we are moral as long as we are rational; hence, we should emotionally disengage ourselves from the world and our individual experiences, as well as from the conditions of life while making rational choices. Critics point out that the ultimate fallacy with all forms of absolute morality is that — since virtually everyone claims they know what constitutes right versus wrong thought and action, and since effectively all moral systems differ from all others to a greater or lesser degree — there cannot be an absolute, universally accepted morality.[1]

---

1. Michael Shermer, *The Science of Good and Evil*, New York: Henry Holt and Company, 2004, p. 160.

Relative morality, on the contrary, is taken to mean a flexible set of rules for right and wrong thoughts and behaviours, derived from how the situation is defined by the social group in which individuals live. The problem with relative morality is that one can justify almost any behaviour and any action as moral — starting from self-sacrifice to human sacrifice. Such morality can be validated from any utilitarian, existential or subjective standpoint. Both absolutism and relativism violate our actual observation that there is a wide diversity of ethical theories about right and wrong moral behaviour. In reality there are disputes about what constitutes right and wrong both between ethical theories and moral systems as well as within them. There are moral principles which are neither absolute (not without exceptions) nor relative (anything goes), yet they are provisionally true for most people in most circumstances most of the time. Therefore any viable ethical theory of morality must account for these observations. The world is more complex than the two exclusive choices typically presented by these two opposite doctrines of absolutism and relativism. We may hold that moral principles are derived from our moral sense and they are not absolute, even if they apply to almost all people in most cultures under most situations at almost all times. Neither they are relative, entirely determined and altered by experiences, circumstances, culture, and history. We are all subject to the laws of nature, and our thoughts and behaviour are largely shaped by the forces of culture, history and civilization, yet we are in some sense free moral agents responsible for our actions. None of us know the entire causal net that determines our individual lives, hence there is no absolute judge to validate our actions and consequences. Nevertheless we work with some generally accepted moral principles and standards, which are founded on general consensus.

Psychological Features of Adolescents

Before we enter into the discussion on communication of moral values, we need to understand who are the receivers of these values. Here our focus is on adolescents. "Adolescence" may be defined as a period within the lifespan of a human being when most of the person's physical, psychological and social characteristics are in a state of transition from what they were in childhood to what they will be in adulthood. Simply stated, adolescence is a period of life characterized by several major changes that bring the person from childhood to adulthood. Since the last century systemic research on moral development of youth has been carried out. Worth mentioning among them are the works of psychologists Jean Piaget (1896–1980) and Lawrence Kohlberg (1927-87), who conducted thorough researches on moral development and education of children.[2]

Piaget was the first to recognize the qualitative differences between a child and an adult's intellectual abilities. His model of four-staged cognitive development explains how a child gradually grows into maturity and reaches the level of autonomy, individuation and abstraction. According to Piaget, human beings construct and reconstruct their knowledge of the world as a result of interactions with the environment. He observed that along with the cognitive development of children there occur certain changes in their moral behaviour. Piaget found that young children are initially egocentric and are unable to simultaneously take into account their own perspective as well as others' perspective. This egocentrism leads children to project their own thoughts and wishes onto others. This is regarded as heteronomous moral thinking. He contended that children start with learning to follow a law

2. William Puka "Moral Development", *The Internet Encyclopedia of Philosophy*, 2005, www.iep.utm.edu/m/moraldev.htm

external to the self, without understanding the reason behind its acceptance. Gradually they internalize the moral conventions existing in the society. As children consider concrete situations in life, they develop ability to consider rules critically, and selectively apply them on the basis of a sense of mutual respect and co-operation. By adolescence, boys and girls reach what Piaget called the stage of formal operations in cognitive ability. Their ability to act from a sense of reciprocity and mutual respect is associated with a shift in the child's cognitive structure from egocentrism to perspective-based reasoning. Thus Piaget viewed moral development as the result of interpersonal interactions through which individuals learn to resolve problems related to morality.

Lawrence Kohlberg, being consistent with Piaget, proposed that children form ways of thinking through experiences which include understandings of moral concepts such as justice, equality and human welfare. He determined that the process of attaining moral maturity is longer and more gradual than Piaget had conceived. Kohlberg identified six stages of moral reasoning grouped into three major levels, viz. pre-conventional level, conventional level and post-conventional level.[3] Stage 1 is characterized by ego-centrism and in stage 2 there is early emergence of moral reciprocity, where one follows the rules only to fulfil her/his immediate interest. Stage 3 brings into children awareness of shared feelings, agreements and expectations which take primacy over individual interests. This is the perspective of family. Stage 4 marks the shift from defining what is right in terms of local norms and role expectations to defining what is right in terms of the laws and norms established by the larger social system.

3. Lawrence Kohlberg, *Essays on Moral Development: Moral Stages and the Idea of Justice,* vol. I: The Philosophy of Moral Development, San Francisco: Harper and Row, 1981.

Finally, the post-conventional level is characterized by reasoning based on principles, using a prior-to-society perspective. In this stage individuals reason on basis of principles which underlie rules and norms, but reject a1 uniform application of a rule or norm. This last level of moral judgement constitutes reasoning which is rooted in the fairness principle of morality, from which moral laws are devised. Kohlberg found that during adolescence individuals reach post-conventional morality, which is the level of achieving self-accepted principles. It consists of two stages: firstly, the individual believes that there should be flexibility in moral beliefs to make it possible to modify and change the moral standards, if it is advantageous to group members as a whole; and secondly, individuals conform to social standards and internalized ideals so as to avoid self-condemnation.[4]

In Piaget's view, children define morality individually through their struggles to arrive at fair solutions; hence the educator needs to provide students with opportunities for personal discovery through problem solving. On the other hand, Kohlberg rejected the traditional character education practices, according to which moral character is comprised of a cluster of virtues, such as honesty, kindness, patience, etc. According to the traditional approach, educators are required to teach the virtues through examples and direct communication of convictions, by giving them opportunity to practise these virtues. However this approach does not provide us with any guiding principle for defining or identifying moral virtues. On the contrary it assumes as values certain attributes which are accepted by community consensus, even if they are conditioned by social, cultural and individual biases. Hence

4. Elizabeth B. Hurlock, *Developmental Psychology: A Life-Span Approach*, 5th edn., New Delhi: Tata McGraw-Hill, 1981, pp. 242-43.

this actually proposes a kind of ethical relativity, which is strongly opposed by Kohlberg. He contends that a better approach to towards affecting moral behaviour should focus on stages of moral development. The stages mentioned by him are critical, as they consider the way an individual organizes her/his understanding of virtues, norms and rules, and integrates them into a moral choice. He further maintained that certain basic moral principles (of justice and fairness) are cross-cultural and are globally accepted in human societies. For Kohlberg the goal of moral education is to encourage individuals to develop to the next stage of moral reasoning. Within any stage of development, the child's thought is organized according to the constraints of that stage. The child interacts with the environment according to her/his basic understanding of the environment. But at some point the child faces information which is not fit to her/his world-view, and is forced to adjust her/his own view to accommodate the new information. This process is called equilibration through which moral development occurs. Kohlberg appreciated the importance of moral dilemmas for educating children, and also acknowledged the need to include experiences which help the child to operate as moral agent within a community. He, with his colleagues developed "just community" schools approach towards promoting moral development of children. In such schools, issues regarding life and discipline are discussed openly and decided upon, valuing the voices of all students and teachers. In such schools teachers play a crucial role of a leader and a guide to help the child to reach the appropriate level of reasoning. However some scholars think that morality and convention are distinct, parallel developmental frameworks, rather than a single system, unlike what Kohlberg thought.

All social events take place within the context of the larger society. There are some factors involved in the healthy development of adolescents. One of the most important tasks for all adolescents is learning the skills that will help them manage their own lives and make positive, healthy choices. Parents and others can help youth develop this sense of self-governance, responsibility, independence, and decision-making. During adolescence an individual becomes able to think in the abstract, weigh options, and look ahead to see the possible consequences of their actions. They also start relying on themselves and recognizing the value of advice from others. This is the time of conformity or what is termed as "peer pressure." It means following the behaviour and opinion of friends or others. Youth are most prone to peer conformity during the middle adolescent years — in about seventh and eighth grades (that is between 11-13 years of age). Younger adolescents are usually more influenced by parents. As they grow older, they learn to make decisions independently of their peers. During this time, teenagers begin to see their parents as different individuals, and to take more and more responsibility for their own choices and actions. Often there are disagreements at this time because adolescents want more independence and parents want more closeness and communication. Yet these arguments do not usually lead to serious problems if they have proper communication.

As evident from Piaget and Kohlberg's views, early adolescence is an important definitional stage in human development during which a person's value system and behaviour code is shaped. If one's value system and behaviour code, which govern moral reasoning and resultant behaviour, are shaped during early adolescence, then they grow up with the values which are inculcated in them. In any case, the ways in which early adolescents reason about moral/value questions are of great importance. It does appear that different modes of moral education exist, including care and justice, prize and punishment, positive and negative reinforcements and in many societies the justice mode is better recognized than others. Traditionally justice mode is ideal for male and care is related to female. By listening to women's experiences, Carol Gilligan offered that a morality of care can serve in the place of the morality of justice and rights, which has been advocated by Kohlberg. In her view, the morality of caring and responsibility is premised in non-violence, while the morality of justice and rights is based on equality. Gilligan states that the care perspective is neither biologically determined nor unique to women; however it is a moral perspective different from that which is currently embedded in psychological theories and measures.[5] We need to help young individuals, female and male, so that they choose their actions sensibly and flexibly depending on the situations. It has been generally admitted that individuals who are flexible and who are capable of using more than one moral decision-making mode, who are capable of understanding perspectives different from their own are better prepared to survive in our society. Since different individuals have different perspectives, tolerance and understanding are necessary if one is to foster the development and learning of all individuals. We shall come back to this care and empathy perspective later in our discussion.

How Can We Teach Values to the Young Minds?

It needs more than a teacher just saying that children should tell the truth, respect the elders, or not harm others. The existing form of education has an in-built hierarchy where the teacher is always superior to the student, irrespective of her/his efficiency and expertise. The student in such a condition is

---

5. Carol Gilligan, *In a Different Voice*, Cambridge: Harvard University Press, 1982.

compelled to accept what is imparted to him/her — be it a fact or a value. Such a kind of education is ineffective for the child. The child is required to experience, think and develop their own meaning of values. Here the role of a teacher is very different from usual. As Socrates said "I cannot teach anybody anything, I can only make them think." Government and educationists, in every nation, prescribe certain set of moral values, yet they do not find it easy to determine how these values are to be imparted. Let us consider three different approaches taken in the West for inculcation of moral values.

Traditionally, adults have guided the younger generation on how to lead happy and productive lives. They used to moralize or inculcate values upon the young, directly or indirectly. The assumption behind such moralizing was that — adults believed that their experience has taught them a certain set of values which would be right for the child. They effectively transferred their own values to their children. One of the problems with this approach is that it is less effective. The direct inculcation of values works when there is complete consistency about what constitutes "desirable" values. But considering the youth of today, we find that parents offer one set of should and should not, teachers offer some other and the peer group offers a third set of values. The young person is ultimately left to make her/his own choice about whose advice or values to follow. But young people brought up by moralizing or imposing of values by adults is not mentally prepared enough to make their own responsible choices. They fail to be independent and hardly learn the way of selection and rejection of options open to them. Thus, too often the important choices in life are made on the basis of peer pressure, unthinking submission to authority, or the power of propaganda and persuasion. Another problem with the direct inculcation of values is that often it results in a dichotomy between theory and practice; theoretically these values are accepted, while behaviour contradicts them. Young people left on their own, experience a great deal of conflict and confusion. Although most young people do not want adults running their lives for them, yet they need considerable amount of help.

Another approach, suggested by psychologists is modelling. If a person is important enough in a child's life, she/he can make an impression by presenting herself/himself as a role model who lives by a certain set of values. This approach acknowledges two realities — first, the importance of setting a living example for a learner to follow; and, second, the necessity in teaching values for the deeds to match the words. But the fact is that the young person is exposed to many models to emulate, such as parents, teachers, politicians, movie stars, friends, and so on. Hence it is difficult to decide or sort out all the pros and cons and achieve her own values among the many models and moralizing lectures given to her. It also becomes hard to understand whether she wants to stick to the old moral and ethical standards or try new ones. In other words such a set-up does not help to develop one's own sense of identity, nor does it help the young in learning to relate to people whose values differ from their own.

A more accepted and effective approach is the value-clarification approach which tries to help young people answer some of these questions and build their own value system. It is not a new approach. There have always been parents, teachers, and other educators who have sought ways to help young people think through value issues for themselves. This approach does not aim to instil any particular set of values. Rather it aims to help students utilize the processes of valuing in their own lives; to apply these valuing processes to already formed beliefs and behaviour patterns and to those still emerging. To accomplish this, the teacher uses approaches which help students become aware of the beliefs and behaviours they prize and would be willing to stand up for in and out of the classroom. She uses materials and methods which encourage students to consider alternative modes of thinking and acting. The teacher also helps the students to consider whether their actions match their stated beliefs and if not, how to bring the two in a harmony. Finally, she tries to give students options, in and out of class; for only when students begin to make their own choices and evaluate the actual consequences do they develop their own values.

Traditional Indian System of Imparting Moral Values

Indian morality, which is identified as *dharma*, primarily aims at the autonomy of the individual, i.e. at making the individual self-sufficient, self-dependent and free from all forms of bondage, be it material, physical, social or spiritual. This ideal of non-social self-autonomy and self-sufficiency is neatly consistent with the Law of *karma* which apportions to each individual their due in accordance with their performed actions. Such objective morality has been accepted as preparatory to the higher moral life of self-purification, which necessarily presupposes the mediation of an objective code of right and wrong. According to the early Hindu ethical concepts and norms, we find there have been several common duties and specific duties. The former included duties which are morally obligatory for every human being. These were steadfastness, forgiveness, non-appropriation, cleanliness, repression of sensibilities and sensuous appetites, refraining from injury to living beings, veracity, purity or sincerity of motive, and restraint of anger. The *Bṛhadāraṇyaka Upaniṣad* sums up a whole ethical philosophy in three words: self-control, charity and compassion. In the *Taittirīya Upaniṣad* the teacher exhorts the pupil to speak the truth, practise virtue, not to be negligent of virtue, welfare and prosperity, to honour the parents and the teacher and so on. *Manu-Smṛti* proclaims: Self-possession, patience, non-violence, self-control, integrity, purity, restraint, intelligence, truthfulness, absence of anger – these ten are the marks of *dharma.*

Ancient Indian educational system focussed on building a disciplined and value-based culture, where emphasis was given on values such as trust, respect, honesty, dignity, compassion and so on. As mentioned in *Taittirīya Upaniṣad* the qualities required to be developed in the students are not very different from the qualities that modern educational systems are trying to impart. This is evident from the following lines:

> Speak the truth. Practise righteousness. Make no mistake about study. There should be no inadvertence about truth. There should be no deviation from righteous activity. There should be no error about protection of yourself. Do not neglect propitious activities. Do not be careless about learning and teaching. There should be no error in the duties towards the gods and manes. Let your mother be a goddess unto you. Let your father be a god unto you. Let your teacher be a god unto you. Let your guest be a god unto you. The works that are not blameworthy are to be resorted to, but not the others. The offering should be with honour; the offering should be in plenty. The offering should be with modesty. The offering should be with sympathy. Then, should you have any doubt with regard to duties or customs, you should behave in those matters just as the wise men do, who may happen to be there and who are able deliberators, who are adepts in those duties and customs, who are not directed by others, who are not cruel, and who are desirous of merit. This is the injunction. This is the instruction. This is the secret of the scriptures. — *Taittirīya Upaniṣad*, I.xi.1-4.[6]

---

6. Panduranga C. Bhatta, "Holistic Personality Development through Education: Ancient Indian Cultural Experiences", http://www.iimcal.ac.in/research/download/cpbhatta.pdf

Some important qualities required for adolescents can be derived from the above. These are:

(a) social consciousness based on love for the humanity,

(b) character, honesty based on moral law, and

(c) discipline based on the sense of duties and responsibilities of an individual.

Ancient Indian system of education played a major role in making students realize their duties and responsibilities and emphasized on the necessity of discipline for an orderly social life. Character and discipline cannot be imparted to an individual by preaching or through speeches. While students can be imparted the knowledge of what is moral and what is immoral, what is discipline and what is indiscipline, they can be made to act in conformity with the required standard of behaviour, only through personal example. The ancient system of education in India prompted the students to utilize their educational attainments and capacities for the benefit of society restricting their own selfish desires and prevented them from acting in a manner harmful and detrimental to the common good. Mere knowledge of what is virtue and what is not does not enable an individual to be virtuous.

A later development of Vedic society is the system of four *āśrama*s or stages of life. The *āśrama*s divide the life of an individual. The first phase is called the student phase (*brahmacarya*). During this time of life the individual goes to the house of the *guru* (*gurukula,* the ancient Sanskrit word for school) and lives a life of celibacy serving the teacher and learning what needs to be learned for later years.[7] India had a traditional method of teaching where the *guru* or teacher was

---

7. Radhagopinath, "Vedic Culture and Varnashrama Dharma", part I-1, http://www.radhagopinath.com/manuals/Grihastha_Manual_Contents.pdf

central. Without serving the *guru* and without his blessings a student cannot accomplish much in life. In imparting knowledge and morality the teacher shows the way by his own example and through his understanding of the scriptures, accompanied by his own experience, practice and deep insight. In ancient India, while parents were responsible for the physical well-being of the child, the *guru* was responsible for their spiritual welfare. It was his sole responsibility to subject them to rigorous discipline and shape them into responsible adults. In *gurukula* students had to live in a very austere environment, practise celibacy and cultivate discipline and virtue. They were required to serve him personally and also undertake many menial jobs in his household to learn the virtue of humility and value the opportunity they have been given to learn under the teacher. The *gurukula* system provided an effective environment to students who got educated under the close supervision of the teachers in an atmosphere of extended family relationships and sense of belongingness, serving as a home away from home. Since a student lived in the house of his teacher he had a great opportunity to observe his *guru* closely and learn from his conduct. He also received ample opportunity to exchange ideas with his fellow students and learn from them, as they all shared similar experiences and competed with one another to gain attention and praise of the teacher. Rabindranath Tagore, who was dissatisfied with the Western model of education introduced a similar system of education in India during the British rule and felt that *gurukula* system had several merits and could prove to be useful in educating young Indians in natural surroundings and building their character and sense of appreciation. However the *gurukula* system had the following deficiencies:

(a) It was a highly centralized system in which the authority of the teacher was final. The parents of the students living in *gurukulas* had little control or voice in their education.

(b) Since most of the teaching was oral and secretive there was no guarantee that the things being taught were correct or authentic, though it was presupposed to be so.

(c) It was a caste-based system, in which students of particular castes were allowed entry (brāhmaṇas). In the long run its emphasis on caste proved detrimental and contributed to the weakness and division of individuals based on hierarchy. Girls were not admitted into *gurukulas*, as it was exclusively meant for teaching male students.

(d) A *guru* had authority to punish his students according to his best judgement and many of these forms of punishment are proved to be harmful for the mental health of the students.

(e) The system of education was based on rigid adherence to the scriptures, and to the unconditional submission to the teacher. The method of education being primarily memory-based, there was little scope for creativity, experimentation and scientific analysis.[8]

From the above exposition it is evident that none of the Western or Indian approaches can be accepted as appropriate for moral education of the present young generation. It is to be noted that the effectiveness of the method of imparting moral values depends upon proper communication of such values with the young recipients. At this point we need to understand what exactly we mean by proper communication with adolescents. Quite related to this is another query as to who are the best persons to communicate moral values to children.

---

8. Panduranga C. Bhatta, op. cit.

Appropriate Method of Communication with Adolescents

Modern thinkers contend that our moral thinking is not completely separated and should not be compartmentalized from emotion, since emotion is an important constituent of our overall thought process. In this connection, psychologists and scientists point out that the architecture of the brain is such that it is possible for emotions to overrule a person's logical and rational thinking. It is through entering into emotionally secure relationships that the child and adolescent could nurture her capabilities and values. Hence there is need for emotional learning and awareness. Present time psychologists and scholars develop theories of human mind and brain, where they propose that the human brain has an in-built value system. Researches show that values, feelings and emotions are central to the function of our brain and to the cognitive development of a child or adolescent. A central part in child's learning consisits in helping the child to develop the sense of values and to balance between emotion and thought. While the choice of values are always personal to every individual, there is often a striking unity within the values that we humans seek to live by. This kind of sharing of values indicate unity of human knowledge and understanding. Hence these uniformly accepted values (love, honesty, respect, co-operation, tolerance, responsiblity, etc.) can be role-modelled and practically instantiated so as to inspire the young minds and help them to spontaneously follow them. The above reality cannot be ignored in any way. Building young individuals of integrity and building bridges between teachers, parents and young individuals are two important goals which can help us to face the present situation. In any case, individualism should not oppose interdependence, and competition must not overrule co-operation. The solution of the problems faced in the present conditions of development of young minds would require not only the individual efforts but also the efforts and co-operation of social organizations, government agencies, and, furthermore, international organizations. In helping adolescents to get the right sense of values and internalize it, what is needed more is right education and enlightenment of citizens based on the guidance of conscience rather than compulsion.

As children grow up they are wished to develop respect and compassion for others, to be honest, decent and thoughtful, to stand up for their principles, to be capable of making moral choices, to co-operate with others and to act with responsibility. For all these to occur, the parents need to play the most unique and significant role of a communicator. In word and deed, parents can immensely help their young children in developing a good moral sense of right and wrong, good and bad. As parents and caregivers, one cannot impose her/his own values on her/his young child, but each parent does have a responsibility to start a conversation about their values and discuss why they hold them as important. They also have a responsibility to listen to children and respect their values as particular to them. They might talk about why it is important to respect other's opinion or not behave violently towards others. Prior to educating young adults, parents need to understand and respect values that are different from their own. To do this the usual method is:

(1) Listening to others without judging them,

(2) Accepting that others are different and one should not try to change them by imposing one's own values on them, and

(3) Trying to understand others by talking with them or reading about their beliefs.

Ideally, the process of communicating values begins early

in a child's development and requires to be revisited occasionally. Parents may start with their core values. For example, parents may hold values such as truthfulness, honesty, respect for self and others, hard work, personal integrity, and community involvement as their core values. Such values are to be discussed and reviewed with other important individuals in the family. Parents can very briefly tell why these values are important to them. As they grow up, children might be asked to make a list of values that they think or find as important. They should also be asked about the reasons for such perceptions. After this is done, parents need to interact and share individual views, discuss similarities and differences in their values. One should be careful not to overwhelm the young mind with too much information that she/he is not ready to understand. It is useful to discuss with young adolescents examples of morally good values and poor values, how these values sometimes change with space, time and culture, why individual moral values differ and conflict. We also have to discuss how emotions, fears, desires, and such can affect the way one assess and respond to values, the situations where a number of values come into play. It is important that these meetings are not "lectures" from parents. They are supposed to be sharing information and helping adolescents in learning through positive, open and lively dialogues.

Let us take the example of the value of sex education. This is very important for adolescents. According to some thinkers adolescents who do not accept the traditional moral stance of sexual abstinence may feel as if there are no clear values associated with sexual activity. Society gives conflicting messages through the media, as well as through the power balance in sexual relations and parents' own confusion on the issue. From birth, children observe and learn from their parents' behaviour and the way parents answer questions and discuss issues related to sexuality. Even avoiding the subject altogether conveys certain information. The absence of sex education by parents is actually an educative process that portrays sex as negative and taboo rather than as a natural part of responsible human behaviour. In reality parents can influence adolescent attitudes through their own attitude to sexual behaviour. Sometimes what is modelled by parents is what is most influential. Another indirect way that parents influence their children's sexual behaviour is through the teaching of coping strategies and the encouragement of personality traits such as the ability to think of the consequences of actions beforehand, and developing a sense of responsibility. Naturally, parents wish to disclose information and provide guidance that is consistent with their values and rules of life. Experts on child development say that parents are often better at providing information about the facts of life than they are at talking about their personal preferences. Parents are the best guide to the adolescents when they start relying on their friends and others for support and guidance. What is important here is to realize that one can respect others' values without necessarily agreeing with them. Every parent faces the possibility that their values will not correspond to those of their child, just as they may have values which are different from their parents. Communicating about those differences can increase understanding and reduce friction.

Good communication is central to working with young people, their families and care-givers. It involves listening, questioning, understanding and responding to what is being communicated by children, young people and those caring for them. Many of the major threats to adolescents today are not a matter of chance, but a matter of choice — choices like drinking and driving, smoking, taking drugs, involving in sex, and dropping out of school. Research shows that young people who engage in one risky behaviour are more likely to participate in others, so parents should help their children understand the potential risks and consequences of their choices — not just for the immediate future but for their lifetime as well. It is important to be able to communicate both on a one-to-one basis and in a group context. Communication is not just about the words we use, but also our manner of speaking, body language and, above all, the effectiveness with which we listen. This requires the involvement of children, young people and those caring for them in the design and delivery of services and decisions that affect them. It is important to consult with them and consider their opinions and perspectives from the outset. A key part of effective communication and engagement is trust, and rapport among the workforce, children, young people and their carers. Unfortunately, parents sometimes make mistakes and treat their adolescent child disrespectfully based on their beliefs and values, or through non-acceptance of their child's values. For example, being verbally or physically aggressive, abusive or treating someone rudely or ignoring them because they think or behave differently than we do — is disrespectful.

Let us now consider some skills which might help in effective communication of values to the young minds:

I. ***Listening and building one's empathy***: This consists in establishing rapport and respectful, trusting relationships with young people, their families and care givers. Parents need to be aware of the fact that young people sometimes do not communicate verbally and hence they need to adapt a style of communication which is at par with their needs and abilities. They must build open and honest relationships by respecting children, young people, and make them feel valued as individuals. Active listening in a calm, open, non-threatening manner and using questions to check understanding and acknowledging what is being said is part of building empathy.

Further, they need to understand the role and value of family members and other care givers in supporting children to achieve positive outcomes. Parents have to explain, inform, involve and help the child or young person to assess different courses of action, understand the consequences of each. Parents and other caregivers need to be warm and loving; at the same time they should be firm and fair. They can use rules consistently, and explain them to their children. Adolescents should be given responsibility for decision-making and leadership in school and in after-school activities, in social and community services. When listening to the opinions of adolescents, one should encourage them to explain the reasons behind their opinions. Meanwhile there is need to watch for opportunities to talk about consequences of their decisions and behaviour, both good and bad, so that they learn to be accountable and experience the connection between behaviours and consequences.

2. ***Communication***: This is a two-way process. It consists of knowing how to listen to people, make them feel valued and involved. Sometimes we have to focus on the individual rather than the group. There are different ways of communicating and many barriers to communication. So one has to be aware that the adolescent may not have understood what is being communicated. Above all parents need to be self-aware about how to demonstrate a commitment to treating all people fairly; be respectful by active listening and avoiding assumptions. Communication has to be done openly. As children grow up and are faced with new decisions, there should be open family discussion about family and school rules and values. The development of self-mastery — in emotions, behaviours, and values — is a basic developmental challenge of the adolescent years.

3. ***Setting up limits***: Another important issue is setting of limits or behaviour boundaries for adolescents. The limits are set for the young individual should be well grounded and well communicated. Adolescents do best when they understand what is acceptable, what is not, and what will happen if they push the boundaries too far. There are times when one needs to be strict as well as flexible about limits. Ideally, it is necessary to set limits ahead of time and make it explicit to the young adult. Through careful listening, adults can come to a better understanding of an adolescent's point of view, and respond in ways that youth can understand and appreciate. Also, adults can help adolescents imagine the results, good and bad, of their behaviours. One should always keep in mind that youth and adults may not see the results in the same way. For example, to an adult, a negative judgement by a friend may not seem like much, but to the teenager this may be a terrible thing. Research shows that adolescents turn to their peers for opinions about social matters, sometimes they turn to teachers and other adults when they want facts, and to parents for advice on moral values, decisions, and future plans. It is important that parents set firm and clear guidelines for children and youth. It is just as important that youth are given chances to think and decide on their own in certain matters, to contribute individual views to their families and communities. Asking their opinions and inviting them to help with decision-making can be done from early adolescent age. Parents can start with assigning easy tasks and allow adolescents to work towards gathering important information and helping to make major decisions. They learn best through practice. Hence they should be given chances to work through difficult decisions before they leave home, so that they can exercise free will while parents are present as a safety net. Today adolescents experience lot more complications and adversities of life than their parents did and they are surely exposed to much adult stuff at younger ages. Due to technological advancement they begin to trespass into territories that were restricted to adults' world before. Hence there is need for collective effort from all fronts — family, school, society and media — to take necessary actions in order to help the adolescents set certain morally desirable goals, and also have clear and consistent expectations.

Role of Philosophy

There is a unique connection between understanding moral values and doing philosophy. Moral values are communicated with the objective of developing the mind and character. Every action and thought leaves an impression in the human mind. These impressions determine one's behaviour at a given moment and one's responses to a given situation. The sum total of all these impressions is what determines one's character. Just as values generate an ought-to-be and an ought-to-do and call forth moral persons, so philosophy invites us to be integrative. This integrative function of philosophy is more an ideal to be achieved rather than a guaranteed role, for philosophy does not impose but springs from the responsible freedom of a human being. Philosophy urges humans to be moral persons, persons of integrity who are self-possessed because their speech, feelings, thinking and actions are one. This unity derives from the individual's commitment to the moral values. Philosophy invites individual minds to be true to the self and to humanity.

Aristotle postulated that if one developed psychologically one would move towards virtue. He tells us that the well being or *eudaemonia* which is the good for man is an activity in accordance with virtue, and each virtue is a disposition to make right choices. A person with practical wisdom would determine what constitutes the virtuous choice, and such a person is good at choosing the means to the end of *eudaemonia*. The dispositions which are generally found to be advantageous to an individual are the virtues which harmonize with knowledge and are based upon some conception of good and with some respect for the way of life of the society in which one lives. The challenge is not about knowing what the virtues are, but in being able to live according to them. We might take from Aristotle the formal sketch of good life and can fill it up with our chosen (more or less uniformly accepted and time tested) content. In Aristotle's view, "the good life will consist in activities that manifest and realize developed dispositions for choice."[9] To be moral it is necessary that we should act to some extent in ways that are not prudentially or egoistically profitable for us. Adolescents need to be shown that their choice of dispositions, characters and overall patterns of life control their choice of actions. Even if they practise some kind of rational egoism then too their actions will be determined by their personality (what kind of person they are) and their objectives or aspirations (what kind of person they want to be). In other words adolescents may identify morality in Mackie's way, as concerned particularly with the well-being of active, intelligent participants in a partly competitive life and the constraints of morality will be set as necessary limits for the benefit of all competitors.[10] Here the flourishing of human life is taken to be the foundation of morality; this implies that the needs well-being of the young generation shall have to be ensured in such a moral set-up.

Our values, both moral and non-moral, are acquired along with language and socialized behaviours at an early age and they come from some very strong traditions that are part of our societies and cultures. Law, religion, family, and peer groups all tell us what we ought to do, but following these

---

9. J.L. Mackie, *Ethics: Inventing Right and Wrong*, Harmondsworth, England: Penguin Books Ltd, 1977, p. 188.

10. Mackie, p. 193.

more traditional "ought" does not necessarily constitute a moral life. A great number of people live long and useful lives without ever consciously defining or systematically considering the values or moral rules that guide their social, personal, and professional lives. However most individuals throughout their lives distinguish what is right and what is wrong. Generally life decisions are taken from self-interest and egoism. Sometimes, however, we face difficulty deciding what is right and what is wrong, and we find our own experience and knowledge is not enough. Sometimes we recognize moral issues but do not have sufficient insight into our value system or sufficient information to make a reasoned, informed decision. That is why we have conflicting values and have difficulty deciding what is more important. And things becomes more difficult when we have to work with other people and their beliefs about right and wrong. In this context philosophy enables us to better understand one's own moral beliefs and attitudes, to make moral decisions, and to work more effectively with others. To choose one's own values or to make one's own moral decision is to philosophize. The attempt to examine one's own values and moral rules, to shape and rethink them in the light of her/his own experience and the dictates of reason, is a philosophical task. Philosophy begins when we systematically reflect on our moral rules or guidelines or the rules and guidelines of our society and ask whether these rules are reasonable or unreasonable and whether good reasons or poor ones support them. Philosophy helps the young adults to get an understanding of the role of cognitive and moral values in world-views, by discussing and writing about the ethical implications in the modern scientific and technological world. It also enables them to recognise the difference between matters of fact and matters of value, while understanding the important ways in which facts influence value assessments and ways in which value judgements shape our vision of "the facts." Further it also explains how ethics plays an important role in science and technology. Scientists and philosophers of science have already begun to acknowledge the need to bridge the gulf between science and value. It is recognized that the development of science should be supplemented by enormous development of the value of human kindness. Bertrand Russell has pointed out that there are two ancient evils that science may intensify by unwise use: they are tyranny and war. His counsel to mankind is to avoid cruelty, envy, greed, competitiveness, search for irrational subjective certainty, and what Freudians call Death-Wish. He states that the key to the solution of all forms of human conflict is love. This simple message should be communicated to adolescents.

If we look back and see the lives of reformers in India such as Raja Rammohun Roy, Devendra Nath Tagore, Rabindranath Tagore, spiritual leaders like Sri Ramakrishna, Swami Vivekananda, Sri Aurobindo, or teachers like Dr Radhakrishnan and Krishnamurti, we find a clear attempt to re-establish and recreate the moral and spiritual foundation of India. However, it is hard to find young adults who consider and follow any of these values seriously. Although life of individuals in the twenty-first century is different in many respects, yet it is practically possible and favourable to consider some of the traditional moral values like non-violence, tolerance and sincerity or purity of motive. All these values can be prescribed for the young adolescents, in India and all over the world.

References

Bhatta, Panduranga C., *Holistic Personality Development through Education: Ancient Indian Cultural Experiences*, http://www.iimcal.ac.in/research/download/cpbhatta.pdf.

Chattopadhyay, Madhumita and Sanyal, Indrani, eds., *Siskhakhetre*

Parasparik Samparka (Bengali), Kolkata: Anjali Publishers, 2007.

Cory, Rachel, *Kohlberg's Stages of Moral Development*, 2006, www.aggelia.com/htdocs/kohlberg.shtml

Doris, John, *Moral Psychology: Empirical Approaches, Stanford Encyclopedia of Philosophy*, 2006, plato.stanford.edu/entries/moral-psych-emp/

Gilligan, Carol, "In a Different Voice: Women's Conceptions of Self and Morality", in Diana T. Meyers, ed., *Feminist Social Thought: A Reader*, New York: Routledge, 1997.

———, *In a Different Voice*, Cambridge: Harvard University Press, 1982.

Hurlock, Elizabeth B., *Developmental Psychology: A Life-Span Approach*, 5th edn., New Delhi: Tata McGraw-Hill, 1981.

Jayaram V., "Hinduism and Education", www.hinduwebsite.com/hinduism/h education

Kohlberg, Lawrence, *Essays on Moral Development: Moral Stages and the Idea of Justice*, vol. I, The Philosophy of Moral Development, San Francisco: Harper and Row, 1981.

Mackie, J.L., *Ethics: Inventing Right and Wrong*, Harmondsworth: Penguin Books Ltd., 1977.

Maitra, S.K., *The Ethics of the Hindus*, 3rd edn., Kolkata: Calcutta University Press, 1963.

McLean, George F. and Frederick Edward Ellrod, *Philosophical Foundations for Moral Education and Character Development: Act and Agent*, 2nd edn., Washington: The Council for Research in Values and Philosophy (CRVP), 1992.

Mohanty, J.N. and Bina Gupta, *Classical Indian Philosophy: An Introductory Text*, Maryland: Rowman & Littlefield Publishers, 2000.

Nayak, G.C., "Philosophy for Value Education", in P. George Victor, ed., *Teaching Philosophy in the Twenty-First Century*, New Delhi: D.K. Printworld (P) Ltd., 2002.

Pearson, K. and A. Love, "Adolescents' Value Systems, Preferred Resolution Strategies, and Conflict with Parents", *Australian Journal of Psychology*, vol. 51, no. 2, 1999.

Puka, William, "Moral Development", *The Internet Encyclopedia of*

Philosophy, 2005, www.iep.utm.edu/m/moraldev.htm

Radhagopinath, "Vedic Culture and Varnashrama Dharma", part 1, http://www.radhagopinath.com/manuals\ Grihastha_Manual_Contents.pdf

Russell, Bertrand, *Marriage and Morals*, London and New York: Liveright Paperback edition, 1970.

Sen, Amartya, *Identity and Violence: The Theory of Destiny*, Allen Lane, London: Penguin Books Ltd., 2006.

———, *The Argumentative Indian: Writings on Indian History, Culture, and Identity*, New Delhi: Penguin Books Ltd., 2005.

Shermer, Michael, *The Science of Good and Evil*, New York: Henry Holt and Company, 2004.

Trissler, Ted, "Should Values be Taught in Public Schools?", 2000, www.newfoundations.com/PracEthics/Trissler.html

11

Values in Politics
An Exploration into Sri Aurobindo's Early Political Thought

Anirban Ganguly

THE question of values in politics continues to be discussed *ad infinitum*. The perception that an acute degeneration has set in our public life because of separation of values from the practice of politics generates intense and, at times despairing, debates. There is frequent reference to the immediate Indian past when the struggle for liberation was waged against the British rule to show that movements and leaders were then value-based and vision driven. It has been suggested that the emulation of those values in the present-day socio-political context may serve to a large extent as a panacea for current ills. My intention here is not to go into an analysis of this debate, but rather to try and show that thoughts of a value-based political action preoccupied Sri Aurobindo during his days as a political revolutionary in Bengal between 1906 and 1910 and that his political action, programmes and formulations were firmly based on certain universal values that provided an altogether original direction to the concept and vision of freedom. An infusion of value in a mass movement context, in case of Sri Aurobindo, always meant evolving the movement to a next progressive stage of unfolding where its effects and sweep would be wider and more comprehensive. A survey of certain value-based stands and initiatives of Sri Aurobindo would therefore be in order to form a preliminary idea of his early efforts in this area of human quest.

Proletariat — The Real Key: Need for a Mass-Based Political Action

In June 1893 just four months after his return to India from England, Sri Aurobindo, then twenty-two years old, began writing a series of articles — *New Lamps for Old* — on political issues of the day in the Bombay Marathi-English weekly *Indu Prakash*. His Cambridge friend K.G. Deshpande edited the paper and the articles were hard hitting indictments of the mendicant policy followed by the then Congress leadership towards the colonial masters. The aim of the series was to "try and awaken the nation to the ideas of the future"[1] and one of the significant new ideas of the future, which Sri Aurobindo projected through the writings, was the demand for the political awakening of the masses and of the need for the movement to work out their salvation. The Congress, Sri Aurobindo firmly held, had to be made into a popular body and "the elite would have to lift up the lower classes; for it was only a broad-based movement, not the palaver of a smug minority, that could bring about the country's liberation."[2] This was a radically new departure for the period in question. Elitism and exclusivity still ruled the proceedings of the Congress and the thought of including the masses was not given priority at all. One of Sri Aurobindo's indictment against the body was that it was not a national one despite its being called as such, "when . . . I said that the Congress was not really national" he frankly wrote, "I simply meant that it did

1. Sri Aurobindo, *Autobiographical Notes and Other Writings of Historical Interest*, 2006, p. 9.
2. Peter Heehs, *Sri Aurobindo: A Brief Biography*, 2005, p. 30.

not represent the mass of the population"[3] and unless this state was consciously altered Sri Aurobindo saw no hope for the movement to widen and command lasting influence. The arrogating attitude of the elite leaders held that "because the masses [were still] unable to articulate definite political demands the function and duty devolved upon their educated and enlightened compatriots to feel, to understand and to interpret their grievances and requirements, and to suggest and indicate how these [could] be best redressed and met."[4] Such an attitude Sri Aurobindo opposed; the masses he argued had to be admitted into the scheme of things, and their voices had to be allowed direct expression because such a move alone could guarantee an effective and lasting public movement that would eventually ensure liberation. "The proletariat among us," he wrote:

> is sunk in ignorance and overwhelmed with distress. But with that distressed and ignorant proletariat . . . resides, whether we like it or not, our sole assurance of hope, our sole chance in the future. Yet he is set down as a vain theorist and a dreamy trifler who would raise it from its ignorance and distress.[5]

The proletariat, he further observed, was "the real key of the situation" and though not an "actual force" at present, he [proletariat] nevertheless remains "a very great potential force, and whoever succeeds in understanding and eliciting his strength, becomes by the very fact master of the future." Thus the only policy that would have a chance of success would be one that would be based upon an "adroit management of the

---

3. Sri Aurobindo, *Indu Prakash,* August 1893, *On Nationalism: Selected Writings and Speeches*, 1996, p. 20.

4. Ibid., p. 21.

5. Ibid., December 4, 1893, Ibid., p. 49.

proletariat."[6] It is interesting to note that long before any of his contemporaries had even made such a demand and realised the essentiality of mass-based public movements, Sri Aurobindo had publicly articulated such a need and became the first political leader in the country to use the term "proletariat" and to apply the nomenclature while discussing prevailing political conditions.[7] He thus championed the cause of the marginalized at a time when such a stand was labelled, as he himself noted, as belonging to vain theoreticians. The foremost political demands of the day were mainly confined to constitutional non-issues *vis-à-vis* the masses, playing with these "baubles" with "Legislative Councils," "Simultaneous Examinations" with the issue of the separation of the "judicial from the executive functions"[8] the leaders omitted any serious reference to them and overlooked their as yet unarticulated needs. This call for the involvement of the masses that Sri Aurobindo made in the early 1890s was finally implemented by the Congress in its programmes nearly a quarter century[9] later allowing the body to assume a pan-Indian character and a greater effective power of action.

Sri Aurobindo's case thus for an inclusive mass action articulated in the pre-mass mobilization Indian political scenario was, it may be said, an addition of values into public action. A public movement that lacked an inclusive character

6. *Indu Prakash,* March 6, 1894, Ibid., p. 59.

7. Haridas and Uma Mukherjee, *Sri Aurobinder Rashtra-Darshan* (Sri Aurobindo's political philosophy) in *Swadeshi Andolon O Banglar Nabayug* [Beng] 2008, pp. 96-97; Prithwindranath Mukherjee, *Sadhak Biplabi Jatindranath* [Bengali] 1990, p. 66; Amalendu De, *Sri Aurobindo's Role in Indian Freedom Struggle,* 2003, p. 8; Rishabchand, *Sri Aurobindo: His Life Unique,* 2007, pp. 100-01.

8. *Indu Prakash,* 4 December 1893, op. cit., p. 49.

9. Peter Heehs, op. cit., p. 30.

was bound to fail, it was devoid of the essential values that would lead the country to freedom therefore the inclusion in it of an inclusive approach was vital for it to be viable. The petitioning policy that the then Congress followed appeared to Sri Aurobindo to be deficient in values because of its isolationism, limited appeal and its being de-linked from the true urges and aspirations of the people, such an approach needed a course correction, the element of inclusiveness was therefore the infusion of a cardinal value which was to eventually bring about that correction.

Alternative Vision of the Country — Growth of an Organic Link with a Living Entity

The *Bhavānī Mandir* pamphlet published some time in August 1905 and authored by Sri Aurobindo espoused publicly as its aim the idea of training *saṁnyāsins* (monks) who would "carry political education and revolutionary action in the country."[10] It spoke of the nation as "a mighty Śakti, composed of the Śaktis of all the millions of units that make up the nation" and not as a "piece of earth," or "a figure of speech," or "a fiction of the mind."[11] It pointed towards the necessity of a "spiritual regeneration" and towards the imperativeness of a live-link with the mother country — it urged the growth and realization among the people of an organic bond with the country and argued that such a link could only evolve when the country would be seen as a living entity. Such an approach was necessary if a binding unity was to be worked out in a till then disparate conglomeration of provinces and nationalities. The colonial administration made a sceptical assessment of the professed aims of this work and saw in it a misinterpretation by the

10. K.R. Srinivasa Iyengar, *Sri Aurobindo: A Biography and a History*, 2006, p. 195.

11. *On Nationalism*, op. cit., p. 71.

author of "Vedāntist ideas for his own purposes, and to adorn his talk and point his moral."[12] That it had made a remarkable impact on the young mind of Bengal was evident when years later the Rowlatt Committee Report on sedition (1917) still recalled its influence and accused it of being a "remarkable instance of the perversion of religious ideals for political purposes."[13] Influenced by this colonial reading of the work a certain school of historians have interpreted a similar motive in it[14] and have completely missed out on the deeper value-inspired vision of the country that it espoused. Its talk of unity, eradication of class distinction, its talk of India spreading the "Eternal religion which is to harmonize all religions, science and philosophies and make mankind one soul,"[15] its vision of combining the strength of technology and science to the power of morality-spirituality, has been mostly overlooked by such partial analysis and yet it is in these very formulations that one perceives an early attempt at value infusion into the public discourse of that period. The project of the *Bhavānī Mandir* never took off, but the ideas it generated initiated in the youth a widening of thought and of vision. Speaking of salvation through the adherence to *dharma* and strength the work did provide a hope for the transformation of the Indian socio-political scene at a time when events were pointing towards a nadir.[16] That such a stance was not simply a clever method of

---

12. Haridas and Uma Mukherjee, *Sri Aurobindo and the New Thought in Indian Politics, Introduction*, 1997, p. xxviii.
13. K.R. Srinivasa Iyengar, op. cit., p. 200.
14. Peter Heehs, *The Bomb in Bengal*, 2004, pp. 69-70.
15. Sri Aurobindo, *Bhawani Mandir, On Nationalism*, op. cit., p. 70.
16. Two months after its publication Bengal was to convulse over the partition issue. Amalendu De, *Banga-Bhanga Andolon-Bishleshatmak Parjalochana* [Bengali], 2005, pp. 4-5. →

public posturing and political rhetoric is clear from the fact that even in a private letter to his wife Mrinalini Devi, written around that time (30 August 1905) in which Sri Aurobindo spoke among other things of his experiencing the country as more than a piece of an inert land, one perceives the depth of conviction in his observation. Terming it as his madness he wrote:

> While others look upon their country as an inert piece of matter — a few meadows and fields, forests and hills and rivers — I look upon my country as the Mother, I adore Her, I worship Her as the Mother . . ..[17]

This intense personal realisation Sri Aurobindo sought to translate into a mass-experience, such an attempt was by itself a step towards a positive remoulding of the political discourse of that period on nation, nationality and self-determination. Though unwilling to publicly accede, the colonial intelligence with its limited intellectual span perhaps understood the value-essence of Sri Aurobindo's political formulations during this period and therefore commented in a secret note that:

> The teachings of Arabinda Ghosh . . . were modelled on the same line as Swami Vivekananda's, but with a more definite appeal to force or *śakti*, which he maintained was necessary for the regeneration of India.[18]

In this assessment the colonial administration was probably right because in a sense Sri Aurobindo did revive "the theoretical teachings of Bankimchandra and [Swami]

→ See this monograph for an alternative assessment of the *Bhavānī Mandir* aims and effect.

17. Letter to Mrinalini Devi, in A.B. Purani, *The Life of Sri Aurobindo*, 2006, p. 82.

18. *A Note on the Ramakrishna Mission*, in Amiya. K. Samanta, ed., *Terrorism in Bengal*, vol. 4, 1995, p. 1350.

Vivekananda and introduced them in the field of practical politics."[19] In fact, exploring the link of his early political thought with Swami Vivekananda's vision slightly further, it can be seen that when talking of a spiritual mission for India — a recurring theme in his political thought, adopted not merely as a political mechanism to instil confidence in a dispirited race but one that stemmed from a genuine conviction — Sri Aurobindo pointed towards the similarity of intent that Swamiji had for India's spiritual mission and of how that could become the principal fountain of inspiration for the emerging Indian nationalism. Discussing the English utilitarian philosopher Henry Sidgwick's (1838-1900) work, *Elements of Politics* (London, 1891), Sri Aurobindo points out that if it was that "physical expansion proceeds from a desire for spiritual expansion . . . [then] why should not India be the first power in the world? Who else has the undisputed right to extend spiritual sway over the world? This was Swami Vivekananda's plan of campaign. India can once more be made conscious of her greatness by an overmastering sense of the greatness of her spirituality. This sense of greatness is the main feeder of all patriotism. This only can put an end to all self-depreciation and generate a burning desire to recover lost ground."[20] This was to form one of the bases of Sri Aurobindo's nationalism — a spiritual nationalism — based not, as some have mistakenly assumed, on an appeal to raw religious emotions but on a more sublimated vision of nationalism and national mission inspired by one of the spiritual giants of arising India. Sri Aurobindo referred to this influence of Swamiji's thought-power on the movement when he recalled later that "The influence of Ramakrishna and Vivekananda worked from

19. R.C. Majumdar, *The Genesis of Extremism in Studies in Bengal Renaissance*, 2002, p. 168.

20. Sri Aurobindo, *Bande Mataram*, 1997, p. 428.

behind" [on the movement] and that the Movement and Secret Society had become "so formidable that in any other country with a political past they would have led to something like the French Revolution."[21] Alluding perhaps to this link and influence of thought and ideas, Bhupendranath Datta (1880-1961), Swami Vivekananda's younger brother and member of the radical group of the early revolutionaries who was imprisoned in the *Yugāntar* sedition case, has aptly observed that:

> The ferment created by Swami Vivekananda in the intellectual plane burst forth after his death into a revolutionary upsurge in Bengal. And later it spread everywhere as a movement led by another great man, in a certain sense his successor — Aurobindo Ghose, who, according to Romain Rolland, "was the real intellectual heir of Vivekananda."[22]

Sri Aurobindo's appeal did not cease at that pamphlet; through his writings later in the fiercely nationalist daily *Bande Mataram* he further developed the idea of the country as a living being which needed adoration, worship and sacrifice. It became clear to him that until this concept of the nation achieved certain permanence in the national psyche no sustained movement could be generated. Sri Aurobindo was interested in this sort of value-based vision of the country as he realized its importance in a movement for national freedom. He observed:

> It is not till the Motherland reveals herself to the eye of the mind as something more than a stretch of earth or a mass of individuals, it is not till she takes shape as a great Divine and Maternal Power in a form of beauty that can dominate the mind and seize the heart that . . . the patriotism that

---

21. Nirodbaran, ed., *Talks with Sri Aurobindo*, vol. 1, 2001, p. 26.
22. Bhupendranath Datta, *Swami Vivekananda: Patriot-Prophet*, 1993, p. 132.

> works miracles and saves doomed nations is born.[23]

Defining this patriotism he wrote that it was one which saw:

> God as the Mother in our country, God as *śakti* in the mass of our countrymen, and religiously devotes itself to their service and their liberation from present suffering and servitude.[24]

There has been much confusion generated on this aspect of Sri Aurobindo's political thought which talks of combining religion and politics but a careful and unbiased reading of his writings of this period does reveal that the religion that Sri Aurobindo spoke of was the religion of *nationalism.* It was to be a religion which saw the nation as the presiding deity, it was not a religion in the conventional sense of the term nor did it espouse the tenets of a certain sectarian creed or school of thought. It demanded a certain self-exceeding and placed an alternative vision of the country before a people then in the throes of near extreme self-depreciation. To some therefore who took "for granted the separation of the political and religious spheres enjoined by post-Enlightenment European secularism . . . any infusion of religious language into political discourse [seemed] illegitimate" and to colonialists who perceived "religious nationalism" as a "challenge to the established political order"[25] such a language and thought seemed to be particularly inciting and perverse. But among the Indian masses, where the religious sentiment pervades, this vision of the country as the Mother, as God to be worshipped was readily accepted, the value of the country,

23. Sri Aurobindo, *Bankim-Tilak-Dayananda*, 1994, p. 13.

24. *Bande Mataram*, op. cit., p. 235.

25. Peter Heehs, "Religious Nationalism and Communalism" in *Nationalism, Terrorism, Communalism: Essays in Modern Indian History*, 2005, pp. 104-05. See this essay for a detailed treatment of this argument.

the *svadeśa,* thus deepened enabling "a deep affective bond with the motherland . . . to [gradually] replace the abstract nationalism of preceding decades."[26] This affective bond was to assign an altogether new role and value to the emotion of love in politics, it was not to be a mere attraction and seeking after position and pelf at the expense and exploitation of the country. "Love," wrote Sri Aurobindo "lyrically" while defining its value in public life:

> has a place in politics, but it is the love for one's country, for one's countrymen, for the glory, greatness and happiness of the race, the divine *ānanda* of self-immolation for one's fellows, the ecstasy of relieving their sufferings, the joy of seeing one's blood flow for country and freedom, . . . The feeling of almost physical delight in the touch of the mother soil, of the winds that blow from Indian seas, of the rivers that stream from Indian hills, in the sight of Indian surroundings, Indian men, Indian women, Indian children, in the hearing of Indian speech, music, poetry, in the familiar sights, sounds, habits, dress, manners of our Indian life, this is the physical root of that love. The pride in our past, the pain of our present, the passion for the future are its trunk and branches. Self-sacrifice, self-forgetfulness, great service and high endurance for the country are its fruits. And the sap which keeps it alive is the realisation of the Motherhood of God in the country, the vision of the Mother, the knowledge of the Mother, the perpetual contemplation, adoration and service of the Mother.[27]

A remarkable vision that is strikingly relevant to the discourse on the necessity for attitudinal course-corrections in

---

26. Sugata Bose, "The Spirit and Form of An Ethical Polity: A Meditation on Aurobindo's Thought", in *Modern Intellectual History*, 4, 1, 2007, p. 134.
27. Sri Aurobindo, "The Morality of Boycott" in *On Nationalism,* pp. 361-62.

contemporary Indian public life. Sri Aurobindo foresaw that such a sublimated emotion, once established in the race consciousness, would provide self-less workers in thousands and give the movement a self-sustaining momentum. Thus a clear perception emerges that Sri Aurobindo's definition or vision of patriotism had a far deeper essential value than the "normal patriotism that everyone is expected to feel for one's country." He looked upon India as a "living and pulsating spiritual entity"[28] and sought to convert that into a fundamental guiding light of the new movement that he had initiated. Years later, writing his social and political thought Sri Aurobindo commented on the "new conception of the nation" pursued by the movement of 1905 in Bengal; drawing its contours of vision, he wrote that the conception was not that of the nation:

> Merely as a country, but a soul, a psychological, almost a spiritual being and, even when acting from economic and political motives, it sought to dynamise them by this subjective conception and to make them instruments of self-expression rather than objects in themselves.[29]

Much has often been asked and discussed regarding the method of identifying with this conception of the nation as a soul; the narration of an experience here, may perhaps provide an empirical insight into Sri Aurobindo's method of identifying with the nation as a pulsating entity and of establishing an organic link with that entity. K.M. Munshi (1887-1971)[30] remembered how as a student at Baroda he once directly asked:

---

28. Karan Singh, *Prophet of Indian Nationalism*, 1991, pp. 74-76.
29. Sri Aurobindo, *The Human Cycle*, 2005, pp. 38-39.
30. Indian freedom fighter, polymath, member of the Constitution Drafting Committee of the Indian Constituent Assembly, Union Minister, Governor, author and founder →

> Prof. Arvind Ghosh, "How can nationalism be developed?" "He [Professor Ghosh] pointed to a wall-map of India and said. . . . Look at that map. Learn to find in it the portrait of Bhāratmātā. The cities, mountains, rivers and forests are the materials which go to make up Her body. The people inhabiting the country are the cells which go to make up Her living tissues. Our literature is Her memory and speech. The spirit of Her culture is Her soul. The happiness and freedom of Her children is Her salvation. Behold Bhārat as a living Mother, meditate upon Her and worship Her in the ninefold way of Bhakti [*Navavidha Bhakti*] . . ."[31]

The suggestions in the above exercise were but the first elementary steps of preparation.

Alternative Concept of Nationalism: A New Force in Politics

To the concept of nationalism, Sri Aurobindo imparted newer dimension and depth. The term nationalism may have been used and abused over the last century and may have inspired predatory political activism mainly by the Western imperial and ideological conquests but its relevance if seen from the interpretation that Sri Aurobindo gave to it becomes evident in the present socio-political context. Sri Aurobindo spoke of nationalism as "a religion divine and sāttvic," he held that "Nationalism survives in the strength of God and it is . . . immortal [it] cannot die, because it is no human thing." For Sri Aurobindo, a nationalist is not one for whom nationalism is "merely a larger kind of selfishness," instead it is one who

---

→ of the Bharatiya Vidya Bhavan, Munshi was Sri Aurobindo's student at Baroda. As a member of the Constituent Assembly Munshi was in touch with Sri Aurobindo and later met him at Pondicherry in 1950.

31. *Bhavan's Journal* (vol. 3, no. 26, 22 July 1962) cited in Roshan and Apurva, eds., *Sri Aurobindo in Baroda*, 1993, p. 85.

wishes to be free not in order to be able to "oppress others," one who has "real faith" [in the greatness and salvation of the country] and not mere "political aspiration," one who holds the source of the newly evolving political creed to be something higher, one who believes that God works through this movement [of liberation] to bring about the salvation of the nation and ultimately one who has realised that he is but an instrument to work out this higher purpose.[32] And a nationalist who believes in a higher source of inspiration and does not seek to be free in order to oppress others can never preach or perpetuate a predatory and hegemonistic nationalism. The nationalism that Sri Aurobindo espoused demanded to be lived and practised in a certain "spirit of humility and dedication." It differed from its European prototype in that it did not emphasize solely the change of an alien rule by that of an indigenous one but also exhorted the "expansion and extension of one's consciousness in order to identify oneself with the activities, feelings, aspirations and happiness" of the vast multitude. Its primary emphasis was on developing a deeper level of "self-transcending fraternization with one's countrymen"[33] and on making sincere efforts to work for their integral well-being. It called for an identification with the nation and its constituent elements in a spirit of sacrifice and self-giving. The new nationalism that had awakened in Bengal, Sri Aurobindo pointed out, was not at heart "guided by any self-interest," it was not "a political self-interest" that was propelling the movement and its leaders. This nationalism was seen instead as a religion which was being tried to be lived, "it is" he stated:

---

32. Sri Aurobindo, *Speeches: On Indian Politics and National Education*, 2005, p. 20.

33. V.P. Varma, *The Political Philosophy of Sri Aurobindo*, 1976, pp. 200-01.

> A religion by which we are trying to realise God in the nation, in our fellow-countrymen. We are trying, some of us consciously, some of us unconsciously, we are trying to live not for our own interests, but to work and to die for others.[34]

Nationalism in Sri Aurobindo's thought is thus perceived to be "not merely a patriotic and intellectual pastime but a deep and fervent religious *sādhanā*"[35] which had as its principal tenets the attitudes of sacrifice, self-giving and self-forgetfulness. This attitude of self-giving and self-abandonment for a larger emancipatory national cause was what was absent in a collective scale in the earlier movements that demanded mere constitutional correctives. At a wider level Sri Aurobindo's nationalism possessed an integrative aspect. In it the nation, the individual and the world were all inter-linked, inter-dependent and striving for a greater harmony and union, and India therefore had to be free for "the sake of humanity," and nationalism was to work for that freedom keeping that higher aim of human welfare and integration as the guiding light. The patriotism that was inspired by this new nationalism would thus proceed "on the basis of love and brotherhood and [look] beyond the unity of nation and [envisage] the ultimate unity of mankind." But it was to be "an unity of brothers, equals and freemen — not the unity of master and serf, of devourer and devoured." The "ultimate brotherhood of humanity" was to be achieved "not by blotting out individual peoples and effacing outward distinctions, but by removing the internal obstacles to unity, the causes of hatred, malice and misunderstanding" and that is why India too demands the "realization" of her "corporate existence" as a distinct race and nation and that is what was the guiding vision

34. *Speeches*, p. 29.

35. Karan Singh, op. cit., p. 78.

and objective of this nationalism.[36] These observations, made when major mass movements had not yet begun in India, when Indians in general could not as yet coherently conceive of a world role for their country, remain significant today — a hundred years after they were made — especially if one looks around at conditions and equations of international relations and global dealings. This idea of human unity as one of the goals of the new nationalism was to also form later "the principal matrix of his [Sri Aurobindo's] integral philosophy." And it is through these significant alternative visions of nationalism that Sri Aurobindo emerged "as a great thinker of world unity who was largely responsible for imparting a spiritual significance to the idea of internationalism beyond Indian nationalism."[37] And the spiritual significance given to nationalism, nation and the individual's role in the nation's emancipation could be said to be a principal factor that worked towards converting the nationalist movement "from an intellectual pastime of the English-educated elite into a mass movement that created in the minds and hearts of the Indian people the will to freedom and the determination to achieve it at any cost."[38] This determination thus was the result of a new value infusion that Sri Aurobindo initiated into certain fundamental concepts and factors that usually inspire revolution and bring about societal-transformation.

"The New Thought": Alternative Methods and Definitions of Resistance and Svarāja

"The New Thought" that Sri Aurobindo introduced in the Indian political discourse between 11 and 23 April 1907 through

36. Sri Aurobindo, "An Open Letter to My Countrymen", *On Nationalism*, op. cit., p. 439.
37. Ramin Jahanbegloo, *The Spirit of India*, 2008, p. 129.
38. Karan Singh, op. cit., p. 78.

his series on the "Doctrine of Passive Resistance" was a new departure for that age. Its tone and tenor of exposition introduced an element of frankness in articulating political demands. It was for the first time that a method of mass struggle was being introduced for implementation in the Indian context. The series were widely read and generated intense discussion, before this "no one had clearly outlined its [passive resistance] objects, methods, [and] limitations."[39] Sri Aurobindo put the whole doctrine on firm scientific foundations and through a progressive delineation demonstrated its structure, uses, efficacy and ultimate goal under Indian conditions and demands. This in itself was a first step and in place of muted constitutional methods till then in vogue the series advocated a bold mass action with the aim of making "administration under present conditions impossible by an organized refusal to do anything which shall help either British commerce in the exploitation of the country or British officialdom in the administration of it — unless and until the conditions are changed in the manner and to the extent demanded by the people."[40] This demand of the people the series articulated as not only "a national government responsible to the people but a free national government unhampered even in the last degree by foreign control"[41] the use of such definitions for freedom — *svarāja* then was far in advance of its time, and has been considered to be the "clearest exposition [of the word] . . . by declaring it [to be] synonymous with independence. . . ."[42] Defining the goals of the "new

---

39. Peter Heehs, *Sri Aurobindo: A Brief Biography*, op. cit., p. 44.

40. *Sri Aurobindo and the New Thought in Indian Politics*, p. xxxi.

41. Sri Aurobindo, *The Doctrine of Passive Resistance*, 1966, pp. 11-12.

42. K.R. Srinivasa Iyengar, op. cit., p. 228. Prof. Iyengar highlights Daniel Argov's position formulated on the →

politics — the politics of the twentieth century" Sri Aurobindo wrote that his advanced nationalist party would cure "a bad and oppressive financial system" by giving "the control over taxation to the people" whose money pays for the needs of the government, it would put "an end to executive tyranny" by making "the people and not an irresponsible government the controller and paymaster of both executive and judiciary" and it would attempt to stop the drain by the only method feasible, by establishing "a popular government which may be relied on to foster and protect Indian commerce and Indian industry conducted by Indian capital and employing Indian labour." The new politics did not believe in "tinkerings and palliatives," it would instead work for the substitution of an "autocratic bureaucracy" which presently "misgoverns" India with a "free constitutional and democratic system of government and [work for the] entire removal of foreign control in order to make way for perfect national liberty."[43] And in doing that it would recognize "no political object of worship except the divinity in" the Motherland, "no present object of political endeavour except liberty, and no method or action as politically good or evil except as it truly helps or hinders [the people's] progress towards national emancipation."[44] At a time when most leaders hesitated to use

---

→ definition of *svarāja* in the latter's *Moderates and Extremists in the Indian National Movement (1883-1930)*, Bombay: Asia Publishing House, 1967. For a detailed analysis of some of the themes and Sri Aurobindo's original defining contributions to them see for instance my *Interventions: Opportunities Given to India*, pp. 327-41, in *Mother India: Monthly Review of Culture*, April, 2009, Sri Aurobindo Ashram, Pondicherry.

43. Ibid., p. 10.

44. *The Doctrine of Passive Resistance*, op. cit., p. 48. Though not a part of the discussion here because of its wide ambit, a word regarding Sri Aurobindo's stand *vis-à-vis* the method of →

such resounding language and make such bold demands and instead nearly always made sure, when publicly talking of "self-government," to add the qualifying epithet "colonial" to it[45] in order to safeguard their twin image of loyalist and "nationalist" such frank assertions were indeed path-breaking. These views were "poles apart from the much less inspiring outlook of the Moderates who hankered after petty administrative and political reforms."[46] They introduced the element of courageous speech, lofty vision and a certain level of self-reliance in action in a race that had by then faced oppression and discrimination and received repeated blows to its sense of the national self. Before the end of 1906 a certain model of passive resistance was being worked out in distant South Africa, probably its originator there and the one who was to later master the art on a mass scale under Indian conditions may have read the series while in action and perhaps therefore wrote to its author decades later that "ever since my return to India I have been anxious to meet you face to face."[47] It had also inspired the Mahatma's foremost political disciple and heir, then a student in England, and led him later, as we find in the following quotation, to reassess Sri

→ armed struggle may not be out of place here. Sri Aurobindo never condemned the use of any method out of moral compunctions, his stand was that "the choice by a subject nation of the means it will use for vindicating its liberty" was "best determined by the circumstances of its servitude" and he considered the path of "armed revolt" to be the "third course open to an oppressed nation" for achieving liberation. [*Doctrine of Passive Resistance*, op. cit., pp. 18-20; also see, Sri Aurobindo, *On Himself*, 1995, pp. 40-41.]

45. Upendranath Bandyopadhyay, *Nirbasiter Atmakatha* [Bengali] (Autobiography of an Exile) [Beng. 1357], p. 1.

46. Karan Singh, op. cit., p. 81.

47. Mahatma Gandhi's letter to Sri Aurobindo, dated 2 January 1934, *Autobiographical Notes*, p. 442.

Aurobindo's contribution to the movement giving it an appropriate historical recognition:

> He [Sri Aurobindo] shone like a brilliant meteor and created a powerful impression on the youth of India. The great anti-partition movement in Bengal gained much of its philosophy from him and, undoubtedly, prepared the day for the great movements led by Mahatma Gandhi.[48]

There were others — to emerge later as pillars of the Indian struggle for freedom — who derived values and thus directions for selfless action from the political thoughts of Sri Aurobindo. The freedom fighter and legendary socialist leader Acharya Narendra Deva (1889–1956) recalled how during his youth he was powerfully influenced by Sri Aurobindo's articles in the *Bande Mataram.*[49] Subhas Chandra Bose (1897–1945?) iconic leader in the Indian struggle for freedom who advocated the policy of military struggle against British occupation could still feel the effects of Sri Aurobindo's action of that period. Decades after Sri Aurobindo had ceased to be active in direct political action, Subhas Chandra wrote to his brother Sarat Chandra Bose of the values that he had imbibed from the words of Sri Aurobindo and from the inspiration of Swami Vivekananda:

> We who have grown up under the influence of Swami Vivekananda on one side and Aurobindo Ghose on the other have fortunately or unfortunately, developed a mentality which does not accept a compromise between points of view so diametrically opposed. It is quite possible that I have been nurtured on a wrong philosophy. But it is the characteristic of youthful minds to have more faith in

---

48. Pandit Nehru's foreword in Karan Singh's *Prophet of Indian Nationalism.*

49. Acharya Narendra Deva makes this observation in his *Bauddha Dharma Aur Darshana* (Hindi), Patna 1956, source: V.P. Varma, op. cit., p. 168.

> themselves than in others. It is perhaps an unfortunate fact but it is a fact all the same.[50]

Referring to the *Bande Mataram* phase of the nationalist movement Subhas Chandra observed that:

> It was in the mouth of Aurobindo that we heard the message of political freedom for the first time. And when Aurobindo wrote in the columns of "Bandemataram" — "we want complete autonomy free from British control" — the freedom-loving Bengalee youth could feel that he had at last got the man of his heart.[51]

---

50. Subhas Bose's letter to his brother Sarat Chandra Bose dated 6 April 1921 in Sisir Kumar Bose, ed., *Netaji Collected Works,* vol. 1, 1980, p. 223. Subhas Chandra Bose (Netaji) like a number of others at that point of time believed that Sri Aurobindo would return to active politics, mortified that this did not happen Subhas Chandra at a certain point of time (1928-all India Youth Congress Session held at Calcutta) questioned the utility of setting up āśramas (alluding to Sabarmati and Pondicherry) and practising passive sadhana (as he understood Sri Aurobindo's *yoga* to be) when the country was still under foreign yoke. But such an attitude of Subhas Chandra may be treated as a passing phase. In another address in 1931 while referring to Sri Aurobindo's role in awakening the masses to the yearning for freedom Subhas Chandra was to observe that "The hankering of the heart had found real expression and the whole country cried out as it were 'Hereafter all is a man after my heart'; Friends, how many leaders of India at the time dared to speak in that strain? Thus developed the present day Nationalism twenty-five years ago." [*Netaji Collected Works,* vol. 6, pp. 11, 201-02,] Subhas Chandra was to maintain a link with Sri Aurobindo through his life-long friend and disciple of Sri Aurobindo Shri Dilip Kumar Roy (1897-1980). For an analysis of Sri Aurobindo and Subhas Chandra see, e.g. Amalendu De, *Sri Aurobindo–Max Muller–Subhas Chandra,* 2005.

51. Address to the Student's Conference at Hooghly, Bengal, 22 July, 1929, *Netaji Collected Works,* vol. 6, 1980, p. 202.

This is corroborated by others who, galvanized by that definition of *svarāja,* rushed in a revolutionary fervour into self-abandoning political action.[52]

Absence of Hatred and Deceit in Political Discourse and Action

Another value-based approach that Sri Aurobindo adhered to while in politics — one that seems especially relevant to the present political climate in India where individual affront overshadows issue-centric discourse and debate — is his refusal to introduce any element of rancour or race attack while upholding a certain political cause, line of action and ideology. Sri Aurobindo "never brought any rancour into his politics [and] never had any hatred for England or the English people," instead he "based his claim for freedom for India on the inherent right to freedom. . . ."[53] The ideal of *svarāja* that he upheld did not preach "hatred of any other nation nor of the administration" in the country, its sole objectives were to alter a "bureaucratic administration" into a democratic one, change an "alien government" into an "indigenous" one and transmute a "foreign control" into an "Indian" one and this aspiration it held did not necessitate hatred but the determination to "suffer and strive, to speak the truth boldly and without respect of persons, to use every lawful means of pressure and every source of moral strength in order to establish ourselves and disestablish that which denies the law of progress."[54] This attempt at igniting the capacity to "suffer and strive" was an infusion of values in the movement that had till then avoided direct confrontation and had adopted instead timid diversionary methods. This capacity was to

52. Upendranath Bandyopadhyay, op. cit., p. 1.

53. *On Himself,* p. 44.

54. *On Nationalism,* pp. 438-39.

demonstrate its usefulness later during the mass civil disobedience movements.

The value-based approach to political action did inspire the youth who had come forward during that period to participate in the movement. And the values they imbibed then were to become, as appears from accounts of that period, an integral part of their life and living. A young worker in the nationalist party had a first-hand experience of Sri Aurobindo's political attitude. The young worker was attending the Hooghly Political Conference on 6 and 7 September 1909, where it "became evident for the first time that Nationalism was gaining the ascendant for it commanded a majority among the delegates." But Sri Aurobindo decided in the interest of a united front [between Moderates and Extremists] to tone down the nationalist resolutions, and "spoke at the public session explaining his decision and asking the Nationalists to acquiesce in it in spite of their victory [in the Subjects Committee where the Moderates resolution welcoming the administrative reforms of the Indian Council's Act of 1909, was defeated] so as to keep some unity in the political forces of Bengal."[55] This decision to forego the advantages of a majority was taken earlier at a closed meeting of nationalist leaders, witnessed by the young worker who remembered the incident for "its great sublimity" — events at the meeting perhaps require quoting in some detail. "Before the start of the Conference," recalled years later Dr V.V. Athalye,

> Aurobindo was seated in his room. He was surrounded by his colleagues, and Dr Paranjpe, though a worker from Vidarbha and not from Bengal, went in because of his acquaintance and got for himself a seat next to Aurobindo. We students stood outside the room and listened to the discussion going on inside. Aurobindo's colleagues were

55. *On Himself*, pp. 32-33.

> making forceful speeches, exhorting him to trounce the Moderates in that Conference, by any and every means. Aurobindo would not agree to this improper method. Seeing that he was not coming round, Paranjpe broke in: "Aurobindo Babu, you don't know politics. You must bring down the Moderates by any means fair or foul, by hook or crook . . .."

Aurobindo was very calm. After everybody had spoken, he said:

> No, I shall never agree to that. Do you have any idea what great work Surendranath Banerji and his Moderate Party have done in Bengal politics? We are standing on their shoulders and because of that we appear tall. Besides this, whatever be anybody's work, I shall not be a party bringing about their downfall by foul means. We shall fully respect the Moderate Party and place before the Conference, in clear terms, our stand of Independence. If our ideal is sacred and lofty and just, the Conference cannot but give its verdict in our favour. If you do not accept this policy I shall withdraw from this Conference.
>
> The sublimity of Aurobindo's advice was so effective that his colleagues . . . shut up as if they had been slapped in the face. . . . Aurobindo's noble yet powerful stand made a great impression on me. In my later life, on many occasions, this teaching has kept me watchful."[56]

Those inspired by these values and exalted aims of the revolution seemed to have never really forgotten their preceptor; decades after he directly worked in Bengal under those who learnt their basics of revolution from Sri Aurobindo, Rashbehari Bose (1886-1945), just before convening the Tokyo Conference in March 1942 to establish the Indian Independence League and to discuss moves to raise an army for Indian liberation, saluted Sri Aurobindo in an open message from

---

56. *Mother India: Monthly Review of Culture*, August, 1972.

Tokyo and remembered his inspiring call which gave "birth to positive Indian nationalism" and pleaded with him to further inspire the new struggle that was to be soon launched.[57] M.N. Roy (1887-1954), later the originator of radical humanism, and once among the early group of revolutionaries who considered Sri Aurobindo to be their "Supreme Commander" in action was to write to the latter a few months before taking the initiative in forming the Communist Party of India at Tashkent on 17 October 1920, asking him to guide the new forces that had been then unleashed on the world stage. Concluding a long letter from Moscow dated 12 August 1920 and addressed to "Arabinda Ghose, Pondicherry, French India," Roy appealed:

> At last I take the liberty of imploring you to come back to active life, to take in your wise hands the direction of the revolutionary forces of India. The forces that are working in India and all over the world today are beyond the understanding of politicians and pacifists. People with great soul and spiritual vision are needed to lead the humanity to its salvation — to real freedom and happiness. How I wish you can come here and see the old corrupted society destroyed, not by brute force, but by the dynamic power of a great idea, and a new world built in its place. This is the goal of every revolution. Anything short of it is not worthwhile to shed blood and add more misery to already suffering humanity.[58]

---

57. Chanda Poddar, Mona Sarkar, Bob Zwicker, eds., *Sri Aurobindo and the Freedom of India,* 1999, pp. 136-37.

58. Prof. Amalendu De includes this interesting extract in his editorial note in the monograph — *Sri Aurobindo and the Mother on Indian Independence and On War and Peace,* 1999. He cites this letter from *The Indo-Russian Relations (1917-1947): Select Documents from the Archives of the Russian Federation,* ed. Purabi Roy, Sobhanlal Datta Gupta, Hari Vasudevan, Kolkata: Asiatic Society.

The historical assessment of Roy here is not important but what concerns us instead is his understanding of the core vision and goal of every revolution — an understanding that he must have imbibed from the receiver of his letter, by then a decade into political exile in a then non-descript corner of India and yet continuing to exercise influence through the power of his values and value-led ideas.

Need for Selfless Political Workers and Value-Oriented Political Training

Sri Aurobindo long realized in his early political days that a different sort of training would be required to sustain a freedom earned through a relentless struggle; he continued to emphasize this aspect even later during his retirement at Pondicherry. "If the country is to be free," he observed, "it must first organize itself so as to be able to maintain its freedom. The winning of freedom is an easy task; the keeping of it is less easy. The first needs only one tremendous effort in which all the energies of the country must be concentrated; the second requires a united, organized and settled strength." It is interesting to note that as early as March 1908 while working for freedom he was also giving expression to this thought of preserving freedom once gained and demanded the formation of groups of selfless workers who would work for organizing *svarāja* and "make it their sole life-work." Interestingly in the same breath he proposed the formation of an institution that would "train and support men to help those" who were then labouring "under great disadvantages to organize education, to build up the life of the villages, . . . to help the people in time of famine and sickness." The ultimate aim of such a training would be to prepare workers who would be "selfless, free from the desire to lead or shine, devoted to the work for the country's sake, absolutely obedient yet full of energy. They must breathe the strength of the spirit, of selfless faith and aspiration . . ." all of these had to be imbibed from the "spiritual guides of the institutions."[59] What he had in mind was not only a political workers' training institution but an institution that would be manned and directed by individuals who had themselves set high standards of conduct in public life. The continuing relevance of this idea may even be traced to present times where such an institution still remains the need of the day and perhaps a possible remedy to a number of imbalances in our performances of public duties. Very few if at all among the leaders then were thinking along these lines and realized the need for a constructive plan and coherent team to organize and maintain freedom.

That the thought of creating genuine workers and of instilling discipline and values in their conduct so as to be effective when *svarāja* eventually came continued to preoccupy him even when he had retired from political into spiritual action is clear from the following conversation that took place at Pondicherry in 1925. It also reveals that Sri Aurobindo did not isolate himself into some kind of passive seclusion inspired by an ideal that would require of him renunciation of active worldly life and action but rather shows that he had a constant concern for the welfare of the Indian nation and the fate of the movement for freedom to which he had provided a momentous impetus. The interlocutors were Sri Aurobindo, Lala Lajpat Rai (1865–1928) and Purushottamdas Tandon (1882–1962), the two nationalist stalwarts who had come to Pondicherry to meet Sri Aurobindo. The discussion was on the then political situation and programmes undertaken and provides an insight into Sri Aurobindo's thinking and to the problems that he had by then identified as paramount in developing a healthy political culture and discourse in the country. The fact that the conversation took place in 1925 and

59. Sri Aurobindo, *Bande Mataram*, pp. 765-66.

had a certain premonitory aspect to it makes it highly relevant for the present and for exploring the infusion of values into politics and the management of public offices. In it Sri Aurobindo identifies discipline and a sense of national honour as necessities for political workers of the country and people in general to cultivate in the interest of the country's future free existence. A superficial aspect of democracy — the chronic compulsion to make tall promises and claims — too emerges from this conversation. Discussing the political programmes initiated at Allahabad Tandon says that he is not in favour of entering local bodies as that would eventually lead "to lust for power and then personal differences and jealousies" and the high hopes that people had reposed in the leaders would then be unjustifiable. The problems of office had already begun to appear among the leaders. Lala Lajpat observes that high hopes have to be given to people, it was one of the modes of functioning in a democratic age, "if you want to enter governing bodies you must make big promises; that is the nature of democracy." This is where Sri Aurobindo interjects and one perceives again the direct appeal for a value-based approach. He questions the very necessity of democracy if it is to thrive on false promise making and says that shunning public office is not the solution to maintaining purity of action.

> Then, why democracy at all? The lust for power will always be there. You can't get over it by shutting out all positions of power; our workers must get accustomed to it. They must learn to hold positions for the nation. This difficulty would be infinitely greater when you get *svarāja*. These things are there even in Europe. The Europeans are just the same as we are. Only, they have got discipline — which we lack — and a keen sense of national honour which we have not got.

The weakness of succumbing to the lures of power and position cannot be prevented, Sri Aurobindo continues, but a certain control and mitigation could be brought about and that needed to be done by bringing about "discipline and [a] sense of national honour in" the people. What is required is not merely an outward action but the need to develop discipline and a sense of national honour and the growth of the habit of exploring the areas and possibilities of "common interest in the midst of conflicting interests."[60] This perhaps was his essential nature when it came to values in political action, a radical adherence and support to values, and for that all established orders and systems could be questioned and scrutinized. The worker must live and act for the nation and the people and the thought and consideration of self ought not to rise at all. Writing as much to one of his disciples, who had been elected to the Bengal Legislative Council in January 1937 and sought guidance in matters of legislative function, Sri Aurobindo observes displaying an acute sense of pragmatism as well as value adherence, that the question of "what to do in a body like the Assembly depends on circumstances, on the practical needs of the situation which can change rapidly. In such a body the work is not of a spiritual character. All kinds of work can be done with the spiritual consciousness behind, but unless one has advanced very far, one must in the front be guided by the necessities of the work itself and its characteristic nature." To the work of the party that the disciple had joined he directs him to bring to it "all the consciousness, ability and selflessness which" he could command,

> . . . a *sādhaka* entering politics should work not for himself but for the country. If he takes office, it should be only when he can do something for the country by it and not until he has proved his character and ability and fitness for the

---

60. A.B. Purani, *Evening Talks*, 2007, pp. 54-56.

position. You should walk by a high standard which will bring you the respect even of opponents and justify the choice of the electors."[61]

The quintessential Sri Aurobindo *vis-à-vis* value-based action in politics had perhaps best expressed himself here.

An exploration therefore of some aspects of Sri Aurobindo's early political thought seem to point towards the fact that he did attempt, in the sphere of his early political action, to evolve certain value-based concepts and actions and these in turn did generate a wide appeal and did bring in a certain level of positive activism and direction to the early phase of the Indian struggle for freedom. Sri Aurobindo's infusion of values into the early Indian political discourse conferred on the movement a certain degree of inclusiveness and dynamism that was required at that point of time in order to widen the scope, aim and reach of the struggle. The dilemma of the political-spiritualist or the spiritual-politician yet confounds political discourse and models of political reforms. Sri Aurobindo, it may be said, provides to a large extent, through his early political thought and action, signposts towards a possible harmonization and integration of that essential dilemma and the eventual unification of values and political action.

References

(Sri) Aurobindo, *Autobiographical Notes and Other Writings of Historical Interest*, Pondicherry: Sri Aurobindo Ashram, 2006.

———, *Bande Mataram*, Pondicherry: Sri Aurobindo Ashram, 5th impression, 1997.

---

61. Sri Aurobindo's letter dated 21.2.1937 written to Birendra Kishore Roychowdhury (1901-72?), *Autobiographical Notes*, p. 448. Birendra Kishore was elected to the Bengal Assembly in January 1937. Later in life he was to excel as a musician and musical scholar and a master of the Dhrupad style.

———, *Bankim-Tilak-Dayananda*, Pondicherry: Sri Aurobindo Ashram, 2nd impression, 1994.

———, *On Himself*, Pondicherry: Sri Aurobindo Ashram, 6th impression, 1995.

———, *On Nationalism: Selected Writings and Speeches*, Pondicherry: Sri Aurobindo Ashram, 1996.

———, *Speeches : On Indian Politics and National Education*, Pondicherry: Sri Aurobindo Ashram, 7th edn., 2005.

———, *The Doctrine of Passive Resistance*, Pondicherry: Sri Aurobindo Ashram, rpt., 1966.

———, *The Human Cycle*, Pondicherry: Sri Aurobindo Ashram, 2nd impression, 2005.

Bandyopadhyay Upendranath, "Nirbasiter Atmakatha" [Bengali] (Autobiography of an Exile) in *Upendranath Bandyopadhyay Granthabali*, Kolkata: Basumati Sahitya Mandir, [Beng. 1357].

Bose, Sisir Kumar, ed., *Netaji Collected Works*, vols. 1 and 6, Kolkata, 1980.

Bose, Sugata, "The Spirit and Form of An Ethical Polity: A Meditation on Aurobindo's Thought" in *Modern Intellectual History*, 4, 1, Cambridge University Press, 2007.

Datta, Bhupendranath, *Swami Vivekananda: Patriot-Prophet*, Kolkata: Nababharat Publishers, 2nd rev. edn., 1993.

De, Amalendu, *Sri Aurobindo and The Mother on Indian Independence and On War and Peace*, Kolkata: Sri Aurobindo Samiti, 1999.

———, *Banga-Bhanga Andolon-Bishleshatmak Parjalochana* [Bengali] Kolkata: Parul Prakashani, 2005.

———, *Max Müller–Sri Aurobindo–Subhas Chandra*, Kolkata: Sri Aurobindo Samiti, 2005.

———, *Sri Aurobindo's Role in Indian Freedom Struggle*, Kolkata: Asiatic Society, 2003.

Heehs, Peter, "Religious Nationalism and Communalism" in *Nationalism, Terrorism, Communalism: Essays in Modern Indian History*, New Delhi: Oxford University Press, 2nd impression, 2005.

———, *Sri Aurobindo: A Brief Biography*, New Delhi: Oxford University Press, 5th impression, 2005.

———, *The Bomb in Bengal*, New Delhi: Oxford University Press, rpt., 2004.

Iyengar, K.R. Srinivasa, *Sri Aurobindo: A Biography and a History*, Pondicherry: Sri Aurobindo International Centre of Education, 5th edn., 2006.

Jahanbegloo, Ramin, *The Spirit of India*, New Delhi: Penguin, 2008.

Majumdar, R.C., "The Genesis of Extremism", in Atul Chandra Gupta, ed., *Studies in Bengal Renaissance*, Kolkata: National Council of Education, Bengal, 3rd rev. edn., 2002.

Mother India: Monthly Review of Culture, August 1972, Pondicherry: Sri Aurobindo Ashram.

Mukherjee, Haridas and Uma, "Sri Aurobinder Rashtra-Darshan" (Sri Aurobindo's political philosophy) in *Svadeśī Āndolon O Banglar Nabayug* [Bengali], Kolkata' Dey's reprint, 2008.

———, *Sri Aurobindo and the New Thought in Indian Politics*, Kolkata: revised 2nd edn., 1997.

Mukherjee, Prithwindranath, *Sadhak Biplabi Jatindranath* [Bengali], Calcutta: West Bengal Govt. Book Board, 1990.

Nirodbaran, ed., *Talks with Sri Aurobindo*, vol. 1, Pondicherry: Sri Aurobindo Ashram, 2001.

Poddar, Chanda, Mona Sarkar, Bob Zwicker, eds., *Sri Aurobindo and the Freedom of India*, Pondicherry: Sri Aurobindo Ashram, 2nd impression, 1999.

Purani, A.B., *Evening Talks*, Pondicherry: Sri Aurobindo Ashram, 4th rev. edn., 2007.

———, *The Life of Sri Aurobindo*, Pondicherry: Sri Aurobindo Ashram, 5th impression, 2006.

Rishabchand, *Sri Aurobindo: His Life Unique*, Pondicherry: Sri Aurobindo Ashram, 3rd impression, 2007.

Roshan and Apurva, eds., *Sri Aurobindo in Baroda*, Pondicherry: Sri Aurobindo Ashram, 1993.

Samanta, Amiya K., ed., *Terrorism in Bengal*, vol. 4, Kolkata: Govt. of West Bengal, 1995.

Singh, Karan, *Prophet of Indian Nationalism*, Mumbai: Bharatiya Vidya Bhavan, 3rd edn., 1991.

Varma, V.P., *The Political Philosophy of Sri Aurobindo*, New Delhi: Motilal Banarsidass, 2nd edn., 1976.

12

The Ideal of Human Relations
Sri Aurobindo's Global Perspective

Aparna Banerjee

IF each of us is found to be foot-firm in our own nation's/community's best interests, then our model of internationalism is likely to be global only from a very limited and interest-oriented point of view. Liberal or non-liberal, both forms of nationalism mostly ignore the need for a global conception of citizenship. But, political philosophers must address some common problems that arise in collective human life, with its needs, aims and complexities. The question is how far our need for a global concept of citizenship in the modern times is realizable. The question of need arises in the context of common environmental problems, problems of international security and economic interdependence. In fact, so far power and interests rather than moral ideals have dominated even nation-building to some extent. The intolerant attempt to assimilate immigrants or minorities to the culture of the majority is a problem that is faced by the minorities of different types all over the world.[1] Just as there are serious inequalities within nation states, the inequalities between the developed, developing and the underdeveloped countries are no less obvious.

1. Will Kymlicka, 2002, *Contemporary Political Philosophy, An Introduction*, see ch. 8.

The issues that are involved are highly complex. The concepts of sovereignty and of law that are central are evaluated in terms of the overarching ideals of justice, equality and freedom. The ideals themselves are not unanimously given equal importance. We need only to note the traditional controversies on this issue between the leftist and the rightist disputants. In between there are others who believe in placing these ideals in still different value scales. Again the ideals of justice, equality and freedom too differ from community to community, since these are in a large measure formulated within particular historical and traditional perspectives. If we add to these issues the hegemonic trends that are still very much operative at both the national and the international levels, then achieving a global community that will be based on moral principles, may appear to be a utopian ideal. However, the increase in awareness of the issues involved in the debate cannot be denied. Similarly, in the modern world, the ideal of democracy seems to have taken a central position, although the world history is full of disturbing events which have occurred in the name of democracy. "Democracy . . . is like a soft, round and straw hat which fits in different heads of very many shapes and sizes."[2] The question is whether all these ideas in their present formulations are sufficient for us to cope with the phenomenon of globalization as it is emerging as a matter of fact rather than as it has been advocated as a moral ideal.

Sri Aurobindo[3] points out that in the modern times, while the ideal of global unity had its roots in the idealistic basis of the French Revolution, it was yet a vague "intellectual sentiment" than a clear idea. In fact, the ideal that definitely

2. D.P. Chattopadhyaya, 2002, *Interdisciplinary Studies in Science, Society, Value and Civilizational Dialogue*, p. 242.

3. Sri Aurobindo, 1950, *The Ideal of Human Unity*, p. 548.

developed out of the French Revolution was a self-conscious nationalism rather than internationalism. It was not until the nineteenth century that it re-emerged as a recognizable force combining with socialism and anarchism. In this form, internationalism seeks to rise above national, cultural and geographical and economic boundaries which create walls between men. This view is futuristic no doubt since it aims to turn away from the prejudices of the past and the present. But its real weakness lies in its abstractness and remoteness from concrete reality. As long as, even at present, man lives mostly by outward rules and customs rather than allowing ideals to take control, these ideals continue to remain remote.

It is more usual for the internationalist to encourage multilateralism with some limited supranational powers so that there is a healthy interdependence between countries. The ideal of a world government is, on the other hand, suspected to be by nature negligent of national identity and freedom. This is comparable to the modern-day preference for democracy as against autocracy or rejection of any form of totalitarianism, at the national level. It should not be assumed that the ideal of internationalism is of recent origin. Just as in the ancient Indian tradition, we have the motto *vasudhaiva kuṭumbakam*, similarly in the West, it is said that the Socratically inspired Diogenes in the fourth century BCE was the first to give explicit expression to Cosmopolitanism. When asked where he came from, Diogenes had replied that he was a citizen of the world (*Kosmopolitês*). However, this is usually taken to imply a denial of his citizenship of Sinope rather than a positive commitment to what one can readily understand as cosmopolitanism.

II

It is amazing that Sri Aurobindo had foreseen the situation in which internationalism turns into a necessity and inevitability, as early as 1915-18, during which time his essays called *The Ideal of Human Unity* had first appeared. The world was yet to witness another world war. Writing about the possibility of "unification of the human race on political, administrative and economic lines," he points out how the need for such unification became manifest. Thus he says:

> (T)his spirit has been created largely by increased mutual knowledge and close communication, partly by the development of wider and freer intellectual ideals and emotional sympathies in the progressive mind of the race.[4]

Now in the twenty-first century the situation remains more or less the same. In spite of tremendous improvements in the technology of communication and hence of mutual knowledge, the spread of the favourable intellectual ideals and especially the emotional sympathies does not seem to have proportionately increased. That the situation would be qualitatively not very different, in spite of pressing practical needs, was not very much unexpected to him.

In the relation between the group and the individual there is the strong possibility of conflict and strife because individualism and collectivism are equally deep-rooted human tendencies:

> Human lives cannot run upon free parallels; for they are compelled by Nature continually to meet, impinge on each other, intermix, and in the ego life that means always a clash. The first idea of our reason suggests that our human relations may be subjected to a mechanical accommodation of interests which will get rid of the clash and the strife; but this can only be done up to a certain point.[5]

Human beings have tried to solve this problem in terms of

---

4. Sri Aurobindo, 1950, *The Ideal of Human Unity*, p. 355.
5. Ibid., *War and Self-Determination*, p. 627.

the ethical ideal of altruism. While often enough, what is practised superficially as altruism hides within itself either egoism itself or some form of collective egoism, even in its sincere manifestation it goes against the true laws of life. This is because, "the law of life cannot be self-immolation; self-sacrifice can only be a step in self-fulfilment."[6]

In fact, the reason why altruism is an ethical ideal is that, it brings about the growth of the self in the process. Its sincere acceptance can be based upon the realization that self-expansion can come only through mutuality. The question is:

> . . . whether this shall be done on the lower basis of the ego, attended by strife, friction and collision with whatever checks and controls, or whether it cannot be done by a higher law of our being which shall discover a means of reconciliation, free reciprocity and unity.[7]

What holds true of the self and the group at the individual level, applies equally well at the global level of choice between nationalism and global justice.

Sri Aurobindo is convinced that nature does not work only at the surface level. The natural sciences are concerned with nature at this level. However, nature has various levels like the physical, biological, mental, spiritual, etc. In fact, he describes Nature as the executrix force (*kāryitrī śakti*) of the Divine.[8] The social and historical phenomena are integral parts of this natural process. In spite of such obviously metaphysical foundation underlying Sri Aurobindo's philosophy, its relevance in throwing light upon the moral issue involved in our discussion cannot be denied; nor can one fail to be

6. Sri Aurobindo, 1950, *War and Self-Determination*, p. 628.
7. Ibid.
8. D.P. Chattopadhyaya, 2001, *Societies, Cultures and Ideologies*, p. 58.

impressed by the extensive reference to the history of different countries and organizations that he makes in support of his theoretical position.

He points out that the main aim of individual life is self-development or self-exceeding. But the reason it is so fundamental in man is because he is not merely a form of mind and body but a living power of the eternal truth; and it is the same eternal truth that expresses itself through the Nation. He refuses to call this just a parallel. To him it is a real identity of nature. The difference is that the group-soul or the nation-soul is more complex.[9] The search for national unity is thus for him the advancement of society from the objective age to the subjective age. At first, the subjective awareness works subconsciously. It may concern itself mostly with national idiosyncrasies, habits and prejudices. But these are the manifestations of the vital soul. We fail to locate the nation-soul, when we mistake the vital ego of a culture as the expression of its true national character. The process of true realization requires a reciprocal soul-searching for both the individual and the society:

> The society has no right to crush or efface the individual for its own better development or self-satisfaction; the individual, so long at least as he chooses to live in the world, has no right to disregard for the sake of his own solitary satisfaction and development his fellow-beings and to live at war with them or seek a selfishly isolated good.[10]

The underlying reason for this is:

> . . . first, that we are a higher self than our ego or our members, secondly, that we are in our life and being not only ourselves but all others; for there is a secret solidarity which our egoism

9. D.P. Chattopadhyaya, *The Human Cycle,* p. 35.

10. Sri Aurobindo, *The Human Cycle,* p. 47.

> may kick at and strive against, but from which we cannot escape. It is the old Indian discovery that our real "I" is a Supreme Being which is our true self and which it is our business to discover and consciously become and secondly, that that Being is one in all, expressed in the individual and the collectivity, and only by admitting and realizing our unity with others can we entirely fulfil our true self-being.[11]

In fact, Sri Aurobindo's view about the nation is far more positive than what he says about the state. For him the state is a soulless machine, which being mechanical and artificial is perishable. Only when a society has discovered its nation-soul can it establish its appropriate political structure.

If we now leave aside the metaphysical underpinnings of Sri Aurobindo's philosophy, we cannot fail to note that what he says is enormously important. Any evaluation of a collective life must be based on an understanding of the basic demands and character of human nature involved in it; for it is through his group affiliations that man realizes his higher potentialities. On the other hand, it is important to note that one's loyalty and identification with one's own group need not stand in the way of having concern and sympathy for the sufferings of people in other parts of the world. Such attitude may not be uniformly spread out in all human beings; nor may it seem possible to most. For our levels of sensitivity differ and grow with the right kinds of information and education. We may also associate this with our reasoning ability. But Sri Aurobindo is sceptical of the autonomy of reason. The inner being of man is conceived of by him as consisting of three stages — the infrarational, the rational and the suprarational. Reason cannot be the guiding principle of human life — either individual or collective — because it does not operate on its own. It mediates between the other two

11. Sri Aurobindo, *The Human Cycle,* pp. 47-48.

strata. In fact, there may be the rare individual who can govern his life in terms of clearly conceived truths. But, just as others are subject to the tyranny of passions and interests, such an individual is subject to the tyranny of ideas. In fact, he turns these ideas into interests. While the ideas are to some extent fulfilled, they also bring disappointment, being insufficient; for ideas are always partial and what is partial cannot be treated as the whole truth of life. We are compelled by nature to apply reason to solve all problems of life. But since we possess only a partial rationality, and that too confused by the lower strata of our nature, it fails. On the other hand, when an attempt is made to take it up to a higher stage of disinterest knowledge, it loses hold:

> The root of the difficulty is this that at the very basis of all our life and existence, internal and external, there is something on which the intellect can never lay a controlling hand, the Absolute, the Infinite.[12]

> Life escapes from the formulas and systems which our reason labours to impose on it; it proclaims itself too complex, too full of infinite potentialities to be tyrannized over by the arbitrary intellect of man.[13]

In his theory of human evolution Sri Aurobindo had accepted the division of society into certain distinct psychological stages following the German theorist Lamprecht. These are the symbolic, the typal and conventional, individualist and subjective. This is, of course, too neat a scheme for understanding the psychology of man and his societies. For these are too complex and synthesize too many factors to fit any rigorous and formal analysis. But these give us some rough ideas of the complex process of human evolution. For the

---

12. Sri Aurobindo, *The Human Cycle*, p. 112.
13. Ibid., p. 108.

primitive man imagination and symbolism was the medium through which he had glimpses of hidden truths. The image to them was a revealer of the unrevealed. But, gradually this stage passes into the conventional in which," . . . the outward expression of the spirit or the ideal becomes more important than the ideal."[14]

When, however, the gap between the conventions and the truths widens, the age of Individualism and Reason comes to predominate men and society. Since all the previous general standards of truth become bankrupt, the individual turns to his own reason to discover the true law of the world and of his own being. It comes as the revolt of critical reason against faith and dogma. Its result is the triumphant progress of physical science:

> In society and politics, it started with a crude primitive perception of natural right and justice which took its origin from the exasperation of suffering or from an awakened sense of general oppression, wrong, injustice and the indefensibility of the existing order when brought to any other test than that of privilege and established convention.[15]

This individualistic stage started in Europe and its questioning spirit led to atheism and secularism. However, as we have already noted, Sri Aurobindo points out that this unrestrained use of reason without any other standard of guidance except itself, ". . . is likely to lead rather to a continual fluctuation and disorder of opinion than to a progressive unfolding of the truth of things."[16]

The twin norms of direct observation and individual reasoning appeal to the rational mind. But, if each individual

---

14. Sri Aurobindo, *The Human Cycle*, p. 11.
15. Ibid., p. 18.
16. Sri Aurobindo, *The Ideal of Human Unity*, p. 19.

followed the dictates of his own rational faculty there would result a relativism of truth on the one hand and anarchism in society on the other. Some universal standard of truth and social order was therefore necessary. In natural science, on the one hand, and socialism on the other, the Individualistic age in Europe found its answer. Science worked as the standard of truth without being dogmatically authoritative. But the drive to govern human life by some order and principles which all can observe and verify leads to the idea of universal laws of which the individual is almost a by-product and by which he must necessarily be governed. This involves:

> . . . a new ordering of society governed by a rigid economic or governmental socialism in which the individual, deprived again of his freedom in his own interest and that of humanity, must have his whole life and action determined for him at every step and in every point from birth to old age by the well-ordered mechanism of the State.[17]

This way of representing socialism is obviously not uncontroversial. Even if the metaphysical presuppositions of Sri Aurobindo's philosophy are not accepted then the socialist ideal of a global social system based on a judicious combination of regimentation and free variation for the development of the lives of the millions of people who live below the poverty line, may seem both worthy and urgent for implementation. Moreover, the principles of socialism may be and have been interpreted in different ways so that there may be different ways of practising socialism. The idea of free variation and unity need not necessarily be incompatible with socialism. Sri Aurobindo, however, firmly believed that any administrative unity that is imposed either nationally or internationally can result only in a superficial unity. As long as man is governed primarily by reason, he looks for a comparatively neat and

17. Sri Aurobindo, *The Ideal of Human Unity*, p. 21.

clear-cut model of unity. But the ideal society is one which is based on a natural unity, which is complex and organic, and not a mechanical unity.

Many internationalists, who are not socialists, want to move towards the ideal of democratic globalization by creating a world government. However, this idea is opposed by those who believe that any world government body would be too powerful to be trusted. They are also sceptical of the measures and policies adopted by such supranational organizations as the League of Nations (that had been formed in Sri Aurobindo's times and was actually criticized by him), and more recently the United Nations and the European Union. Sri Aurobindo would agree with them. In fact, what he says in the context of discussing the difficulties of the League applies generally:

> Law is necessary for order and stability, but it becomes a conservative and hampering force unless it provides itself with effective machinery for changing the laws as soon as circumstances and new needs make that desirable. This can only happen if a true Parliament, Congress or free Council of the nations becomes an accomplished thing.[18]

According to Sri Aurobindo "[T]he quarrel between law and liberty stands on the same ground and moves to the same solution." This is because their meeting point has to be natural. The principle of nature is such that no rule is imposed from outside. ". . . she impels life to grow from within and to assert its own natural law . . .."[19]

The law for the individual is to perfect himself by free development from within. But in the process he needs to respect, help and gain help by a same free development of

18. Sri Aurobindo, *The Ideal of Human Unity*, p. 532.

19. Ibid., p. 425.

others. Similarly, the law for the nation is to perfect its own existence by a free development from within, no doubt. Yet, it too needs not only to aid but to be aided by the individuals within. What is more, it should respect, help and be helped by a corresponding development of other nations. In fact, socialism owes its defects to its origin. For, it came as a revolt against the individual ego which it seeks to subordinate to the collectivist ideal. Thus far, the move was justified. "But this element of truth is neutralized, in fact overcome, by the collectivist attempt to eliminate all individual freedom."[20] In fact, no form of collectivism can offer the solution to human unity if it is guided only by reason and its mechanical solutions.

The failure of individualism, in the opinion of Sri Aurobindo, was due to its confinement to two conceptions of the individual — the vital and the rational. But, the Subjective Age that comes after the Age of individualism attempts to delve deeper into the true nature of the individual. However, even subjectivism may fall into error. Thus, while "nationalism" is a subjective phenomenon, it may centre on geographical similarity alone of men, which is actually more objective than subjective. Here, group identity is narrowly confined to a few individuals. Another narrow form of group-subjectivity is its identification with the habits and idiosyncrasies of a nation. In fact, true subjectivism would miss its goal if it confined itself to the national ego. For, nation-soul is, according to Sri Aurobindo, different from nation-ego. Just as the true route to one's soul is through unity with the others, similarly a true nation-soul seeks to stand in a relation of harmony with others, keeping intact the identity and the diversity of the people at the same time, both within and without.

That a free union of individuals is easier to achieve in a

20. Mohanty, p. 145.

small community cannot be doubted. Sri Aurobindo points out that a democratic equality is almost inevitable in a small community. The phenomenon of strong class distinctions and superiorities may establish itself during the military period of the clan or tribe, but it cannot be maintained for long in the close intimacy of a settled city-state except by artificial means. It may be noted that by democracy he means non-Marxist democracy, just as by socialism he primarily means Marxism.

III

Until quite recently democratic theorists would not venture to extend their realm of concern beyond the state. But with the spread of globalization there has been a profound shift in modern democratic theories. Thus, for example, insofar as democracy is a system of rules concentrated within the territory of a state, the inequalities generated by the operations of global markets and the international corporate powers fall beyond its scope. While the cases of public dissatisfaction with the operations of democratic governments keep growing it cannot be denied that in the modern world democracy is the only universal political ideal. It is no wonder that the need for new global institutions combines with the claim for making them democratic.

The ideal and the emerging network of an international civil society are very relevant in this context. This ideal has one of its bases in the concern about the democratic credentials of the existing systems of global relations. The need for new institutional foundations of democracy beyond the limits of the state is being increasingly felt. But, spelling out its meaning and scope with the attending problems of specifying the issue of accountability gives rise to much theoretical debate. However, each party in the debate has the ideal of political cosmopolitanism in mind and the vision of a world in which the interests of the individual and the small group are not overlooked in the interest of states and other bigger political organizations.

In its earlier development, liberal nationalism has considered economic interdependence between different states as the primary route through which a world order would come about in which states would gradually disappear. However, in its present formulations this conviction of a complete transformation of the world has given way to the more moderate hope of reform of the world. In fact, the liberal pluralists point out the need for a more pluralistic world order, with the necessity for a rule by consensus. The necessity for a more representative and accountable government is increasingly being felt not only at the state level but also at the international level.

In contrast, radical democratic pluralism is advocated primarily through the multiplicity of various social movements that question the authority of states and international organizations. It challenges the existing global institutions and political classifications like the foreign/domestic, public/private.[21] In the various such social movements, it traces underlying tendencies towards the transcendence of the sovereign state as the basic prerequisite of democracy. However, such hopes of transcendence have their own attending difficulties. For example, without some conception of sovereignty as a cornerstone of appeal, it may be argued that it is confusing how the competing claims of plurality of communities could be settled, even within a limited geographical area. On the other hand, when one thinks globally in terms of transnational democracy, the debates and clashes of interest generated, once again, would crucially

21. J. Burnheim, in Held and Pollitt, C., 1986, *New Forms of Democracy*, pp. 218-39.

require some authority of law so that there is neither oppression of the strong on the weak nor victory through organized political violence. Democracy, even if pluralistic, seems to involve the rule of law and sovereignty as its very condition. Yet, it is no less true that in actuality international law has been so far established by the most powerful states in their own interests. They encourage international laws only where these enhance their own interests directly or indirectly. One crucial test is whether any democratic state is prepared to sacrifice its natural self-autonomy for a more democratic world order. The answer for all such states is invariably in the negative. Hence, the ideal of a democratic world unity remains a utopian ideal.

Sri Aurobindo has clearly pointed out that as long as man takes Reason to be the primary guide, he cannot accept anything which is imposed conventionally as the social norm. It cannot be the Reason of a few — the ruling class:

> Hence arises the principle of individualistic democracy, that the reason and will of every individual in the society must be allowed to count equally with the reason and will of every other in determining its government, in selecting the essential basis and in arranging the detailed ordering of the common life.[22]

But, unfortunately it develops by its own nature into a perpetual strife, which turns gradually into "an impotent and sterilizing chaos of names, labels, programmes, and war-cries."[23] In fact, ultimately any established order must end in imperfection. While a free association and unity is the final goal of our development, in the present state of human egoism, every proposed order remains imperfect:

---

22. *The Human Cycle*, op. cit., p. 196.
23. Ibid., p. 198.

> In the absence of a general idealistic outburst of creative human hope which would make such changes possible, the future will be shaped not by the ideas of the thinker but by the practical mind of the politician which represents the average reason and temperament of the time . . ..[24]

Modern technology and commerce have cleared the ground for what is a natural human urge for unity. This is not the growth out of some consideration for convenience. It arises out of the realization that neither the growth of the individual, nor the growth of the group can be complete without ". . . parallel development of both, in which each helps to fulfil the other."[25] Now, this may appear to be too utopian a dream. As D.P. Chattopadhyaya remarks:

> (O)ne wonders whether this lofty ideal has any operational significance at all. Even if we assume with Sri Aurobindo that man is a growing godhead, the question remains whether he has grown enough to accept this ideal as a practical proposition. Otherwise, we can hardly draw a line of distinction between practical idealism, which we are for, and utopianism, which is of no consequence in solving the problems of mankind and shaping its destiny.[26]

No doubt, this is a very strong criticism, which it is difficult to solve. But, a few supportive arguments may still be offered. First, although there is no unanimity about man's basic characteristics among people so that Sri Aurobindo's view can be accepted as uncontroversial, there can be no doubt that man has always the project of self-exceeding both personally and socially. Secondly, a deep urge to overcome conflicts and misunderstandings with others is basic in human beings.

---

24. *The Ideal of Human Unity*, op. cit., p. 386.
25. *The Human Cycle*, op. cit., p. 60.
26. D.P. Chattopadhyaya, 1988, *Sri Aurobindo and Karl Marx*, p. 188.

Rabindranath Tagore, a contemporary of Sri Aurobindo speaks of "an abyss of separation" in each of us, in his Bengali essay, *Meghadūta*.[27] He also makes reference to an English poet, whom we can identify as Mathew Arnold, as referring to this same painful separation felt by us (as if by an angry god's curse) in life. In his poem *To Marguerite*, Arnold refers to our human longing for uniting with others as supported by our conviction of oneness. He says:

> For surely once, they feel, we were Parts of a single continent![28]

Since continental drift is not an imaginary phenomenon, but a geographical fact, perhaps our unity would not have appeared so unachievable to us had we been members of the same continent.[29] This knowledge of an original unity of the earth may perhaps make the ideal of a more united world appear as a realizable dream.

References

Aurobindo, Sri, *The Human Cycle, The Ideal of Human Unity, War and Self-Determination*, Pondicherry: Sri Aurobindo Ashram, 1962.

Chattopadhyaya, D.P., *Sri Aurobindo and Karl Marx: Integral Sociology and Dialectical Sociology*, Delhi: Motilal Banarsidass, 1988.

———, *Interdisciplinary Studies in Science, Society, Value and Civilizational Dialogue*, Shimla: Indian Institute of Advanced Study, 2002.

———, *Societies, Cultures and Ideologies*, Mumbai: Bharatiya Vidya Bhavan, 2001.

---

27. "Prācīna Sāhitya", in *Rabindra Racanabali* (1989), pp. 113-15.
28. Mathew Arnold, 1964, in *The Golden Treasury*, p. 364.
29. I owe this argument to a discussion I had with Shri Arabinda Pal of Maulana Azad College, Department of Economics.

Held, D., and Pollitt, C.C., *New Forms of Democracy*, London: Sage Publications, 1986.

Kymlicka, Will, *Contemporary Political Philosophy*, New Delhi: Oxford University Press, 2002.

Mohanty, J.N., *Essays on Indian Philosophy*, New Delhi: Oxford University Press, 1993.

Thakur, Rabindranath, "Prācīna Sāhitya", in *Rabindra-Rachanābali*, Daśam Khaṇḍa, Prabandha, Paścimbaṅga Sarkar, Mahakaran, Kolkata: Sri Saraswati Press Limited, 1989.

The Contributors

Aditi Dasgupta is a Senior Lecturer in Philosophy at West Bengal State University. She is the author of several articles in applied ethics and social and political philosophy.

Anirban Ganguly is a reasearch scholar with the Centre for Sri Aurobindo Studies, Department of Philosophy, Jadavpur University. He is the author of several articles on Sri Aurobindo's educational and political philosophy in various journals.

Aparna Banerjee is Reader in Philosophy at Calcutta University. She is the author of *Explanation and Understanding in Social Science* (2002).

Arun Mahata is a Senior Lecturer in Philosophy at Jadavpur University. He is the author of several articles in social and political philosophy, and existentialism.

Atashee Chatterjee Sinha is Reader in Philosophy at Jadavpur University. She is the author of *The Many Faces of Reason and Violence* (2005).

Indrani Sanyal is Professor in Philosophy at Jadavpur University. She is the author of *On Essentialist Claims* (2002), and co-editor of *Wittgenstein: Jagat Bhasa O Cintan* (1998), *Understanding Thoughts of Sri Aurobindo* (2006), *Sri Aurobindo and His Contemporary Thinkers* (2007), *Siksaksetre Parasparik Samparka* (2007), and *Dharmaniti O Shruti* (2009).

Jhuma Chakraborty is Reader in Philosophy at Jadavpur University. She is the author of several articles in philosophy of language, and social and political philosophy.

Krishna Roy is a former Professor in Philosophy at Jadavpur University. She is the author of *Hermeneutics: East and West* (1993), *Subjectivity in Science: Interpretation of Cartesian Project,* (2009), and editor of *Fusion of Horizons: Socio-Spiritual Heritage of India* (2000), and *Political Philosophy: East and West* (2003), and also co-editor of *Language, Knowledge and Ontology* (1988), *Essays in Social and Political Philosophy* (1989), *Theory and Practice: A Collection of Essays* (2003), *Understanding Thoughts of Sri Aurobindo* (2006), and *Sri Aurobindo and His Contemporary Thinkers* (2007).

Madhumita Chattopadhyay is Professor in Philosophy at Jadavpur University. She is the author of *What to do with the Liar?* (1998), *Ratnakirti on Apoha* (2002), and *Walking along the Paths of Buddhist Epistemology* (2007). She is also co-editor of *Ethics: An Anthology* (2002), and *Siksaksetre Parasparik Samparka* (2007).

Ratna Dutta Sharma is Professor in Philosophy at Jadavpur University. She is the author of *Philosophical Discourse* (2002) and also co-editor of *Patient-Physician Relationship* (2007), and *Dharmaniti O Shruti* (2009).

Rubai Saha is a Senior Lecturer in Philosophy at Jadavpur University. She is working on Hindu ethics.

Sashinungla is Reader in Philosophy at Jadavpur University. She is the author of *Environment Preservation: A Philosophical Critique* (2005) and also co-editor of *Patient-Physician Relationship* (2007).

Shefali Moitra is a former Professor in Philosophy at Jadavpur University. Her books include *Feminist Thought: Androcentrism, Communication and Objectivity* (2002), and *Naitikata O Naribad: Darshaner Prekshite Nana Matre* (2003) and editor of *Women, Heritage and Violence* (1996), and *Kalyaniyasu: Letters written to Shefali Moitra between 1973-84 by Kalidas Bhattacharyya* (2005). She is also co-editor of *Wittgenstein: Jagat Bhasa O Cintan* (1998), and *Communication, Identity and Self-expression* (1984).

Index